IMAGINING WALES

A View of
Modern Welsh Writing in English

JEREMY HOOKER

UNIVERSITY OF WALES PRESS
CARDIFF
2001

British Library Cataloguing-in-Publication Data.
A catalogue record for this book is available from the British Library.

ISBN 0–7083–1635–2 hardback
    0–7083–1636–0 paperback

THE *A*SSOCIATION FOR
*W*ELSH *W*RITING IN *E*NGLISH
*C*YMDEITHAS *L*ÊN *S*AESNEG *C*YMRU

Typeset at University of Wales Press
Printed in Great Britain by Dinefwr Press, Llandybïe

Contents

Acknowledgements

Chapter 1, 'Natives and Strangers: A View of Welsh Writing in English in the Twentieth Century', is a revised and expanded version of a paper which I gave at the Fourth International Conference on the Literature of Region and Nation, held at the University of Wales, Swansea in 1992, and which was published in *Writing Region and Nation*, ed. James A. Davies and Glyn Pursglove with M. Wynn Thomas and Andrew Varney (University of Wales, Swansea Department of English: A Special Number of *The Swansea Review*, 1994). Chapter 7, '"God is Who Questions Me": A Portrait of Roland Mathias', draws substantially upon Chapter 7, 'Roland Mathias: "The Strong Remembered Words"' in my book *The Presence of the Past* (Bridgend: Poetry Wales Press, 1987) and my 'Profile: Roland Mathias', *The New Welsh Review*, No. 4.

Chapter 2 and Chapter 6 both originated in conference papers, which I gave at Birkbeck College, London and Pembroke College, Cambridge respectively, and I am grateful to the organizers for the invitations which instigated my work on these chapters.

My thanks are due to colleagues in the School of English and Creative Studies at Bath Spa University College, whose support afforded me the teaching relief which helped me to work on the book.

I am grateful to Professor M. Wynn Thomas for reading an earlier version of my chapter on Emyr Humphreys's 'Land of the Living' sequence of novels, and for the critical insight of his comments, which helped me to revise the chapter.

Introduction

In this book I look closely at the work of some of the most vital and challenging modern Welsh writers in English. These include Emyr Humphreys, John Cowper Powys, David Jones, R. S. Thomas, Alun Lewis, Gillian Clarke, Roland Mathias, Tony Conran and Hilary Llewellyn-Williams. My critical engagement with these writers has developed over a period of thirty years, and is rooted in excited recognition. As an English poet and critic who first came to live in Wales in 1965 my involvement with Welsh writing in English has entailed a dual process of learning. As I have educated myself in the writing so the writing has taught me more about aspects of Welsh culture and identity. The excitement of recognition has been partly 'that thrill of excitement' to which T. S. Eliot refers in 'A Note of Introduction' to *In Parenthesis*. This excitement, 'from our first reading of a work of literature which we do not understand', is, Eliot says, 'itself the beginning of understanding'. My excitement has also been partly that of participating in the pioneer work of criticizing and teaching Welsh writing in English. The desire to share discoveries in this valuable but, until recently, relatively neglected field is one of my principal motives as a critic.

It follows from this that it is not my aim to provide a comprehensive survey of the subject. Two areas in particular are largely outside my focus on the present occasion. One is the literature of urban, industrial and post-industrial Wales, an important area requiring detailed consideration in its own right. The other is the work of younger writers who have come into prominence in recent years. If my aims were more comprehensive I would also have included a chapter on Dylan Thomas and attempted a much fuller treatment of R. S. Thomas. I could say that these omissions are simply due to the fact that this book is not meant to be a survey of the whole field. And that would be true. There are other truths that should be recorded, however. As a critic of 'poetry of place' I have concentrated on the work of writers who have constructed imaginative 'worlds' from their knowledge of predominantly rural communities and landscapes, or provincial 'centres'; and that is what I know most about. My primary focus here is consequently upon writers who construct ideas of Wales based mainly, though not exclusively, on the land, on life lived in relation to the land, and on areas of Wales outside the industrial and post-industrial south. It is also my aim to illuminate the work of important writers who have yet to receive extensive treatment or full recognition, rather than those who have been written about in detail and in depth, or those still at an early stage in their careers.

What I provide is, inevitably, a personal view. This is as it should be: the kind of criticism I write is based on close personal engagement with the text perceived as another person's construction of an imaginative world. There is a need for treatments of Welsh writing in English that deploy new theoretical approaches; and these have begun to appear in recent years. There is also a need for criticism based upon the engagement of one person's mind with the imaginative work of another, reader with writer's constructed 'world'. My critical values are based on patient, close reading, of specific writings but also of lifework, a writer's body of writing. This does not mean ignoring the socio-historical matrix or the impersonal elements which go to the making of our humanity. It means prioritizing the writer's struggle to shape a coherent vision from the conscious and unconscious elements that have shaped him or her as a person. David Jones's 'one is trying to make a shape out of the very things of which one is oneself made' stands as a succinct epigraph at the head of my thinking on this subject.

Through detailed readings of particular works, I explore the uses certain writers make of the different possibilities available to them by virtue of the fact that they are *Welsh* writers in *English,* with access to Welsh and English literary traditions. While recognizing the opposing elements within these traditions, I am concerned mainly with the sense of imaginative possibility that different writers find in the 'border' or 'frontier' situation between their Welsh and English inheritances.

Imagining Wales is concerned above all with the different ways in which certain writers form ideas or shape visions of Wales in their work. As I have explained, I am not concerned here with the whole of Wales; nor are most writers – in poems and stories, it is often a part of Wales that is made to represent a particular tradition, or to stand in some sense for what the writer regards as the 'essential' Wales, as in R. S. Thomas's 'true Wales of my imagination'.

The historical relationship between England and Wales is notoriously problematic. One literary consequence of this is that it has not been easy for Welsh writers in English, or their critics, to acknowledge debts to English influences. This is more understandable than the general English ignorance of the Welsh literary tradition in both its tongues; but it is still a limitation. Here, I attempt to right the balance. One of my recurring themes is the interaction in Welsh writing in English between influences drawn from English Romanticism and communal values deriving from Welsh history and Welsh-language literary traditions. Another is the relationship between history and myth, and writers' use of Welsh myth, and figures such as Arthur and the fabulous Taliesin, in shaping responses to modern dilemmas. The theme of identity recurs: personal identity, national or cultural identity, ultimately human identity.

As my understanding of Welsh writing in English has grown over the years, I have found myself increasingly using the word 'religious' to describe my findings. This is not merely a vague counter, however, or a synonym for 'serious' or 'deep'. In the present book I show that the religious traditions of Wales, Catholic and Nonconformist, have continued to exert a strong and, in the main, positive influence upon major Welsh writers in English. Specific religious commitments have a shaping influence on the work of writers such as Emyr Humphreys and Roland Mathias and David Jones. In other Welsh writers in English religious influences occur in more diffuse forms, and appear, for example, in the need for some kind of religious belief that was an important element in Alun Lewis's quest, and in the metaphors for liminality that recur in modern literature from Wales. There is abundant evidence that ideas of the Otherworld continue to haunt the secular imagination in Wales. This persistence of a sense of the numinous connects also to the new 'feminine sensibility', which I discuss, together with the rise in Wales of a new nature poetry that responds to the ecological crisis. Rather than saddling any writer with an abstractable dogma or creed, my aim is to illuminate what actually happens in particular writings, through the work of the transformative imagination.

It is my intention, then, to show how different elements – Welsh and English – work together, whether harmoniously or in opposition, to make the distinctive weave of a literature that is important for its own sake, and makes an invaluable contribution to our understanding of Wales. The book is a summation at *this point* of my findings as a critic who has been long involved with Welsh writing in English. The emphasis reflects my conviction of the value of rereading as a critical activity, rereading in which the critic shares his or her discovery of new depths in writings, and learns – and helps others to learn – from misreadings or earlier partial readings. The point is not the critical performance, but to share an enlarged awareness of the richness and complexity of the literary work. I referred earlier to the excitement of doing pioneer work. This was especially my experience as a teacher during the later 1970s, when I taught with Ned Thomas on a course on Welsh writing in English that he founded at University College of Wales, Aberystwyth. This was, I believe, the first course, or one of the first courses, of its kind in Wales. For me, the communication of discoveries made in their reading by teachers and students remains a model of the collaborative critical process. I would like to communicate something of the spirit of that endeavour in this book.

On occasions in what follows I refer to, and in a few instances reproduce passages from, my earlier critical writings – always, however, in the context of later understanding. My chapter on Roland Mathias is to a large extent a reworking of earlier material, in a new attempt to do justice to the achievement of this demanding writer who has yet to receive due recognition. It would be totally contrary to the spirit of *Imagining Wales* to claim that it is the last word – even my last word – on the subjects with which it is concerned. It offers views by which I see further, greatly extending my explorations in the field. Its new readings of major writers open a new perspective upon the subject of modern Welsh writing in English. I hope it will help to illuminate a valuable subject for others, as I have been helped by discussions and repeated rereadings in learning about some writings which construct imaginative versions of Wales, and about the Wales they reveal.

~ 1 ~

Natives and Strangers: A View of Welsh Writing in English in the Twentieth Century

The opening of what is known as 'Dai's Boast', from David Jones's *In Parenthesis*, offers a good starting-point for an overview of Welsh writing in English in the twentieth century:

> My fathers were with the Black Prinse of Wales
> at the passion of
> the blind Bohemian king.
> They served in these fields,
> it is in the histories that you can read it, Corporal – boys
> Gower, they were – it is writ down – yes.
>   Wot about Methuselum, Taffy?
> I was with Abel when his brother found him,
> under the green tree.
> I built a shit-house for Artaxerxes.
> I was the spear in Balin's hand
>   that made waste King Pellam's land.[1]

David Jones was born in Brockley in Kent in 1895, and lived for most of his life in London. His father was Welsh from a Welsh-speaking family, and his mother English. Even in old age David Jones bitterly regretted that he did not speak Welsh. It is interesting to reflect that one of the conditions of his particular literary achievement was precisely that he did not speak Welsh, or at least that he did not think and feel and write in Welsh, as his friend Saunders Lewis did.

Dai is a Welsh soldier of the First World War, but his speech is a boast based on ancient models, English and Welsh, especially 'the boast of Taliessin at the court of Maelgwn'.[2] In form and style *In Parenthesis* is modernist, of the same world as *The Waste Land* and *Ulysses*. Like the work of T. S. Eliot and James Joyce and Ezra Pound, it mediates ancient things. In the case of *In Parenthesis*, these are things belonging to the Island of Britain, and Dai does not discriminate between myth, pseudo-history, and history. All these together constitute the imagined past, which lives in Dai. Evidently, in David Jones's view this is a distinctively Welsh way of apprehending a cultural identity. Dai 'articulates his English with an alien care', and his poetic speech is contrasted with the Cockney's humorous interjection: 'Wot about Methuselum, Taffy?' It is not, however, Dai's accent and speech rhythms alone that make him Welsh – if it were, one might as well claim that Shakespeare's creation of characters, who speak in a distinctively 'Welsh' way, makes him an Anglo-Welsh writer. It is what sounds in Dai's voice that makes him Welsh. Not accent and speech rhythm alone, but also the things that he loves and knows. Later, in writing about his making of *The Anathemata*, David Jones was to say: 'one is trying to make a shape out of the very things of which one is oneself made.'[3] This is what Dai does in his Boast. It is also what David Jones did in writing *In Parenthesis*: he made a 'shape in words' not only of his war experience, but of the things that constituted his sense of cultural identity. The things are, to a significant degree, Welsh, the words are English. It seems reasonable to call the resulting work Anglo-Welsh.

The term Anglo-Welsh was first used in a literary sense by H. Idris Bell in 1922, but was not employed regularly until later. It was then used to describe English-language writers of Wales who began to publish their work in the later 1930s, in the magazines *Wales* and *The Welsh Review*. Already, in 1894, O. M. Edwards had recorded 'a strong desire for a literature that will be English in language but Welsh in spirit'.[4] Later positive definitions of Anglo-Welsh literature have hardly improved on that for succinctness. For some Welsh writers in English, however, the term had (and has) the negative implication of only being half Welsh and they rejected it. Generally, its adoption by a writer has been a mark of humility as well as an act of self-definition – a recognition that only writers in Welsh, the first language of Wales, can properly be called Welsh writers. This sense of awe in face of the Welsh language, and exile from the Wales for which it spoke, was particularly strong in some Anglo-Welsh writings of the 1960s and 1970s, when a Welsh nationalist consciousness prevailed among Anglo-Welsh writers. In recent years, the term has been dropped by many of the younger writers to whom it could be applied. This is particularly ironic in view of the 'drift towards provincialism' that John Barnie and other critics of Anglo-Welsh writing have condemned, and the fact that the ability of the English language to mediate Welshness is more in question now than it has ever been in modern times.

Behind the question of the term lie the pressures of a history, a complex social experience, and a fear of loss of identity. No modern literary term can have been more agonized over than 'Anglo-Welsh'; a war of feeling and ideas has been fought over it, a war all the more violent and painful for being a civil war, and not infrequently a war within the mind of an individual writer. It is easier, perhaps, for an outsider to appreciate the imaginative opportunites produced by the conflict or interaction of English and Welsh – to see, for example, the poetic good fortune of Harri Webb in being able to stand by Dafydd ap Gwilym's grave at Ystrad Fflur on 'the day that Eliot died', and draw upon both traditions.[5] With few exceptions, such as that of Tony Conran, it is easier for an outsider to speak positively of the Anglo-Welsh situation. Insiders usually describe it as a predicament.

Attempts have been made during the past twenty years or so, most notably by Raymond Garlick and Roland Mathias, to define an Anglo-Welsh tradition which begins before the Act of Union in 1536 and extends to the present. Garlick and Mathias do acknowledge, however, that 'Anglo-Welsh literature in its fullest flowering is essentially a modern phenomenon'.[6] Their researches into the Anglo-Welsh past have considerable literary and historical value. But it is fair to note that they were also an expression of a particular phase or movement of Anglo-Welsh literature. This may be said to have begun with the publication of R. S. Thomas's first book of poems, *The Stones of the Field*, in 1946, and to have ended with the débâcle, from the nationalist point of view, of the referendum on Devolution in 1979. It was a movement in which Anglo-Welsh writers were most conscious of the problematic nature of their identity. They looked back to the achievement of Dylan Thomas and his generation of Welsh writers in English – some of them were of that generation – but they also sought consciously to relate their writing to the Welsh literary tradition. In the organic metaphor prevalent at the time, they were much concerned with their 'roots' in Wales. Significantly, the first major study of Anglo-Welsh literature, Glyn Jones's *The Dragon Has Two Tongues*, was published during this period.

The Anglo-Welsh situation, the situation of a person who writes in English, but feels him- or herself to be Welsh, is part of a process of social change which gained a massive impetus in the second half of the nineteenth century. Anglicization in language occurred through the movement of people from outside Wales into the south Wales coalfield, but especially through the influence of state secondary education following the Education Act of 1889. It is easy to talk about social and historical forces acting upon people, but harder to realize the mixture of coercion and choice, attraction and guilt, which constitutes a process of language loss and language gain. Here we are considering a complex social experience, which different writers have felt and interpreted differently. There are, however, common factors uniting the first generation of modern Anglo-Welsh writers. Glyn Jones, who was born in Merthyr Tydfil in 1905, has argued that his generation inherited a common tradition. This was Welsh in language, Nonconformist in religion and radical in politics.

Glyn Jones was born into a Welsh-speaking family but was educated in English. He returned to the Welsh language in his twenties, and was influenced in his English writing by aspects of Welsh poetic style and form. This pattern of experience has been repeated by some other Anglo-Welsh writers, beginning in the period between the wars. Some Anglo-Welsh writers are bilingual, but usually as a result of acquiring Welsh after their most format-ive years, the period – adolescence, in Glyn Jones's view – during which the imagination becomes rooted in a particular language. Others, while not speaking or reading Welsh, acknowledge its primacy in forming what they regard as Welsh identity. Hence the sense of exile from the culture which it voices, the sense of being a stranger at home, that torments some Anglo-Welsh writers. What Glyn Jones's generation also shared, and many Anglo-Welsh writers have since, is the sense of belonging to a community. This, however, is not as simple as it might seem, in a situation of language loss or conflict between languages.

Gwyn Jones, in *Being and Belonging*, has said: '"Anglo-Welsh" . . . in everything save language means "Welsh".'[7] But the exception is a great and highly problematic one, since a language is deeply implicated in a people's sense of identity. At another extreme, Emyr Humphreys in *The Taliesin Tradition* writes of 'the ancient anti-pathy towards each other inherent in the two languages', and 'the fundamental incompatibility of two cultures and the responses they engendered to the very nature of human existence'.[8]

For an Anglo-Welsh writer who agrees that the incompatibility
is fundamental, self-division can result in self-hatred. The classic
expression of this is R. S. Thomas's 'It hurts him to think' in *What
is a Welshman?* Here, Thomas offers a potted history of Wales in
the period before and after his birth. 'The industrialists came,
burrowing / in the corpse of a nation / for its congealed blood.' He
describes learning English as sucking 'their speech / in with my
mother's / infected milk'. 'Whatever / I throw up now', he says, 'is
still theirs.'[9] This is a grotesque poem, all the more when one
considers that it speaks the mind of one of the finest modern lyric
poets in the English language. It speaks, nevertheless, with a voice
of authentic bitterness, which may be compared with Gwenallt's
'Rhydcymerau' which (in English translation) refers contemptu-
ously to the English spoken in south Wales as 'the South's
bastardized English'.[10] The difference between the poems is that
Thomas has internalized the cultural disease, while Gwenallt
condemns it as a Welsh poet immune to its infection. In contrast
to this bitterness, John Tripp in 'Irony' strikes a sadder note:

> Think. One day this dry
> English pen, this arrogant
> instrument, will no longer
> be required. Then my short
> modest task will be done.[11]

For R. S. Thomas, English is a disease sucked in with his mother's
milk; for John Tripp, it is an instrument of the interloper, to be
laid aside when Welsh speech returns to the whole of Wales.

In an atmosphere that produced such contempt for the English
language in Wales, it is not surprising that other writers came
angrily to the defence of those who spoke it – their family and
friends, themselves, their people. John Davies's witty and acerbic
'How to Write Anglo-Welsh Poetry' should be understood in this
context. 'First, apologise for not being able / to speak Welsh', he
says. 'Go on: apologise. / Being Anglo-*any*thing is really tough.'[12]
The emotions energizing a poem like this are familial, democratic.
It is written in part on behalf of a maligned people, and in defence
of a reality and an identity that an exclusive passion for Welsh-
speaking Wales denies. John Davies's poem helps to remind us that
a sense of belonging to 'my people', as also in Tony Curtis's

'Pembrokeshire Seams',[13] for example, is frequently as strong among Anglo-Welsh poets as it is in their Welsh counterparts, and that both impart to the words a quite different connotation from that which Caradoc Evans gave to them. But still one might say that the tension expressed in 'How to Write Anglo-Welsh Poetry' is a tension within the family. It is a tension within individuals, too. John Tripp's poetry, for example, rather than implicitly condemning his English-speaking compatriots, generally breathes a democratic spirit, and may be seen to belong to the tradition, in Welsh and Anglo-Welsh poetry, which celebrates human brotherhood.

Not all Anglo-Welsh writers feel English to be a cause of national division or self-division. Gwyn Jones is one who expresses a strong sense of unity:

> When I talk with my friends from Welsh-speaking and English-speaking Wales, I am very conscious, whichever the language of our childhood, how much we had in common, and how little we stood apart in my own Sirhowy Valley, Jack and Glyn Jones's Merthyr, Tom Parry-Williams's Eryri, the Sir Benfro of Waldo Williams, Gwyn Thomas's Meadow Prospect, T. Glynne Davies's Hiraethog, Cwm Rhondda, Cwmdonkin, Cwm Eithin and Cwm Tydu.[14]

Wales, in Gwyn Jones's experience, is a conversation of Welsh-speaking and English-speaking friends. But, it seems reasonable to ask, in which language do they talk to each other? Probably, both; although that does not resolve the problem of priority. What can be said for certain is that Gwyn Jones, in affirming a common tradition, appeals to childhood and incants a litany of place-names: which are among the most familiar reactions of the Anglo-Welsh writer asserting his or her Welsh identity. Gwyn Jones, however, does acknowledge a division between his socialism, born in the Valleys, and the priorities of 'our contemporary Welsh-language patriots'.

It would be a simplification to say that the division between Welsh and Anglo-Welsh writers is between socialists and nationalists, or between urban and rural loyalties and values. The division is, however, an element within a complex experience, in which tension between secular and religious feelings also plays a significant part. With the rise in recent years of the new Welsh history a further polarization has occurred, between the traditional view of the organic community, based on 'the interpenetrative marriage of language and land',[15] and the idea that Wales is a construct made by the Welsh people. The former idea is represented eloquently by the philosopher J. R. Jones with his concept of *cydymdreiddiad*, the latter by the historian Gwyn A. Williams, whose key idea has been, significantly, rendered in free verse form by an Anglo-Welsh poet:

> Wales is a process.
> Wales is an artefact which the Welsh produce.
> The Welsh make and remake Wales
> day by day, year by year, generation after generation
> if they want to.[16]

But while the polarization between these ideas of Wales is to be observed in individuals and groups, writing is usually produced in English-speaking Wales from complicated mental and emotional cross-currents.

Writing in *Planet* 16, the prolific Welsh poet Bobi Jones,[17] who had learned the language as a schoolboy in Cardiff, argued that Anglo-Welsh writing originates in and is inspired by the 'colonialist predicament'. Anglo-Welsh writing, he says, is 'a perversion of normality, it is a grunt or a cry or an odour rising from a cultural wound of a special kind'. The view acknowledges the energies released by the predicament in Anglo-Welsh writing – in Gwyn Thomas, for example, 'the delightful masochism, the gusto in delineating demented and unnatural characters . . . the inexhaustible vigour in embodying an inferiority complex in a milieu of torrential cultural decadence'. The situation is perverted, nevertheless, the normal one being that 'the dragon can only have one tongue, and that Welsh'.

Some time later, in the same magazine, Tony Conran[18] published a piece on the English translation of Bobi Jones's *Selected Poems*. The review-article is called, mischievously, 'Anglo-Welsh Manqué?' In praising Bobi Jones as 'a very un-English poet indeed', Tony Conran also pays tribute to a complexity that is 'probably more Anglo-Welsh than Welsh, an acknowledgement of a discontinuity between the generations, a guilt and a healing'. Conran and Jones are of the same generation, and in effect

Conran is comparing the poetic virtues which Jones gained from writing in Welsh with the sense of loss which he himself and their Anglo-Welsh contemporaries have experienced. But the comparison is not to the disfavour of the latter.

> For most of us, Wales was a journey into an exile we were born with. We were heirs to a richness we could only apprehend as memories of childhood. We were third-generation immigrants into our own land, easier with English people, very often, than with our still Welsh-speaking compatriots. Threatened by both the ruling-class English intelligentsia we were trained to serve, and by the native Welsh culture that we felt had the birthright, we tried to make room for ourselves. We wrote elegies for lost Wales. We proclaimed that the Dragon had two tongues. We translated Welsh poetry.

To my mind, not the least interesting thing about this catalogue of woes is that it is also, in context, a boast of achievements. There is an indirection about it, of course. Largely because of their feelings of guilt and respect towards the Welsh language, it is almost impossible for Anglo-Welsh writers to speak well of themselves, except indirectly. But while some have at times exhibited a garrulousness and idiosyncrasy that plays Taffy to an English audience, Conran is surely right to imply that Anglo-Welsh literature is significant because it is not innocent of the complexity of experience, but responds to it. Indeed, Conran's criticism has shown an increasing confidence in developing this point, as he has done through his definition of Anglo-Welsh literature as the product of 'frontiers'.

> It is the literature of a March. These days the March is not a geographical feature. It can be anywhere – through my backyard in Bangor where my children are Welsh-speaking but I am not – through a Cardiff shop or a Llangollen office. Most people in Wales live lives that at some point or other are different because of this insidious March, snaking along between them and the complacency of being completely Welsh or completely English.[19]

Conran describes the March as 'insidious'. Yet it is clear that he thinks it better for a writer to respond to the pain inflicted by living on the March than to rest in complacency on either side of it. I shall say more later about different interpretations of the 'frontier' or 'border' situation of Anglo-Welsh writers.

In *The Cost of Strangeness* Tony Conran speculates that, in the Gwent of W. H. Davies, 'there was some seepage between the speakers of the two languages . . . about the right and proper things poetry should be used for, the right way to set about being a poet'.[20] Within a few pages he expands the idea to claim 'that what I have called "seepage" took place on all cultural levels between the two language-groups in Wales, and that this "seepage" is one of the reasons why Anglo-Welsh poetry belongs to us, the people of Wales, and is not to be simply hived off as interesting but minor English verse'. Other Anglo-Welsh critics, including Glyn Jones and Roland Mathias, have developed versions of the same idea. The Anglo-Welsh poet, it is argued, inherits the Welsh tradition of praise poetry, in which the poet is a craftsman and a member of the community, who uses his gift to honour and celebrate his people. By contrast, the English poet is an individualist, a bohemian playing his part on the fringes of his society, a purveyor of essentially private experience. Whatever exceptions there may be to the idea, on either side of the March (and providing we eliminate its original gender bias to include women poets), it is in general a useful one for delineating the field of choice open to the Anglo-Welsh poet.

One weakness of the idea is that it underestimates the positive influence of English literature on Anglo-Welsh writing. There is, for example, the influence of Wordsworth both on the pre-occupation with the solitary figure of poets like W. H. Davies and R. S. Thomas, and on the honouring of common experience which distinguishes poets as diverse as Idris Davies and Jean Earle. In its fear of contamination by Englishness, the dominant Anglo-Welsh ideology highlights the baleful influence of English models on Anglo-Welsh writing, and underplays the positive interaction of English and Welsh elements. We should be aware, for instance, of the influence of Anglo-American modernism on poets as distinctively Anglo-Welsh, and as different from each other, as David Jones, Dylan Thomas, Lynette Roberts, Tony Conran, and Gerard Casey in *South Wales Echo*.[21] The influence of elements of English Romanticism on Anglo-Welsh literature is a recurrent theme of this present book.

In Emyr Humphreys's view, 'the great choice of the twentieth century' is 'to be an exile or a native'.[22] The words are quoted from his answer to an interviewer who had asked him whether he, like Stephen Dedalus in *A Portrait of the Artist as a Young Man*, was trapped in 'the "triple net" of nationality, language and religion'. Humphreys replied that he was willingly trapped in the net. He acknowledged the 'enormous attractions' which exile holds for the artist, and described it as 'the rock' on which the modernist 'was able to perform and experiment'. But he is certain that 'the torch of creativity is in the hands of the natives now'. What is important in a shrunken world, in which 'exile has become meaningless', is 'standing in the one spot, exploring in depth what you have within the square mile'.

This is an important statement. Rather than being taken at face value, however, it should be understood in the context of the native as modernist, which is what Emyr Humphreys in his novels is. His absorption of lessons learnt from James Joyce and Virginia Woolf, among other modernist writers, and from film and modern painting, is evident in his use of interior monologue, ellipsis, juxtaposition, structural myth, cinematic techniques and other modernist strategies. In *Outside the House of Baal* and in the 'Land of the Living' sequence, he has emerged as a great social novelist, a novelist concerned, like the great Russian novelists of the nineteenth century, with the souls of his characters and the soul of their nation. Humphreys's major characters are persons, men and women with spiritual and sexual needs; they are whole human beings, acted upon by historical forces, responding to the pressures upon their society and nation. It would be a half-truth, though, to say that Humphreys employs modernist techniques to subvert modernist ideas of cellular individualism and isolated sensibility. It is clear that he knows how sharply the cords of the 'triple net' can cut into flesh and blood, and (especially in his preoccupation with the figure of Lloyd George) how individual ambition can subvert the values of Welsh community and nationhood. He knows also the cost of idealism, to both men and women, but especially to women who bear the cost of male dreams and impracticality. It is clear from his work as a whole that he understands the condition of the native who is an exile at home in Wales. Detachment is integral to his way of seeing, but he is equally effective at dealing with intimacy, so that we see his characters against the historical and religious background of their society, at the same time as we are made inward with their desires and ideals and betrayals.

Welsh-speaking Wales has proved to be a potent and mysterious 'other' for English-language writers. This imagined Wales has many different manifestations. One of them is a Wales which is not England, but which, on the whole, the English have constructed. I refer to a Wales invested with 'Celtic Magic'; Wales wrapped in Celtic twilight; picturesque Wales, which is a scenic route for romantics, but also a great source of imaginative potential, a cauldron of rebirth.

Matthew Arnold was an enemy of the Welsh language but a friend of the Celts and their 'natural magic'. What Arnold saw in Wales, and recorded in his lectures as professor of poetry at Oxford in 1865–6,[23] was a 'mystic' landscape, a country 'where the past still lives', and where 'tradition' and 'poetry' are identified with place. He recognized in *The Mabinogion* personages who are not medieval, but 'belong to an older, pagan, mythological world'. True to the contradictions of the idea of progress, he made a fatal distinction between material power and spiritual power. For Arnold, the 'Celtic genius' was virtually the lost soul of the Saxon body politic. His view of Wales was that of an outsider; it was compensatory; it had more to do with what he felt England was not, than with Wales. It was a distant view, a version of the mountain view, which is not only from a high place, but represents social and cultural differences.

Emyr Humphreys is a fierce critic of Matthew Arnold's idea and of its influence in Wales: 'It is not too crude a simplification to maintain that the Institutions of Wales, old and new, were prepared to abandon the mother tongue in exchange for a mess of pottage with Celtic Magic.'[24] Humphreys contrasts Arnold and Owen M. Edwards, both of whom made their 'appeal to a landscape'. Edwards, however, 'laid the foundation for a brilliant literary revival because he re-established the links between the Welsh people and their own past and made a new beginning possible'. Humphreys quotes a wonderful passage in which Edwards may sound, superficially, like Arnold describing the view westward from Llandudno, 'the eternal softness and mild light of the west; the low line of the mystic Anglesey':

It is all sacred. Every hill and every valley. Our land is a living thing, not a grave of forgetfulness under our feet. Every hill has its history, every locality its own romance, every part of the landscape wears its own particular glory. And to a Welshman, no other country can be like this. A Welshman feels that the struggles of his forefathers have sanctified every field, and the genius of his people has transformed every mountain into hallowed ground. And it is feeling like this that will make him a true citizen.

The difference of this from Arnold's appeal to Welsh landscape is, Humphreys says, that Edwards 'belonged to it'.[25]

Belonging, however, as Emyr Humphreys knows, is not a simple matter. John Cowper Powys, for example, had his family background in the English gentry, but made a great deal of his father's claim to an ancient Welsh heritage. As a young man living in Sussex in the first years of the twentieth century, and feeling himself to be a misfit in English society, Powys 'acquired a passion for everything Welsh'. His imagination had been fired by his father's tales of ancestral Wales. Now, 'the *idea* of Wales and the *idea* of Welsh mythology' drummed in his soul 'like an incantation'. Later he felt that, if he had been able to learn Welsh, 'perhaps the mysterious Invisible Presences of that land of enchantment would have helped me to renew and transform my being'.[26] He regarded Wales as a refuge, and he identified Wales with his idea of himself as a magician. Eventually, in 1935, after years of lecturing in America, he went to live in north Wales, where he remained until his death in 1963. Even before this move, however, in his romances set in Wessex, Powys had drawn a large measure of support for his magical view of life from Welsh mythology. Now, in *Owen Glendower* and *Porius*, he drew on ancient and medieval Welsh history and pseudo-history as well as myth. In a sense, Powys recreated Wales in his own image, as is evident in the following passage from *Owen Glendower*:

> The very geography of the land and its climatic peculiarities, the very nature of its mountains and rivers, the very falling and lifting of the mists that waver above them, all lend themselves, to a degree unknown in any other earthly region, to what might be called the *mytholology of escape*. This is the secret of the land. This is the secret of the people of the land.[27]

It would be easy to criticize Powys as one who used Wales for 'escapist' purposes. In a larger perspective, though, we can see that he found in Wales his spiritual home, a home for his mythopoeic imagination. This in turn may be described as a form of the religious sense, a form which requires an 'otherness', a numinous landscape haunted by 'mysterious invisible Presences'.[28]

Arthur Machen may be compared to Powys in this respect. As he grew older, Machen came to ascribe

> anything I may have accomplished in literature . . . to the fact that when my eyes were first opened in early childhood they had before them the vision of an enchanted land. As soon as I saw anything I saw Twm Barlwm, that mystic tumulus, the memorial of peoples that dwelt in that region before the Celts left the Land of Summer.

After many years of living in London, he looked in memory towards his childhood landscape in Gwent, towards the Holy Mountain by Abergavenny. 'It would shine, I remember, a pure blue in the far sunshine; it was a mountain peak in a fairy tale.'[29] The sense of enchantment is not dissimilar to Powys's, or to that which Dylan Thomas evokes in poems such as 'Fern Hill', 'In Country Sleep' and 'Poem in October'. In Dylan Thomas, the sense is heightened. It is a pagan sense, with a strong element of paganized Christianity. Religious language becomes integral to the landscape. Herons priest the shore, water prays, rain falls 'over the sea wet church the size of a snail'.[30] This Wales is a sacred country, like that described by Owen M. Edwards. But there is a difference. In Dylan Thomas's poems, and, despite their religious preoccupations, in Vernon Watkins's Taliesin poems and other poems set in Welsh landscapes, religion has lost its social function. The feeling engendered by the landscape has little to do with making a Welshman 'a true citizen'. Religion no longer binds together the members of a community in one body, as it does in the poems of Waldo Williams, for example. Instead, religion has become part of the natural world; it 'colours' Welsh landscape rather than expressing the mind of a people; it is a linguistic energy of the individual imagination rooted in childhood. It has become poetry, as Matthew Arnold said it would.

Some mountains are holy, as Arthur Machen reminds us. Mountains are also places of temptation. A poet may look down from on high on the people in the valley, feeling alienated, or knowing himself part of them. He may feel tension between the pull of the community below, and freedom to dream on the heights. The view from the mountain may present a choice between solitude and society. In 'The Mountain over Aberdare',[31] Alun Lewis looks down on a place full of social activity, or, haunted by its absence, a place in the grip of economic depression. But what he really sees is a kind of negative religious vision: 'Grey Hebron in a rigid cramp'; 'the church / Stretched like a sow beside the stream'; mourners 'singing hymns / That drift insidious as the rain'; women hugging 'Huge grief, and anger against God'. As the dusk falls,

> that white frock that floats down the dark valley
> Looks just like Christ; and in the lane
> The clink of coins among the gamblers
> suggests the thirty pieces of silver.

Significantly, he hears no other sound – the insidious drift of the hymns seems more a visual than an aural experience. The only sound he hears is a suggestion of ultimate betrayal. But whose? And of what?

What he sees, finally, is enigmatic:

> I watch the clouded years
> Rune the rough foreheads of these moody hills,
> This wet evening, in a lost age.

A rune is a human mark, a letter with associations of magic. But what does it mean? The place is dumb; its silence is like distance, a great distance between the place and the poet on the mountain. It is a silence which he fills with his deeply troubled, alienated view. Nothing speaks to him with its own meaning, its value within the community. No voice sounds in the poem except the poet's own. Yet it is clear, from this and other poems, that Lewis has internalized aspects of his community's religious and social values. His idealistic conception of 'love' recalls the world of the chapel. So also does the sense of guilt with which, here and elsewhere, Lewis torments himself.

The emotional drama of Glyn Jones's 'Merthyr'[32] is less complex than that of 'The Mountain over Aberdare'. There is a verbal and imagistic relish in his description of 'The vale, pink-roofed at sunset, a heavenly acre / Of tufted and irradiated tooth-paste'. He sees 'the liquid coal / Of rivers', hears 'the hooter's loud liturgic boom', smells 'Pit-clothes and rosin fragrant in a warm room'. To strangers, the poet says, 'Such sensations deck a ruinous scene': they ornament it gaudily. He then turns from the sensations:

> But far more than the scene, the legendary
> Walkers and actors of it, the memory
> Of neighbours, worthies, relatives . . .

Thus, Glyn Jones both sees as a stranger – and defamiliarizes by his way of seeing – and sees and feels as a native who honours his people, the people of the place. As Matthew Price, in Raymond Williams's *Border Country*, says of his native valley: 'The visitor sees beauty; the inhabitant a place where he works and has his friends.'[33] And, he might have added, the native who is also a 'borderer', like Glyn Jones and Williams himself, sees both, and sometimes feels the dual vision as an inner rift, that causes guilt.

Idris Davies, who was born in Rhymney in 1905, became a miner in the pit after he left school at fourteen, but later qualified as a teacher, and taught for some years in primary schools in England. He was both a Welsh-speaker and a lover of English Romantic poetry. The latter influenced his mountain view, which is, so to speak, one pole of the experience recorded in his sequences *Gwalia Deserta* and *The Angry Summer*:

> There in the mountain dusk the dream was born,
> The spirit fired, and the calm disturbed
> By the just anger of the blood.
> Wilder than the politician's yellow tongue
> And stronger than the demagogue's thunder,
> The insistent language of the dream would ring
> Through the dear and secret places of the soul.[34]

But he also wrote powerfully in the poems from within the communal experience of the Depression in south Wales. Consequently one of the most remarkable things about *Gwalia Deserta* and *The Angry Summer* is the balance they maintain between detachment and intimacy, between a mountain view and mountain language and Valley voices, and between romantic idealism and prophetic anger. Sadly, after *The Angry Summer*, Idris Davies lost his balance between detachment and solidarity, and prophecy and dream. *Tonypandy* voices his isolated and disorientated spirit more than it speaks for his community. Towards the end of his life, in 'Beyond the Black Tips', he tried to introduce the supernatural into his work. He may have been influenced in this by Vernon Watkins's *Ballad of the Mari Lwyd*, but Davies had none of Watkins's poetic confidence in his handling of the theme of the living and the dead. The achievement of his major sequences surely owed something to the fact that they were written outside Wales and some years after the events from which they seem to speak. But now the distance separating the poet from his subject is too great. It is a distance audible in the voice, which speaks of 'common cares / Of all the common days and common nights',[35] but in a language emptied of common experience, and incapable of a new transcendence.

One 'voice' of the Anglo-Welsh short story may be heard in Caradoc Evans's 'Be This Her Memorial':[36]

> Mice and rats, as it is said, frequent neither churches nor poor men's homes. The story I have to tell you about Nanni – the Nanni who was hustled on her way to prayer-meeting by the Bad Man, who saw the phantom mourners bearing away Twm Tybach's coffin, who saw the Spirit Hounds and heard their moanings two days before Isaac Penparc took wing – the story I have to tell you contradicts that theory.

It is a detached narrative voice – detached, that is, from its subject; with its audience, it is confiding. The story is 'about Nanni', who is at once identified as superstitious, simple-minded, belonging to a backward rural community. Hers would not be the voice of amused epigram with which the story begins, or of an interest in theory with which the second sentence ends. We can be sure from the tone that Nanni's own story would not be like this one. For the voice of the narrator is literary, intellectual and in distancing himself from Nanni the storyteller persuades the reader to collude with his superior knowingness. His is a voice familiar in English literature: humorous at the expense of its subject, and capable of wit and biting satire. It is a voice that uses a word like 'peasantry' to describe the rural Welsh, and is honed for a 'superior' audience.

The story skilfully exploits the distance between two different worlds.

Gwyn Thomas's narrative voice is quite different, as the beginning of 'And a Spoonful of Grief to Taste' immediately reveals:

> You know how it is in our part of the valley. They are mad for singing in choirs. If you can sing a bit, you get roped into a choir and if you can keep your voice somewhere near the note and your morals facing due north where the cold is, someone with pull is bound to notice you and before you know it you are doing a nice steady job between the choir pieces. If you sound like a raven and cause the hair of the choir leader to drop out like hail when you go for a hearing, you mope about in the outer darkness acting as foot-warmer for the boys in the Exchange.

The tone and speech rhythms are quite different from Caradoc Evans's. At first, though, it may seem as if 'you' is being appealed to at the expense of 'they', as Evans divides the reader from Nanni. But in the next sentence 'you' becomes almost indistinguishable from 'they': both are of the same community, and the story is being told for them as well as about them. The voice here is characteristic of Gwyn Thomas's narrative voice, which speaks for an individual or a small group of individuals – his 'dark philosophers' – who live in and share the hardships and to some degree the values and way of life of a community, but also keep a critical distance from it. Thus the speaker is irreverent, disrespectful towards the people 'mad for singing' and their morality, and towards religious language ('outer darkness'). Nevertheless, he is familiar with the people and their ways and beliefs, and he speaks their language.

Gwyn Thomas's art is based on his gifts as a great talker. It is excitingly unpredictable; you never know what is coming next, what extraordinary, hilarious flight of fancy, what wry wisdom, what bitter or tragic note. Thomas ascribed his art to his people, who 'spoke with a boisterous artistry'. He derived from them both what is comic and what is sombre in his work. The way in which he played down his individual talent shows his solidarity with them.

> Humour is a sense of the incongruous or absurd, an aggravated sense of the contrast between man's divine promise and his shambling,

shabby reality. There was enough incongruity between the way my people lived in the Rhondda of my early manhood, and the way in which they would have wanted to live, to have nourished at least ten thousand humorists of the first rank. But of course about the humour produced from such a situation there will be hints of the most extreme savagery; and the artist into whose spirit it may have entered too deeply will find his main task to be the rendering of his anger bearable to himself and acceptable to others.[37]

These are moving words, but there is something in them that may give us pause. Is it always desirable that anger produced by such a situation of deprivation should be made acceptable to others? And who are the others: the people themselves or an external audience? In Gwyn Thomas's case, the answer is both. He was an exuberant humorist, with a vein of tragedy. His writings entertain English and Welsh, without betraying the latter to the former as figures of fun. It is sometimes a near thing, however, in his narrative voice: a touch too much exaggeration, a fraction too much critical detachment, and the people become a comic turn for the superior amusement of outsiders.

In writing and rewriting *Border Country*, Raymond Williams took great care not to write in what had come to be seen in England as a 'Welsh style'.[38] This was a style of extreme verbal inventiveness, using highly coloured figurative language, which derived in part from an aspect of James Joyce and was identified most famously with Dylan Thomas. In Raymond Williams's view the style served a version of what he sought in all his writing and thinking to avoid: escapism. Williams did not want to escape from the working class and the struggle for social change, and he did not want to escape into the past of childhood and an abstracted, static pastoral world.

Border Country expresses a strong feeling for the land, for what was indeed the country of Raymond Williams's childhood. He sees it, however, not as a closed world, but in terms of complex living experience.

To Harry and Ellen, this was not strange country. Harry had been born in Llangattock, only seven miles north-west, and Ellen in Peterstone, three miles farther north. A river runs between Llangattock and Peterstone, and that is the border with England. Across the river, in

Peterstone, the folk speak with the slow, rich, Herefordshire tongue, that could still be heard in Ellen. On this side of the river is the quick Welsh accent, less sharp, less edged, than in the mining valleys which lie beyond the Black Mountains, to the south and west, but clear and distinct – a frontier crossed in the breath.[39]

For Matthew Price as a man, son of Harry and Ellen, 'border country' is not only his loved childhood landscape; it is also an interior division, the 'border' which Williams described elsewhere as 'that border country so many of us have been living in: between custom and education, between work and ideas, between love of place and an experience of change'.[40] This is 'the real Hardy country' and Williams, with his attention focused on social experience, only gradually came to emphasize the Welshness of his experience. *Border Country* dramatizes the tension within Matthew between native and exile, child and man, one who belongs and the intellectual who has learned to measure the experience of change; but it shows the tension in terms of the connections within the 'border' situation. Williams's achievement in the novel depends crucially upon his creation of a voice that crosses the frontier 'in the breath', connecting past and present, and linking different levels of experience.

It is futile to define 'Anglo-Welsh' narrowly. Is the author of *Border Country* Anglo-Welsh, or Welsh? Or is he English, because he writes in English and concerns himself with social experiences that are common to England and Wales? And does it matter? Is it not enough that we can read him with pleasure and profit? But who are 'we'? This is a question that arises repeatedly with Anglo-Welsh literature, which is a literature concerned with identity, consciously or unconsciously. Rarely with the identity of an autonomous individual, in ways familiar in post-war English and American fiction; usually with a person who relates to a people, a community, a society, a nation. As I have argued in this chapter, it is by voice and what sounds in the voice – what 'things' the writer is made of – that we may know Anglo-Welsh writing. It is by how the voice incorporates or interacts with other voices; how it crosses frontiers within the person, between one and others, between the living and the dead.

A kind of dialogue between the living and the dead frequently occurs in Anglo-Welsh literature. But talk across that frontier is rarely comfortable, as the living feel responsible to the dead, and guilty for having survived. It is a situation that releases strong emotion, as in poem XXII of *Gwalia Deserta*:

> I stood in the ruins of Dowlais
> And sighed for the lovers destroyed
> And the landscape of Gwalia stained for all time
> By the bloody hands of progress.
> I saw the ghosts of the slaves of The Successful Century
> Marching on the ridges of the sunset
> And wandering among derelict furnaces,
> And they had not forgotten their humiliation,
> For their mouths were full of curses.
> And I cried aloud, O what shall I do for my fathers
> And the land of my fathers?
> But they cursed and cursed and would not answer
> For they could not forget their humiliation.[41]

Here it is the poet who is dwarfed by the mountain view. The ghosts he saw are ghosts of 'slaves' wandering among ruins, but he also saw them as giants, 'Marching on the ridges of the sunset'. With its invocation of the curses and silence of his 'fathers', this is one of the great heroic statements of modern Anglo-Welsh poetry. Its heroism is that of a tradition of defeat, which raises questions of ultimate meaning. As often happens in Anglo-Welsh writing, emotional and imaginative power springs from a sense of political or national humiliation, and the poet is guilt-stricken at what he feels to be the condemnation of his dead fathers. In the work of poets such as Idris Davies and John Tripp and Roland Mathias, guilt is compounded by the feeling that the cost of their individual vision is betrayal, and Tripp and Mathias in particular, acutely aware of their lack of the Welsh language, often present themselves not as strangers only, but as trespassers in their native land.

A gentler mountain view, which connects the living and the dead in a Welsh landscape, may be perceived in the work of women poets who have come into prominence in the past thirty years. In that of Gillian Clarke, for example, who, in her published talk 'The Voice of the Tribe', describes what she sees from a window of her home in Ceredigion:

> From where I write I see a landscape open like a book, a landscape of
> valleys and hills typical of the view from the study window or writing

desk of many a Welsh writer from any of the seven counties of Wales. I can see a hamlet a mile away, and when night falls I will see its lit windows, and the lights of cars coming and going from the farms. I know the names of all the farms and cottages, and those who live in them. I can name the fields on my side of the valley, and a few on the other side. Valleys, and a land that is tilted to face its neighbour, makes for tight communities and open lives.[42]

If there is a suggestion of romantic idealism here that would make the cynical reach for their Caradoc Evans, it is well to remember that this is the language of gratitude. Here, the writer is giving something back to her home ground. More realistic, it seems to me, are the social and personal differences between Welsh people that Emyr Humphreys depicts 'in one of the four corners of Wales' in *A Toy Epic*.[43] But gratitude is one of the abiding motives of Welsh writing in English, and it may, understandably, gloss over divisions within the society. Anne Cluysenaar is not untypical when she describes her motive in writing a poem as wanting 'to give something back',[44] and although Cluysenaar is not Welsh, it is perhaps significant that she has written her strongest poetry – a poetry of connection to the land and of relationships across the generations – since moving to Wales. Ruth Bidgood, also, uses her poetry to speak for others:

> I am a latecomer, but offer
> speech to the nameless, those
> who are hardly a memory, those
> whose words were always faint
> against the deafening darkness
> of remotest hills.[45]

The land that is seen as the ground of native solidarity, a kind of material memory in which the dead still live, can also be used for offensive purposes, to repel intruders, as it is by Lynette Roberts, a poet of an earlier generation, in 'Fifth of the Strata':

> And before tomorrow
> England will be
> For thousands of years
> Lying below us
> A submerged village

> . . .
> And sharp shell and shale
> Will arise for our freedom . . .[46]

More often in Anglo-Welsh writing, however, the land is used as a defence against intruders and the dilution of Welsh identity.

It is in a feeling for the land of Wales that Welsh writers in English with different and even opposing views – socialist and nationalist, secular and religious, traditionalist and modernist – come close together. In *The Fight for Manod*, the third volume of Raymond Williams's trilogy, Matthew Price speaks of his occasional sense of 'something other' in the land: 'Some particular shape: the line of a hedge, the turn of a path round a wood, or in movement sometimes, the shadow of a cloud that bends in a water-course, or then again a sound, the wind in wires, wind tearing at a chimney.' 'What I really seem to feel', he says, 'is these things as my body. As my own physical existence, a material continuity in which there are no breaks. As if I was feeling through them, not feeling about them.'[47] Some people would describe the feeling as religious, but Williams (who is thinking with his character here) insists on its material nature. Indeed, the feeling is very much part of his socialist imagination, and it helps to shape his narration of almost 25,000 years of human experience in *People of the Black Mountains*. The feeling is not abstracted from the historical making of communities, but is all of a piece with Matthew Price's sense of 'something else' that has moved through the people, and 'belongs to this country: a pure idea, a pure passion, for a different world'.

It is interesting to set the passage from *The Fight for Manod* alongside one from the conclusion of Ned Thomas's *The Welsh Extremist*:

> Nor is this a bad place and time to live; there is an attraction about the modern Welsh culture and its resistance to the inhumanity of the machine. The fields are greener and the sea bluer because of past generations. There is a kind of intensity here that flows below the slack surface of British normality, a constant pressure on the individual to contribute something to the community, to do something for it.[48]

Some years after writing this Ned Thomas realized that the central, poetic sentence – 'The fields are greener and the sea bluer because of past generations' – was an unconscious 'translated semi-quotation' from a poem by Waldo Williams.[49] Ned Thomas's unconscious memory is a nice instance of the way in which physical identification with the land belongs with a strong sense of community through the ages in writing from Wales: he had felt it, as Waldo Williams had done, and many generations before them. The passage from *The Welsh Extremist* had a special importance for John Tripp, and it is gratifying to think of the three writers, the Welsh and the Anglo-Welsh, meeting, as it were, in those words. But it is hard to draw clear-cut boundaries round creative meetings. In his poem 'Pa Beth yw Dyn?' ('What is Man?') Waldo Williams wrote: 'Beth yw gwladgarwch? Cadw tŷ? / Mewn cwmwl tystion' ('Patriotism, what's that? Keeping house / In a cloud of witnesses').[50] Who, then, is to number the witnesses and say which ones are to be excluded? Raymond Williams's feeling for the land of Wales is not less Welsh for being, also, in the tradition of John Clare and Thomas Hardy, any more than Waldo Williams's is for his love of certain English Romantic poets. There is, though, among the things that link the Welsh and Anglo-Welsh writers and distinguish them from their English counterparts, a sense of creative possibility, which is identified with the land and the people. This may take the form of political utopianism or religious hope, or both.

Finally, it may be recalled that Raymond Williams's border country is also the focal landscape of David Jones's 'The Sleeping Lord', a poem that identifies *all* hope with the land of Wales and the cultural and religious renewal that it symbolizes. But the 'border' as David Jones apprehends it is different from Raymond Williams's border 'between custom and education, between work and ideas, between love of place and an experience of change'. For Jones, 'man is a "borderer", he is the sole inhabitant of a tract of country where matter marches with spirit, so that whatever he does, good or bad, affects the economy of those two domains'.[51] The March land is metaphysical territory, with a culture and politics that are integral to it. When all hope seems lost, it is impossible to predict what may awake in that region. As the Saxon sentinel fears:

> you never know *what* may be
> – not hereabouts.
> No wiseman's son *born* do know
>   not in these whoreson March-lands
>   of this Welshry.[52]

'The True Wales of my Imagination': Welsh and English in the Poetry of R. S. Thomas, David Jones and Gillian Clarke

R. S. Thomas's view of Wales as a young man was self-confessedly a romantic one. Wales was where he had lived, in Holyhead from the age of five. Now, as a theological student in Llandaff in the mid-1930s, Cardiff did not correspond to his vision of Wales. Travelling home to Holyhead on the railway line that runs along the Marches, he would look 'Westwards' where

> the sky would be ablaze, reminding one of the battles of the past. Against that radiance the hills rose dark and threatening as if full of armed men waiting for a chance to attack. To the west, therefore, there was a romantic, dangerous, mysterious land.[1]

The view may suggest an English rather than a Welsh way of seeing Wales. It is reminiscent, for example, of Matthew Arnold looking at 'mystic Anglesey' and invoking 'Wales – Wales, where the past still lives, where every place has its tradition, every name its poetry, and where the people, the genuine people, still knows this past, this tradition, this poetry, and lives with it, and clings to it', which Arnold contrasts with 'the prosperous Saxon' who has lost his cultural memory.[2] Thomas's view from the train seems closer to this than to the view of any Welsh-language poet, for traditionally the Welsh poet writes as a member of a historical community, not as an outsider. We may recall, however, that the young Thomas did assume the privilege of addressing himself to his people, which implies, to some degree, a sense of belonging. For example, he wrote a poem called 'Welsh History' beginning 'We were a people';[3] another, equally well known, 'Welsh Landscape', begins with romantic imagery:

> To live in Wales is to be conscious
> At dusk of the spilled blood
> That went to the making of the wild sky

and ends by describing the Welsh as

> an impotent people,
> Sick with inbreeding,
> Worrying the carcase of an old song.[4]

Thomas's role in such poems is both priestly and prophetic, and therefore more Welsh than English, though he writes from an elevated position above his society, rather than as a man who intimately belongs.

In the autobiographical 'No-one', in which he speaks of himself in the third person, Thomas tells us that, during the Second World War, the parish at which he was curate at that time (1940–2), Hanmer in the Marches,

> was in the flightpath of the German aeroplanes as they made for Merseyside. Every night, weather permitting, the aeroplanes would pass overhead on their way in, and they soon started getting on the curate's nerves, not because of fear so much as disgust and despair at the thought that they were on their way to drop their fiendish loads on helpless women and children. (*As*, 49)

In sentiment and expression this recollection is curiously conventional. In this it accords, perhaps, with Thomas's non-involvement as a pacifist. It certainly indicates that his centre of passionate concern lay elsewhere.

On the next page of 'No-one', we read:

> So hateful was it to the curate to think of the destruction occurring almost every night, and such was his *hiraeth* for the hills in the distance (Moel Fama could be seen quite clearly to the north-west), that he decided to learn Welsh as a means of enabling him to return to the true Wales. (*As*, 50)

Thomas turns, then, from thoughts of the war and its destructiveness to 'the true Wales', which recalls what he also describes as 'the true Wales of my imagination' (*As*, 10). The words and his description of his *hiraeth* acknowledge his Romanticism, but, as far as 'the true Wales' is concerned, not in order to subject it to critical scrutiny.

The mission of the German bombers inevitably recalls the earlier description of the sky 'ablaze'. But the blaze to the west is different from that of a city burning as a result of the blitz. The traveller on the railway line along the Marches had been thrilled by a view in which danger was subsumed by romance and mystery. Past battles had given a radiance to the sky over Wales. The images were more glorious and awe-inspiring than they were threatening. They betokened a Wales that defended itself against invasion from England.

In 'No-one' Thomas ascribes the depopulation of the Welsh hill-country and poverty and social deprivation to 'English oppression' (As, 58–9). He tells us this caused 'a great deal of bitterness' in his earlier poems. The conflict that emerges in these poems is between this idea of English oppression and his idea of the true Wales. This is especially marked in poems he wrote after the war, when, in an atmosphere of heightened Welsh nationalist feeling, he became more political, participating, for example, in a protest aimed at preventing the army from extending its camp at Trawsfynydd.

The conflict from which the poems spring was complicated by psychological tensions, and widened into a conflict between an old order based on the land and the modern world of the machine, and, in Coleridgean terms, between imaginative and mechanical modes of apprehending reality. Thomas says that it was at Manafon, Montgomeryshire, where he became rector in 1942, that he 'became conscious of the conflict that exists between dream and reality'. Here, the 'little bourgeois, well-bred, with the mark of the church and library upon' him, found himself 'amongst tough, materialistic, hard-working people, who measured one another by the acre and by the pound, Welshmen who had turned their backs on their cultural inheritance' (As, 11). He wondered what was in the minds of 'solitary beings in the fields hoeing or docking swedes, hour after hour'.

But if the story of Thomas's earlier poetry, from The Stones of the Field (1946), to Pietà (1966), is a story of conflict between dream and reality, it is not possible to make a conventional distinction between these terms, in which one represents Wales and the other England. For Thomas revolts not only against England but against the Wales he sees in the twentieth century – Anglicized, urbanized, eager to sell its heritage to gain commercial advantage – in the name of a Welsh-speaking Wales which corresponds to his idea of a national culture. 'The true Wales of my imagination' is neither Anglicized nor bilingual present-day Wales.

The conflict is complicated by Thomas's ambivalent attitude towards the figure of the 'peasant'. Iago Prytherch is represent-ative not of an ideal Welsh culture but of men who work the soil and are close to it. 'A Peasant'[5] introduces Iago Prytherch as 'an ordinary man of the bald Welsh hills', whom Thomas depicts 'Docking mangels . . . / . . . with a half-witted grin / Of satis-faction', or ploughing. But the ordinariness is problematic.

Picturing Prytherch by the fire at night Thomas says: 'There is something frightening in the vacancy of his mind'. Thomas's fear and repugnance then receive reproof. Prytherch is Thomas's teacher, his 'clothes, sour with years of sweat / And animal contact, shock the refined, / But affected, sense with their stark naturalness'. Refinement and affectation, one might think, describe also the view of the young romantic who rejected the reality of Wales in favour of his dream. But Thomas evidently did not think of it in this way. And it would be simplistic to do so. What after all is the reality of Wales? Welsh identity is a contested site. Between Welsh separatism or an independent Wales that is part of Europe at one extreme and absorption into Britishness at the other, there are a number of competing ideologies and aspirations.

Thomas proceeds to hold Prytherch up for our admiration:

> Yet this is your prototype, who, season by season
> Against siege of rain and the wind's attrition,
> Preserves his stock, an impregnable fortress
> Not to be stormed even in death's confusion.
> Remember him, then, for he, too, is a winner of wars,
> Enduring like a tree under the curious stars.

As these lines show, 'A Peasant' is a war poem. But Thomas naturalizes and universalizes the war, making Prytherch endure 'like a tree' against the forces of nature, including death.

Prytherch is 'a peasant' and 'your prototype', a stark, natural being, but he is more ambiguous than he may appear. Thomas says of himself that he 'had to show that he was a Welshman by using names that could not possibly be English ones. He called his first character . . . Iago Prydderch, spelling it Prytherch so that his English readers would pronounce it correctly'(As, 54). Prytherch is a Welshman, and his naming is a political act, albeit a compromise on Thomas's part, since he is aware of the needs of English readers. Clearly, it is not meant to exclude the latter, but it puts them in their place, ensuring that they accord Prytherch respect. But Prytherch also represents 'Welshmen who had turned their backs on their cultural inheritance'. Hence, in part, the vacancy of mind Thomas ascribes to him.

Another Thomas war poem, 'The Evacuee',[6] is also really about the conflict between mechanical civilization and the old rural order. The girl evacuated from the city wakes and comes downstairs in the farmhouse:

> The sounds and voices were a rough sheet
> Waiting to catch her, as though she leaped
> From a scorched story of the charred past.

The pun on story/storey transposes her from being a victim of the blitz to a figure in the myth that opposes country to city. 'And so she grew,' we are told, 'a shy bird in the nest / Of welcome that was built about her, / Home now after so long away / In the flowerless streets of the drab town.' She has suffered, it seems, not from an air-raid, but from deracination: uprooting and removal to the homeless, flowerless town.

Thomas's romantic lineage is plain to see in such a poem – ultimately Wordsworth, but more immediately Edward Thomas, whose idea of 'home', and unrealized longing to belong, was identified with Wales. A stronger influence on the earthiness of the Prytherch poems was probably Patrick Kavanagh's *The Great Hunger*. But detecting influences is less important than realizing that for Thomas Prytherch was not only a teacher but a liberator. It was not just that the very 'vacancy' of his mind enabled Thomas, as it were, to construct his poetry in that emptiness, finding his deepest concerns in Prytherch's life on the land in Welsh border country, and using Prytherch to conduct a quarrel with himself.[7] It was also that the figure helped him to emerge from the shadow of W. B. Yeats.

What Prytherch liberated Thomas from may be seen in 'Homo Sapiens 1941':

Murmuration of engines in the cold caves of air,
And, daring the starlight above the stiff sea of cloud,
Deadly as a falcon brooding over its prey
In a tower of spirit-dazzling and splendid light,
Pedestrian man holds grimly on his way.[8]

The last line here plods in the down-to-earth way that was to characterize the Prytherch poems, in which Thomas exchanged 'the stiff sea of cloud' for 'a stiff sea of clods', but the preceding lines are a chamber of echoes, mainly of Yeats. Indeed, Yeats's language and imagery so dominate the poem that it suggests *his* attitude towards heroic daring, and *his* mysticism of action, contrary to its ostensible message and to Thomas's pacifism.

It was however a linguistic, and not entirely an ideological, liberation from Yeats that Thomas found in the elemental language associated with Prytherch. The lyricism characteristic of Thomas at his best works in terms of a spare, 'pure', natural imagery – a language analogous to the Welsh mountain streams which, indeed, he invokes as metaphors for Welsh speech   and is not Yeatsian in the way that 'Homo Sapiens 1941' is. Yeats was, nevertheless, as a poet speaking to, and to some extent for, his people, a powerful model for Thomas. It is evident that Yeats's example, as an Irish poet writing in English, encouraged Thomas in his aspiration to fulfil a traditional role of the Welsh poet. And in this respect, R. S. Thomas did indeed play a leading role in creating an English-language literature based on the model of the Irish literary renaissance, with the aim of bringing what were perceived as Welsh cultural values to a non-Welsh-speaking audience.[9] This was, however, a role which, for Thomas, with his negative view of 'Anglo-Welshness', was fraught with a sense of painful contradiction.

From the beginning, Thomas's quarrel with the Welsh people, on the grounds of what he sees as their betrayal of their heritage, is also a quarrel with himself, with everything that makes him less than truly Welsh. At times this results in self-hatred – most painfully in 'It Hurts Him to Think' in *What is a Welshman?*[10] The strength of disgust at himself as an 'Anglo-Welsh' poet has to be registered; but there is no reason to suppose that this entails for Thomas a rejection of 'the magic of English as a medium of poetry',[11] while his prose makes abundantly clear his gratitude (not just his debt) to English Romantic poets and thinkers, especially Wordsworth, Coleridge and Keats, and the American Wallace Stevens.

The organic metaphor of 'the corpse of a nation' in 'It Hurts Him to Think' exemplifies Thomas's disgust at Anglicized Wales. It looks back, for instance, to 'an impotent people, / Sick with inbreeding, / Worrying the carcase of an old song' in 'Welsh Landscape' and 'the putrefying of a dead / Nation' in 'Reservoirs'.[12] Given Thomas's sense of English as an infectious disease in Wales it is no wonder that he speaks of this 'diabolical bilingualism' (As, 21) or feels that 'An Anglo-Welsh writer is neither one thing nor the other. He subsists in no-man's-land between two cultures' (As, 22). While in some writings (such as the poem 'The Old Language' in An Acre of Land) he blames the English for the plight of Wales, his quarrel is more often with his own people. 'Reservoirs' is typical:

> I have walked the shore
> For an hour and seen the English
> Scavenging among the remains
> Of our culture, covering the sand
> Like the tide and, with the roughness
> Of the tide, elbowing our language
> Into the grave that we have dug for it.[13]

Thomas's animosity towards England on political grounds, however, should not be glossed over. As he wrote in 'A Year in Llŷn', at the time when the Berlin Wall came down:

> England has been far more cunning than the Communists. Instead of crushing us with an iron fist, what she has done is erode our identity inch by inch, sugaring the pill at the same time. (As, 166)

It is his engagement with his people that distinguishes Thomas as a poet from his English contemporaries, and relates him to the central tradition of Welsh poetry. A sketch of this would show its origination in the sixth century with Aneirin and Taliesin, celebrants of heroic deeds in a warrior princedom, and its adaptation to changes in Welsh society over the centuries, so that an idea of the poet as a voice of the tribe continues into the twentieth century. I am not concerned here with the details and complications of this history, or with the great differences between poets or thought-worlds belonging to different ages; I want only to emphasize the continuity of an idea of poetic function, which is available to Thomas and other Welsh poets (in either language) for them to adapt to their needs in the modern period.

Thomas's pastoral role fits into this tradition, albeit uneasily, as we see in 'A Priest to His People'. The uneasiness is present in a savage, but uncertain, humour, in references to 'men of Wales' as 'wantoners' and to 'your sweaty females', and in the way in which the poet turns the men's 'scorn even / of the refinements of art and the mysteries of the Church' into scorn for his own 'invective'. He sees the men now as part of the land ('Men of bone, wrenched from the bitter moorland'), and asks whether they detected 'My true heart wandering in a wood of lies', in which the lies were, presumably, his initial romanticism. It is a poem in which one romantic myth drives out another, a myth which enables a poetry that draws its life from an idea of the people replacing the myth of an embittered if dream-clouded isolation:

> I have taxed your ignorance of rhyme and sonnet,
> Your want of deference to the painter's skill,
> But I know, as I listen, that your speech has in it
> The source of all poetry, clear as a rill
> Bubbling from your lips;[14]

The organic metaphor of speech containing 'the source of all poetry' implies a close connection between people, language, and land; indeed that a culture is part of the land, as natural as water.

'The Bush' is a later development of this romantic concept:

> in this country
> of failure, the rain
> falling out of a black
> cloud in gold pieces there
> are none to gather,
> I have thought often
> of the fountain of my people
> that played beautifully here
> once in the sun's light
> like a tree undressing.[15]

The poem speaks of 'this country / of failure' and locates the organic unity of people and land, which was the source of beauty, in the past. This is ultimately a romantic concept, and Thomas deploys the traditional romantic symbols of fountain and tree. There is, however, a danger of overstating Thomas's Romantic (or romantic) leanings at the expense of his mysticism, which is the informing spirit of some of his finest poems, and appears in his prose, at least as early as 'Dau Gapel' ('Two Chapels' (1948)).[16] There, Thomas contrasts two 'visions', called up by two different chapels. At Maes-yr-Onnen, he 'realised that there was really no such thing as time, no beginning and no end but that everything is a fountain welling up from immortal God'. At Soar-y-Mynydd, he 'saw the soul of a special type of man, the Cymro or Welshman'. 'Here, in the soil and the dirt and the peat do we find life and heaven and hell, and it is in these surroundings that a Welshman should forge his soul.' Thomas chooses this latter vision over 'mysticism and other-worldliness', but his feeling for the former is palpable. In my view it is not so much that he has to make a choice between the visions, but that he needs to reconcile them, uniting timelessness with an earth-rooted, religious Welsh culture, and this is what his poetry attempts, with stresses that result from his own sense that the visions may be incompatible, together with the extreme difficulty of reconciling either vision with the Wales in which he actually lives. The important essay 'Abercuawg', to which I shall return, is a later, much more philosophically sophisticated, but equally mystical, treatment of the validity of vision.

It is interesting to note the place of Christianity in Thomas's theme of Welsh culture and nationality as it emerges in his earlier poems. One thing that can be seen is that his favourite image of the Tree takes precedence over the Cross. That is to say, the specific Christian meaning is one among many, and not the most important. In 'The Tree', the speaker, Owain Glyndŵr ascribes 'the thought' that grew in his mind to his harpist's song: 'The thought grew to a great tree / . . . The far tribes rallied to its green / Banner waving in the wind; / Its roots were nourished with their blood.'[17] Once more a Thomas 'war' poem works through organic metaphor, and is about the binding relationship between a Welshman, his people and the land.

'You cannot live in the present, / At least not in Wales', Thomas says in 'Welsh Landscape'. In fact the poet shows no wish to live in the present, if that means living in 'the contemporary world of the machine', whether the machine be aeroplane or tractor. The early poem 'Cynddylan on a Tractor'[18] would seem to identify Thomas as a backward-looking pastoralist. Thomas here employs the familiar strategy of ironic contrast, naming his 'new man', who is 'part of the machine, / His nerves of metal and his blood oil' after the seventh-century king of Powys, subject of 'Canu Heledd', the great Welsh cycle of poems, which, in the manner of Welsh elegy, memorializes a destroyed culture. Ned Thomas is right, however, to claim a philosophical basis for R. S. Thomas's 'critique of technology', which 'is seen, long before it becomes hardware, as a powerful but imprisoning mode of thought'.[19] Rather than being nostalgic for the horse-drawn plough, 'Cynddylan on a Tractor' regrets the 'new man's' lack of vision: he does not see the sun 'Kindling all the hedges' or hear the birds singing. Birdsong is integral to the timeless 'place' which in 'Abercuawg' R. S. Thomas will later present as a vision of his once-and-future Wales. It is to this that Cynddylan is blind and deaf. 'Cynddylan on a Tractor' *may* be seen as reactionary, nostalgic pastoral, but is better understood, I think, as an early and relatively crude poetic statement of R. S. Thomas's belief that the true Wales *is* a vision, a place of creative being.

Acknowledging the bitterness in his poems about the political and social problems of Wales, Thomas adds: 'And yet behind and around everything there was the beauty and freshness of nature' (*As*, 55). Thomas's use of organic language, which is rooted in his love of nature in Wales, may be seen as limiting the range of his poetry, by virtually necessitating his rejection of urban civilization. But it is also the means of his survival and, to an extent, his creative reinvention as a poet. In the later poetry (beginning with *H'm*, 1972), his use of language drawn from nature forces him to confront its own decay in face of the advance of the machine.

> Among the forests
> Of metal the one human
> Sound was the lament of
> The poets for deciduous language.[20]

He meets the crisis of meaning in religious language rooted in organic metaphor by turning simultaneously to a theology of the *via negativa* and to the language of the new physics.

His organic language also enabled him, in his poetry written after his move to Aberdaron in 1967, and especially after his retirement from the priesthood in 1978, to achieve a sense of belonging to the Wales he had long sought. As he said of himself in *Autobiographies*, 'finding himself in a totally Welsh community in Aberdaron, he no longer felt it necessary to emphasize his Welshness, only to accept it as a completely natural fact' (*As*, 77). 'Natural' is the key word. He described living on the Llŷn as being 'as if we had crawled along a branch suspended in time' (*As*, 114). Now, the tree imagery allows him to figure himself as part of the 'tree' of Wales; as he says in 'The Small Country', 'I grow old, / . . . breaking my speech / from the perennial tree / of my people and holding it in my blind hand.'[21] At a profound level, a poet's destiny is enfolded in his language, seeded in his resources of metaphor and symbol. Not surprisingly, Thomas's prayer is that his grave will be

> somewhere within sight
> of the tree of poetry
> that is eternity wearing
> the green leaves of time.[22]

What he had perceived earlier in the land of Wales, as well as its beauty, was the result of past conflict, wars other than the Second World War: sacrificial blood, blood of the Welsh 'tribes'. He had seen that, in a sense, this still flows:

> To live in Wales is to be conscious
> At dusk of the spilled blood
> That went to the making of the wild sky,
> Dyeing the immaculate rivers
> In all their courses.[23]

In the words of another poem, 'Welsh History', Thomas gestures towards his people arising to 'greet each other in a new dawn', or arising 'Armed, but not in the old way', as the earlier and later endings have it.[24] But in attacking English oppression the pacifist Thomas is careful to place his celebrations of violent action in the past. In this respect, he can be said to play variations on the ancient Celtic 'defeat-tradition', which is also a staple of later romantic views of Wales. Past sacrifices have helped to create the spiritual relation between people and land. In a sense, the spirit itself is present in the land, like blood dyeing the rivers. Wales is a richly poetic reality, but at the expense of present political power. Matthew Arnold had said the same thing; the difference is that R. S. Thomas bitterly regrets it.

Another significant difference is that Thomas's vision of Wales contains hope for the future. It is in terms of his Coleridgean belief in imagination as that which enables us, as creative beings, to approach God, that R. S. Thomas defines Abercuawg:

> [Man] is always on the verge of comprehending God, but insomuch as he is a mortal creature, he never will. Nor will he ever see Abercuawg. But through striving to see it, through longing for it, through refusing to accept that it belongs to the past and has fallen into oblivion; through refusing to accept some second-hand substitute, he will succeed in preserving it as an eternal possibility.[25]

This, surely, is, among other things, Thomas's answer to his own romantic nostalgia, with its inclination to idealize a pattern of Welsh rural life belonging to the past; and, here, it is vision that displaces the romantic dream, depicting 'the true Wales of my imagination' as an object of striving and longing, which is also an implicit judgement upon every 'second-hand substitute'.[26]

An aim of R. S. Thomas's poems addressed to his people is, therefore, to awaken them to a sense of their special identity, which is different from that of the English in particular. In this respect, Thomas fulfils another traditional role of the Welsh poet, which may be identified with reference to David Jones's words about the Dying Gaul, from which he 'sensed a continuity of struggle and a continuity of loss'. 'Celtdom', Jones says, meant to him works 'of relentless resistance culminating in defeat. But from each defeat came the living embers to feed the fires of resistance yet to be.'[27] R. S. Thomas, like David Jones himself, is a voice of resistance.

David Jones was born at Brockley in Kent and lived most of his life in London, but his father was Welsh. 'From about the age of six,' Jones said, 'I felt I belonged to my father's people and their land.'[28] The feeling was reinforced by his service with the Royal Welsh Fusiliers during the First World War. Ten years after the war he began a writing based on his experiences on the Western Front, which was published as *In Parenthesis* in 1937. In the meantime Jones, who had always been religious, had become a Roman Catholic convert, and had lived for a time in Eric Gill's community, including periods during the 1920s at Capel-y-Ffin in the Black Mountains.[29] Here, through his paintings, he had acquired a strong sense of the rhythms of Welsh landscapes, while his reading in myth, which began in childhood with his fascination with stories of King Arthur, and his literary and historical studies, enhanced his feeling for Wales as a many-storied land.

The importance to David Jones of a sense of belonging may be gauged from the experience of John Ball, the character with whom he is most closely identified in *In Parenthesis*, as he moves with his companions into the trenches:

> . . . you know the homing perfume of wood burned, at the termination of ways; and sense here near habitation, a folk-life here, a people, a culture already developed, already venerable and rooted.
> . . .
> And you too are assimilated, you too are of this people – there will be an indelible characterisation – you'll tip-toe when they name the place.[30]

Private John Ball is not Welsh; like Jones he is a Londoner, and his name, after the poor priest (also from Kent) who was a leader of the Peasants' Revolt, signifies his status as an Everyman. In this capacity, he has the longing for 'home', as a communal but also a metaphysical sense of belonging, that is especially strong among English-language Welsh poets in the twentieth century – poets who, in R. S. Thomas's terms, subsist 'in a no-man's-land between two cultures', with the outsider's desire to belong.

This, in fact, is essentially what *In Parenthesis* is about. I do not mean by this to denigrate its achievement as a war book, or to disparage its treatment of the horror and pity of war. My aim, rather, is to emphasize that its emotional centre lies in the community of the men in the trenches. The community is a culture – already in *In Parenthesis* we see Jones's Spenglerian opposition between earth-rooted, form-making culture and mechanical civilization, which was to become more fully developed in his later writings.[31] The men, 'mostly Londoners with an admixture of

Welshmen' (*IP*, x), constitute 'a folk-life, a people here, a culture'. This, in turn, invokes the shared myths and history of an older unity, a Britain created under the Romans. The irony of the situation (which is not Jones's subject) is that this unity is recovered outside the British Isles, as the result of a murderous technological war.

Jones's use of 'texts' from *Y Gododdin* underlines the antiquity of the culture present in 'the mind and folk-life' (*IP*, x) of Londoners and Welshmen. *Y Gododdin*, the early Welsh epical poem attributed to Aneirin, Jones says in the General Notes, 'connects us with a very ancient unity and mingling of races; with the Island as a corporate inheritance, with the remembrance of Rome as a European unity' (*IP*, 191–2). Jones's Catholicism is a shaping factor in all his poetry and art, but is more implicit in *In Parenthesis* – an imaging rather than a structuring presence – than it is in his more explicitly devotional later work. Nevertheless, the 'European unity' refers ultimately to that of the Church, which Roman imperial power prefigured and to some degree prepared the way for.

In 'A Note of Introduction' to *In Parenthesis*, T. S. Eliot described David Jones as 'decidedly a Briton' (*IP*, vii).[32] The reference was not to his Welsh patrimony alone, but to his espousal of 'the Island as a corporate inheritance'. To give a brief sketch of a complex subject: Jones's endeavour was to use his historical and mythological knowledge to reverse the effects of the Tudor myth. Whereas the Tudors had used their British or Welsh connections ultimately in the interests of the English nation state, Jones seeks to restore the 'corporate inheritance' of the Island. He found 'the Matter of Britain' embodied in his 'companions in the war'. 'These came from London. Those from Wales. Together they bore in their bodies the genuine tradition of the Island of Britain' (*IP*, x). It would be entirely misleading if my description of Jones's endeavour should make him seem humourless and didactic. What I want to emphasize is that he was an artist of enormous ambition: metaphysical and incarnational, anti-Reformation, in the Catholic tradition, his thinking centred upon the Mass.[33] But *In Parenthesis* works not as a religious tract, but as a poem in which the humour and the humanity of the men, and their diverse and vivid speech, together with the wealth of cultural memory they bear, make the corporate inheritance a rich and diversely textured 'shape in words'.[34]

Jones's idea of the significance of the Arthurian material for the Welsh accords with his idea of unity.

> What makes the Arthurian thing important to the Welsh is that there is no other tradition at all equally the common property of all the inhabitants of Britain (at all events of those south of the Antonine Wall), and the Welsh, however separatist by historical, racial and geographical accidents, are devoted to the unity of this island.[35]

Given the Welsh nationalist thinking that permeates a large part of Anglo-Welsh writing in the period since the Second World War, and which (with a difference) was a shaping influence upon Jones's own work, this is a surprising statement. Indeed it can only be understood in the context of Jones's large historical vision, which seeks to restore the Island of Britain to all its people; as he insisted publicly, in for instance a letter to *The Times* reprinted in *Epoch and Artist*, 'the complex and involved heritage of Britain is a shared inheritance which can, in very devious ways, enrich us all'.[36]

As I have said, Jones's devotion to 'the unity of this island' was religious, specifically Catholic. This determines the significance of his use of the language of *lebensraum*. In his essay 'The Myth of Arthur', he describes St David

> training his shock-troops in the technics of an offensive which had for its objective a true *lebensraum*, the *limes* and boundaries of which march with and impinge upon mundane lands, but which had extending frontiers the other side of time.[37]

The metaphor recurs in 'Art in Relation to War', where he speaks of 'the human species' with 'its rightful *imperium*, its native *Raum*, its double homeland along all the frontiers and uncertain borders of matter and spirit'. 'Man', he says, 'is Lord of the Two Marches, and must keep the difficult dignity of his dual role.'[38]

David Jones shares with John Cowper Powys a strong awareness of the symbolic borderland of Welsh myth and legend. This is a supernatural dimension; as Alwyn and Brinley Rees say in *Celtic Heritage*, 'boundaries between territories, like boundaries between years and between seasons, are lines along which the supernatural intrudes through the surface of existence'.[39] In the

Preface to *In Parenthesis*, in a characteristic metaphor derived from his subject, Jones tells us that the Celtic cycle 'lies, a sub-terranean influence as a deep water troubling, under every tump in this island, like Merlin complaining under his big rock'(*IP*, xi). He is particularly effective when invoking the setting of the Celtic Otherworld, which is

> amphibious, a place of islands, and necks of land, of crystal towers, of transparency and extreme cold, unstable, with lights shining, which (like those familiar Very lights slowly gyrating over a 1916 or, I suppose, a 1940 Flanders field) coldly illumine, but do not clarify the scene.[40]

In the same essay, 'The Myth of Arthur', he writes:

> The folk tradition of the insular Celts seems to present to the mind a half-aquatic world – it is one of its most fascinating characteristics – it introduces a feeling of transparency and interpenetration of one element with another, of transposition and metamorphosis. The hedges of mist vanish or come again under the application of magic, such as Geraint ab Erbin encountered, just as the actual mists over peat-bog and tarn and *traeth* disclose or lose before our eyes drifting stumps and tussocks. It is unstable, the isles float, where was a *caer* or a *llys* now is a glassy expanse.[41]

This is a marvellous evocation of a Welsh landscape. It is also a metaphorical description of David Jones's art – transparent, composed of interpenetrating elements, metamorphotic – in his Welsh landscape paintings, in the palimpsests of myth and literature and history that are his Western Front, in the cultural landscapes of Wales in *The Anathemata* and 'fragments' in *The Sleeping Lord*. Its rendering of 'the application of magic' helps us to understand the sense in which the battlefield in *In Parenthesis* is magical – a place of malign enchantment, on the border between life and death.

Wales for David Jones was, therefore, a March, a sacred land, or border of matter and spirit. The land of Wales was this, and the Matter of Britain, which embodies the unity of the Island, was a repository of myth and magic, history and legendary history, in the keeping of the Welsh. The tradition was symbolized for him by

Arthur and Arthur-type figures, such as Cronus, whom Plutarch associated with these islands,[42] and Brân the Blessed, whose head 'buried under the White Tower' was 'chief protector of London and of the Island, in Welsh tradition'.[43] This tradition of latent powers, guardians of an underlying unity, is the context of the Lady of the Pool's words in *The Anathemata*, when she urges the ship's captain she is addressing to 'let sleepers lie':

> For should these stir, then would our Engle-raum in
> this Brut's Albion be like to come to some confusion!
> > You never know, captain:
> What's under works up. (*Ana*, 164)

The Lady speaks here for the English *imperium*, but with an ironical invocation of the powers that would destroy its narrow base and replace it with the foundations of a holy city. It is a sensitive moment in the historical context in which the poem was written, during and after the Second World War. The idea of the Matter of Britain 'working up' refers to the blitz, which literally exposed foundations, and the immediate post-war concern with Britain's heritage. In this context, 'Engle-raum' is a bitter comment on a narrow and oppressive Englishness which has no regard for the unity of the Island. It defines a frame of mind that Jones associates with 'megalopolitan technocracy . . . indifferent to the ancient language and the ancient sites',[44] and represents 'the placeless cosmopolis of technocrats',[45] to which his muse stands opposed. His muse at this moment is the Lady of the Pool, but throughout his work Jones has a strong sense of the 'feminine' principle, which he identifies ultimately with the Virgin Mary, who for him is mother of 'the holy diversities': 'She that loves place, time, demarcation, hearth, kin, enclosure, site, differentiated cult, though she is but one mother of us all'.[46]

Welsh continuity, for Jones, connects us 'with the remembrance of Wales as a European unity', and therefore, as I have shown, with the sacred. His true Welshman is Lance-Corporal Aneirin Merddyn Lewis who 'had somewhere in his Welsh depths a remembrance of the nature of man', and who 'brings in a manner, baptism, and metaphysical order to the bankruptcy of the occasion' in *In Parenthesis* (1–2). Lewis, as his Christian names imply, is both bard and magician. Bardic memory and bardic honouring of the heroes,[47] and magic as the supernatural, the presiding spirit of the borderland situation of human life, are the qualities that David Jones identified with his fatherland, and interpreted in terms of his Catholicism. It is evident, however, that his idea of the fatherland is in no way patriarchal, and that his vision emphasizes the necessary interdependence of male and female principles in human creativity. The qualities he celebrates embody a continuity which Wales has preserved, and England, by and large, has buried and denied.

Gillian Clarke, who made an immediate impact in Wales with her first collection of poems in 1971, and has subsequently established herself as one of the leading English-language Welsh poets, also has a sense of continuity that is both natural and religious. This she perceives especially in the lives of women, in their cultural and domestic rituals, and their biological functions, and their values. While the women and the values of which she writes are not exclusively Welsh, her main focus of concern is Wales, where, as David Jones said, 'the language, tradition and type of culture are closely knit with a continued rural tradition'.[48] A source of strength in her writing is her ease of movement between her home, which is now in rural west Wales, and Cardiff, where she formerly lived for many years, and generally between country and city in Wales, and, latterly, in England too. (She is also a well-travelled poet who has written poems set in different parts of the world.) Thus, while her feeling for her home in Ceredigion resembles R. S. Thomas's feeling for the Llŷn, Clarke embraces more of the reality of interdependent rural and urban environments, or, in a word, of modern Wales.

Clarke's attitude to both her Welsh inheritance and her social role as a woman has a creative ambivalence. In her long poem written originally for radio, 'Letter from a Far Country', for instance, she writes both of her own confinement in a domestic role and that of women in a traditional Welsh rural society. But at the same time she values the securities of the old way of life, in rural occupations, the sense of communal belonging, the Welsh language. This makes for a tension that is present throughout the poem, as in the following passage:

> I hear the dead grandmothers,
> Mamgu from Ceredigion,

Nain from the North, all calling
their daughters down from the fields,
calling me in from the road.
They haul at the taut silk cords;
set us fetching eggs, feeding hens,
mixing rage with the family bread,
lock us to the elbows in soap suds.
Their sculleries and kitchens fill
with steam, sweetnesses, goosefeathers.[49]

There is no doubt about the rage, or about the sense of imprisonment in domesticity and in a patriarchal society that permeates the
poem. The fact that the 'cords' are 'silk' as well as 'taut', and that
it is 'soap suds' that 'lock us', suggests the 'softening' effects of the
dead grandmothers' appeal; the love that turns the key on the
women in their kitchens. But there are genuine 'sweetnesses' here
too, and the list of activities and things – fetching eggs, feeding
hens, family bread, soap suds, steam, goosefeathers – has the
sensuous plenitude that characterizes Gillian Clarke's poetry.
Thus, even in writing her (unposted) letter of farewell she is
celebrating the way of life, present and past, that has helped to
make her the poet she is.

'Letter from a Far Country' ends with a song:

Will the men grow tender and the children strong?
Who will teach the Mam iaith and sing them songs?
If we adventure more than a day
Who will do the loving while we're away? (CP, 56)

The woman is the one who stays at home, minds things, teaches
the language (Mam iaith, 'mother tongue'), does the loving. It is a
role which, as the poem shows, has a considerable cost, but it is
also an immensely important role, not only for individuals and
families, but for the culture and the language. There is no reason
to suppose Gillian Clarke's view of traditional women's work
would differ significantly from that of her older contemporary,
Jean Earle, who in 'Visiting Light' writes of cleaning 'my step':

Rubbing with bluestone in the old way.
My scour against the world's indifference

> To important symbols – the common roof,
> Likeness of patterns.[50]

Celebration of the common task and the common object is not, of course, exclusively a tradition of women's poetry – on the contrary, it was reaffirmed in *Lyrical Ballads*, and looks back to roots in pagan and Christian values. It makes a difference, however, that poets such as Clarke and Earle write out of an experience of doing domestic work on which life depends, while the knowledge of such things on the part of male poets has frequently been more theoretical. It should also be said, however, that Clarke has written impressive poems, such as 'Harvest at Mynachlog', about men working, in situations in which the woman poet is actually or in memory a privileged casual participant.

Unlike R. S. Thomas, Gillian Clarke does not see bilingualism as diabolic, but as one of 'the first / Necessities for a high standard / Of civilised living'.[51] But she has too, like both R. S. Thomas and David Jones, a feeling for the primacy of Welsh as the language of Wales. Like Thomas, she uses organic metaphors which assimilate culture to nature, language or speech to the land. In 'The Water-Diviner', for instance, water 'shouts through the hose // a word we could not say, or spell, or remember, / something like "dŵr . . . dŵr"' (*CP*, 71). In 'Llŷr' she speaks of 'the river and the king with their Welsh names' (*CP*, 68), reminding us of the Celtic names of our rivers and of the ancient British myths and legendary history on which Shakespeare drew. The very source of life, water, and the originary myths of 'Brut's Albion', such as the story of Llŷr/Lear and the story of Brân the Blessed, are one with the ancient tongue. In a poem from her latest book, *Five Fields*, Clarke describes watching 'ourselves' on television 'disputing our language in the other tongue' with a 'government messenger' – a familiar experience for Welsh-speaking intellectuals obliged, even in their own country, to defend their language. The poem ends:

> We switch off the news, listen
> to the rain falling fluent, filling
> the Bwdram, the Glowan and the Clettwr,
> finding its tongue in the ancient dark
> of the deepest aquifers.[52]

Once again, the Welsh tongue is a language with a deep source, at one with what lies under.

This metaphor is not without dangers. For one thing, it can become repetitive, automatic. For another, it can gloss over social reality and the political and economic forces that threaten the survival of a minority language, however venerable. Clarke is perhaps more inclined than either Thomas or Jones to render the romantic identification between language and land as a permanent underlying condition. But she is also more open to the world of industrialized, urban Wales, which is also part of her own past. Thus, in 'East Moors' (*CP*, 38) she experiences the demolition of the steelworks as both personal and social loss, as well as environmental gain. With this emphasis, she is closer to a younger generation of English-language Welsh poets, such as John Davies and Robert Minhinnick, who defend their homegrounds in Anglicized areas not only against the deprivations of a market economy and Anglocentric attitudes, but also against the nationalism that identifies Welshness with the Welsh language, as R. S. Thomas does. There are moments when Clarke sounds like a parody of Thomas, however – a particularly unhappy one occurs in 'Fires on Llŷn' (*CP*, 92–4), where the matter-of-fact line 'Three English boys throw stones' seems meant to be portentous – but when she writes most as herself, her human sympathies are most inclusive.

Despite her knowledge of the urban world, Clarke is essentially a poet of rural Wales, a poet of nature and neighbourhood, and territory in which memory lives. She grounds herself imaginatively upon her home, Blaen Cwrt, in the countryside of west Wales, as R. S. Thomas in his old age grounds himself upon the Llŷn. But from Blaen Cwrt she visits the outer world, and listens to it. Up to a point, she enlarges the embrace of the Welsh poetic tradition, extending it globally. But her attitude towards this new openness is ambivalent, as the conclusion to 'Neighbours' shows:

> Now we are all neighbourly, each little town
> in Europe twinned to Chernobyl, each heart
> with the burnt fireman, the child on the Moscow train.
>
> In the democracy of the virus and the toxin
> we wait. We watch for bird migrations,
> one bird returning with green in its voice,

glasnost
golau glas
a first break of blue. (CP, 86)

There is something new here, although the openness itself is perhaps not as new as I have suggested. Both in the Christian and socialist traditions, Welsh poets have felt compassionately or angrily for the hardships of other peoples, as well as their own. What is new, though, is this sense of a vulnerable global democracy, as distinct from a utopian universalism. The conclusion also finds a new use for an old poetic figure. The biblical imagery of the Flood and its aftermath, the hope of a new Creation, modulates into the Russian word which spread around the world to symbolize a new political openness. This in turn conjures up a Welsh image: 'golau glas' ('blue light'), which, with a suggestion of the blue planet, is at once an image of vulnerability and hope.

The meaning here is not far perhaps from R. S. Thomas's 'everything / on this shrinking planet favours the survival / of the small people'.[53] In 'the democracy of the virus and the toxin', in which the destruction of human life is a possibility, small peoples with deep cultures are newly viable as centres of resistance to dehumanizing forces. Similarly, David Jones's Sleeping Lord offers a latent power which is a symbol of hope. In the case of each poet the vision is romantic, drawing upon the idea of a culture as an organic whole, something that has grown rather than been constructed. Each poet is also adapting an ancient poetic tradition to his or her purposes – 1,500 years during which the function of the Welsh poet has been to defend a people and a territory.

3

Emyr Humphreys's 'Land of the Living'

Emyr Humphreys's seven novels comprising the 'Land of the Living' sequence were published between 1971 and 1991.[1] Broadly speaking, they tell the story of a group of Welsh characters between the early years of the twentieth century and 1969. The central figures are Amy Parry and the man who becomes her first husband, the poet Cilydd (John Cilydd More), who has achieved early success as a 'national winner' at the Eisteddfod. Both are orphans, brought up in families that strongly affect their choices in life, largely through their reactions against them. The fact of their being orphans, therefore, is an additional strong motivation in their search for an identity, which is a major theme of the sequence. Other key figures are Amy's best friend, Enid Prydderch, who becomes Cilydd's first wife and dies in childbirth, Val Gwyn, his best friend and a leading Welsh nationalist who dies young, and Pen Lewis, a communist activist who is killed fighting in the Spanish Civil War. Principal characters in the period after the Second World War are Peredur, the son of Amy and Cilydd, and his elder brothers, Bedwyr, son of Enid and Cilydd, and adopted by Amy after her friend's death, and Gwydion, son of Amy and Pen.

There are numerous other important figures in the novels, that are memorable for their own sakes, but their primary significance may be said to be cultural: in revealing aspects of Welsh society and culture, they throw light on the choices facing the principal characters. It would be untrue to suggest that Humphreys's characters that do not maintain a fairly central position in the narrative are therefore minor characters. Certainly this is not the case with, say, Esther Parry or Richard Parry. Indeed, I would argue that almost the only minor characters in the sequence of novels are non-Welsh, and especially English characters, and that is because they are stereotypes. They serve a thematic function; they do not belong to the society – indeed, to the civilization – which is the focus of concern. One of Humphreys's great strengths as a novelist is his portrayal of women. This is as true of the 'little scullery maid' in *The Best of Friends* as it is of the principal women characters. In the case of Esther Parry, Humphreys portrays a woman with great powers of endurance, and loving loyalty. She supports her husband and Amy through their impoverished existence, and sustains herself and Lucas through their difficulties and his disappointments. Her life is remorselessly physical through work in and outside the home. Humphreys is the equal of Thomas Hardy in his depiction of women working. Esther, moreover, like Hardy's labouring women, is far from being a drudge. With her sparse use of words, she is at least as much a person of principle as her husband with his sermons. Her human qualities shine in everything she says and does. If she is a product of Welsh Nonconformist culture, she is also, together with other women, an essential part of its foundations. Indeed, Humphreys conveys the impression that without such women Wales would be in danger of evaporating in words.

This broad sketch of the story and characters necessarily leaves out a lot, but it also helps to indicate patterns within the sequence: patterns of relationships, patterns between generations and patterns of choices – between Welsh nationalism and communism, for example. It also helps to suggest that the many stories constitute one single story: an epic narrative, involving history and myth, which recounts the struggle for Welsh identity in the twentieth century. It is an epic which, through its concentration on the lives of individuals in a particular society, examines personal and national destinies, and illuminates the human condition.

There are distinct advantages in treating the sequence as an epic, rather than as seven separate novels, but there are also limitations. One is that each novel is an individually crafted work of art, and in a complete reading would need to be discussed and judged as such. Another arises from the fact that the novel which is sixth in the chronological sequence, *National Winner*, was written first, and consequently has a somewhat unbalancing effect on the sequence as a whole. It is a more schematic novel than the others. It is also a sort of watershed between Amy Parry's life experience, which is central to the first five novels, and the shift of attention to the inner lives of her late husband, Cilydd, and their son, Peredur, in the last novel. While this shift is perfectly justifiable in terms of Emyr Humphreys's vision and techniques, the reader may well feel cheated of his human interest in Amy Parry during what are virtually the missing years of her life between 1952, when the fifth novel in the sequence, *Open Secrets*, ends and the late 1960s, when *National Winner* begins.

In my view, however, the advantages of treating 'Land of the Living' as one epic story outweigh the disadvantages. Above all, it enables the sequence to be seen as a whole: a complete vision of the human condition in the twentieth century, as revealed in the experience of a group of Welsh men and women whose individual destinies are bound up with the destiny of their nation. Emyr Humphreys is concerned with his main characters as whole human beings. They are products of a society and a culture and they are deeply affected by historical movements and events. They are sexual beings and beings with religious needs. Their individual identities are closely bound up with their Welshness, with the language and the fate of Wales. They influence each other, for better or worse. They have ideals to which they are loyal or which they betray. They make choices that shape their lives. Emyr Humphreys's sense of the wholeness of the human being in his or her world makes for a complex vision. In attempting to illuminate it, therefore, I shall concentrate on three central and related issues, beginning with Humphreys's treatment of Welsh Nonconformity: 'The chapel, that key institution which had been brought into existence for the salvation of Welsh souls and therefore for the unspoken affirmation of Welsh identity.'[2] I shall then discuss the uses of myth in the sequence, and the portrayal of Cilydd, the poet who should compose the modern Welsh epic, but is too entangled in the story to be able to tell it.

In the early years of the twentieth century Lucas Parry, the lay preacher, describes the Welsh as 'a pattern-making people' (*FB*, 118). The reference is clearly to the religious and communal pattern that was the product of Nonconformity. There is a certain irony in the words even at this time, however, since Lucas's experiences reveal strains within the pattern. Mainly as a result of his lack of an academic education, Lucas is frustrated in his sense of a calling to become a minister. Having spent his life resisting the encroachments of the modern world in the forms of Anglicization, mechanization and secularism, he meets his death under the wheels of an army lorry while working as a watchman at a holiday camp used for army training during the Second World War. Emyr Humphreys depicts a patterned way of life centred upon the chapel, and he shows it breaking down during the early twentieth century, and especially as a result of the First World War, but he does not simplify either the original pattern or the manner and outcome of its fragmentation.

Humphreys depicts the world of the chapel with great understanding. He neither celebrates nor criticizes it as uniform and monolithic, but shows the doctrinal differences and other divisions that produced tensions in Welsh Nonconformity. The following description of the chapel the Parrys attend does, however, represent the Nonconformist tradition as it stands on the brink of the modern world, which will fragment its pattern:

> It was hot inside the chapel. The pews were occupied by whole families who had come to chapel prepared to face bad weather. Their clothing would protect them on the journey home. The wind had been rising all through the evening service. Impetuous gusts raced around the stout square walls searching for a gap in the defences. But Siloam was built solidly of stone quarried from the same hillside on which it stood. In spite of its exposed position above the road which led down to the sheltered centre of the village, the chapel was nailed safely to the hillside. The congregation sat drowsy with comfort and security. (*FB*, 31)

The description strongly suggests an 'organic community'. The chapel, built from the stone of the hill on which it stands, serves the community. 'Whole families' attend it, safe in the knowledge that it will protect them from 'bad weather'. Everything about Siloam bespeaks safety and security. In fact, however, its security is false. It is threatened by external forces, for which the rising storm is a metaphor. More insidiously, it is in danger from within. Humphreys alerts us to this fact with the word 'nailed'. Is it the function of the religion based on Christ's death on the Cross to offer 'comfort and security'? Should not the image of the torturing nails drive home the message of sacrifice? But complacency is far from being all the chapel as an institution offers – on the contrary, it continues to inspire those who seek to defend a Welsh identity based on a patterned way of life in the chaos of the twentieth century; but it is a force for good through sacrificial action, not through the adaptation of Christianity to cosy traditionalism.

Towards the end of the Second World War Amy Parry speaks urgently of 'a new world taking shape'.

> The Russians within forty miles of Berlin. The Americans over the Rhine. The last stand in the Apennines. And what is happening here in

this tiny patch of ours, it's all part of the same great terrible pattern. Great is small and small is great. If it isn't, we count for nothing at all. (*OS*, 225)

The passion for making 'a new world' is endemic to Humphreys's idealistic Welsh men and women. However transformed by political ideology, its ultimate source is Nonconformity. Amy, at this stage, has identified the cause of the future with British Labour politics. She is, nevertheless, 'the residual legatee of a complex Welsh Nonconformist family inheritance' (*OS*, 10), and her focus on the world of power politics outside Wales is a denial of the pattern in which she has been brought up. In terms of her political perspective, her idea of the 'great terrible pattern' is the opposite of the commitment of those who, like her husband, put Wales first. For them, small is great, because Wales stands for civilization, and its defence starts at home: the crisis threatening Welsh identity is a particular instance of the general crisis in Europe. This is implied in Enid Prydderch's answer to the Englishman who asks what use the Welsh language is: 'Ask yourself, what use is civilization[?]' (*BF*, 67). On another occasion, Val Gwyn argues:

is not art by definition proceeding from the particular to the universal? Therefore, is not the artist under a primary obligation to master the particular? And is not this particular in almost every case that particular society that gave him birth, in all its strengths and weaknesses? (*BF*, 234–5)

The fate of civilization in the twentieth century is central to 'Land of the Living'. The theme is summed up most succinctly by Saunders Lewis, the political thinker to whom Humphreys is most indebted: 'Civilization must be more than an abstraction. It must have a local habitation and a name. Here, its name is Wales.'[3]

The Nonconformist inheritance is complex. Its fate in twentieth-century Wales is not that its pattern is simply broken, for, as it fragments, it continues to have a deep effect upon people's lives. Whether negatively or positively, most of Humphreys's Welsh characters are influenced by Nonconformity. Indeed, whether they accept or reject it, they are largely shaped by it. Above all, it remains bound up with Welsh identity, with language-based cultural nationalism and its sacrificial and heroic ideals. The situation is further complicated,

however, by the fact that, rather like the idea of the organic community in England, the chapel can be used to project an idea of the
past that is a temptation to escapism.

Some of Humphreys's most vivid characters, in this sequence and
in *Outside the House of Baal*, are ministers. They are not all cut
from the same cloth. Some are shown to be at least as concerned
with their appearance and professional advancement as with their
religious calling. Others, such as Nathan Harris and Tasker
Thomas, may be perceived as good men. The practice of 'goodness',
however, is not to be easily separated from self-delusion in
Humphreys's ministers, nor is it an unqualified blessing. Good men
can make impossible demands upon others, especially women.
Real virtue can act as a singleness of purpose which blinds its
possessor to life's complexities. Nevertheless, goodness is a force in
Humphreys's world and there is no reason to suppose the mature
novelist would not endorse what he wrote as a young man: 'A soul
cannot make progress *in vacuo*: many men are better for the
existence of one good man, and one good man is the product of
some kind of progress that was both individual and social.'[4]

It is a strength of Humphreys's moral vision that it makes easy
judgements impossible. He is at once compassionate and acutely
perceptive of self-deception. At his best, as in the portrayal of J. T.
Miles in *Outside the House of Baal* or Tasker Thomas in this
sequence, he gives us a sense of a whole life, revealing both its overall
tendency to goodness and the errors and blind spots involved in its
pursuit. Nonconformity also introduces a particular language into
the novels. It is an irony of the historical context, of course, that in
'Land of the Living' we are frequently reading a kind of 'translation', since the dialogue and thought-processes of Welsh characters
would 'originally' be in Welsh. The irony of these being rendered in
English is especially marked given the importance of the language
issue to Welsh identity. My present subject, however, is not
Humphreys's decision to write his epic of Welsh life in the twentieth
century in English (and it certainly was a choice given his bilingualism and writings in Welsh), but what his use of the language of
Welsh Nonconformity brings to his novels.

Put simply, the chapel provides a poetic dimension. But such a
simple statement begs the question of the relationship between
religious language and poetic language, and it would be truer to say
that Humphreys is a writer acutely sensitive to the poetry of

religion, where the word 'poetry' refers not to fancies and unrealities but to a language capable of expressing the entire relationship between the human and the divine. Thus, religious language encompasses the whole of life, and is spoken equally by the 'man of principle' Lucas Parry, the mystical Nathan Harris, the social activist Tasker Thomas and the idealist Val Gwyn. It continues to pervade Welsh society, even after the 'pattern', which we see on the brink of collapse in the description of Siloam, has broken down.

Religion is bound up with myth, which does not mean, of course, that religion itself is myth, in the weak sense of the word, meaning fiction, untruth. The world of the chapel has a mythological dimension whose most potent expression is the Garden of Eden, the story of the prelapsarian creation, a state of original innocence, which Humphreys shows deeply affecting both the psychology and the social ideas of chapelgoers or those who inherit the tradition. Its centrality to the world of the chapel is nicely pointed up when we learn that Cilydd, at fourteen, 'beat his uncle Gwilym on the subject of the "Garden of Eden" at the Geboah Eisteddfod' (*BF*, 153). The influence of the story of the Garden of Eden takes different forms. It provides the incentive or stimulates the desire to create a new world – the aim that Humphreys's politically engaged characters pursue in response to the chaos of the twentieth century. It also has the capacity to indulge an uncreative nostalgia for the past. Nathan Harris, talking about Tasker Thomas to Amy, describes both forms:

> You see one of the side-effects of that terrible war was to turn our poor old Nonconformity out of its own home-made earthly paradise. Now you can argue that our worthy forefathers had no business to attempt making one in the first place. That's not the point. The point is, whether we like it or not, we are turned out of the garden. We are in a new and frightening desert. A wilderness. And in the wilderness only the men who practise what they preach have any hope of leading the remnant of the faithful to the distant water-hole. (*SOE*, 54)

The old minister does not reject the idea of the earthly paradise, because in the past it has led to misguided results. His reasoning uses it, instead, as a future goal ('the distant water-hole') to which being 'turned out of the garden' points. He is living inside a religious language, a language with its myths and metaphors and moral vision; but it may be argued that, instead of being trapped within it, the language provides him, and his society, with a link between past and present and the means to create a meaningful future.

Myth is a kind of patterning which modernist writers have frequently employed. T. S. Eliot described 'the mythical method' which James Joyce, in *Ulysses,* 'in manipulating a continuous parallel between contemporaneity and antiquity', used as 'a way of controlling, of ordering, of giving a shape and a significance to the immense panorama of futility and anarchy which is contemporary history'.[5] Humphreys's view of the possibilties of history is more positive than Eliot's, and he does not hold Joyce's cyclic view of history, but his use of myth shows their influence. It is the differences, however, with which I am here concerned. Humphreys is aware of myth not just as a way of ordering history but as an energy within history, a force that helps to shape, and to defend, national identity. This is the subject of his *The Taliesin Tradition,* subtitled *A Quest for the Welsh Identity,* which was first published in 1983, and was written during the period when he was writing his epic sequence. There, he argues that: 'The manufacture and proliferation of myth must always be a major creative activity among a people with unnaturally high expectations reduced by historic necessity, or at least history, forced into what is often described as a marginal condition.' 'In Wales', he goes on to say, 'history and myth have always mingled and both have been of equal importance in the struggle for survival.'[6]

Elsewhere Humphreys has said: 'All Welsh storytelling in any language should begin with *Y Mabinogi.*'[7] One implication of this is that myth is, as it were, part of the very land of Wales. That is to say it is in the place-names, and in the stories about places. Myth, together with religion, is a shaping force of the culture, and it lives on in the language and in the poetic tradition (to which the storyteller belongs) as a powerful force of resistance to the external and internal enemies of Welsh identity. Rather than being only an ordering of materials that already exist, as is suggested in Eliot's idea of 'the mythical method', Welsh myth, in the terms of one of its own images, is a cauldron of rebirth, in which identity is renewed from age to age.

Humphreys makes use of specific mythical materials, from *Pedair Cainc y Mabinogi* and other Welsh sources, in 'Land of the Living'. There is, for example, the significance of the severed head, a gruesome motif associated with the admirable Captain Herbert, blown to bits in front of Cilydd as he serves as a private with the Royal Army Medical Corps in the trenches during the First World War (*BA*, 178), and the woman Peredur idolizes, Wenna Ferrario, blown up when planting a bomb intended as a political gesture against the Investiture of the Prince of Wales in 1969 (*BA*, 347). The mythical motif to which the bloody objects refer is the head of Brân, the semi-divine figure from the Second Branch of *Pedair Cainc y Mabinogi*, whose severed head has sacred properties and is a symbol of protection for the Welsh. The proverb derived from Brân's story, '*A fo ben bid bont*' ('Let him who is leader be a bridge'), further reinforces the significance of the severed head for Cilydd and Peredur, since both men are seeking a leader. Cilydd sees Captain Herbert as a man 'born, bred and built to sustain the semblance of order even in the foulest chaos' (*BA*, 175). Interestingly, the words are an echo of, and possibly an allusion to, David Jones's description, in *In Parenthesis*, of Lance-Corporal Aneirin Merddyn Lewis as one who 'brings in a manner, baptism, and metaphysical order to the bankruptcy of the occasion'.[8] Occurrences of the motif in *Bonds of Attachment*, together with the allusion to Aneirin Lewis, deepen our awareness of the significance of events involving father and son separated by more than fifty years and cast an ironic light on those events. Cilydd's and Peredur's need for a leader is not only psychological, but relates to 'metaphysical order'. The deaths of Captain Herbert and Wenna are both, in a sense, sacrificial and, therefore, have the quality of true leadership on the model of Christ's sacrificial death. But both are also deaths that seem to justify violence: Captain Herbert (though his mission is mercy) is serving the violence of the state, and Wenna is turning from the pacific methods of Welsh nationalism to 'armed struggle' (*BA*, 206). Humphreys uses the myth of the severed head, therefore, to raise some very awkward questions about leadership and sacrifice in the service of a cause: both Captain Herbert and Wenna fulfil the sacrificial pattern, but has the captain given his life in an unworthy cause? And does Wenna, by espousing violence, harm a good cause?

It seems to me that the following words from Emyr Humphreys's lecture *The Crucible of Myth* are applicable to his own practice:

Underlying the narrative surface of *Y Pedair Cainc* there is a symphonic structure equipped with figures and melodic phrases and almost

Wagnerian *leitmotif*. These make fresh music from the hazards and splendours of marriage, whether mediaeval or modern: from the delicate relationship between honour and friendship: the dire consequences of irresponsible quarrelling and internecine warfare: the dangerous side-effects of heroic age ideals: the absolute necessity of organic law and the habits of self-discipline.[9]

In one way or another, the leitmotifs named here sound throughout 'Land of the Living' too. Their recurrence, moreover, is not mechanical, but musical, in ways that this description suggests. As M. Wynn Thomas has noted in discussing the form of *Outside the House of Baal*, Humphreys himself felt the technique he developed in that novel 'was similar in some ways to the exploration of consonances and dissonances in modernist music'.[10] Something similar needs to be said, I think, about Humphreys's experimental use of the mythical method. It is quite in accordance with his modernism that the themes and patternings are both ancient and modern.

Parallels between 'Land of the Living' and *Y Pedair Cainc* emerge from the epic story and are reabsorbed into it. Occasionally, they give the impression of being the author's imposition upon the material, rather than the product of a character's mind. This is more often true in *National Winner*, the first of the novels to be written and the most schematic, than in the other novels. Thus, Peredur tells Maxine the story of Blodeuwedd: 'She was given in marriage to an ice-cold man doomed by his mother to live without power and without love' (*NW*, 33). A parallel, though it is not exact, is suggested between Peredur's mother and father. The fact that such references occur frequently in the sequence, but usually with more subtlety than in this instance, is due mainly to two factors: that the land of Wales is imbued with myth and legend, as I have already mentioned, and that most of Humphreys's Welsh characters share what Gwydion calls 'my mythological Welsh mind' (*NW*, 210).

In many cases, myth is integral to the character's self-understanding. This is the significance of Val Gwyn's question to the communist, Pen Lewis: 'What's your name?' Pen replies, 'Penry Aneurin Lewis', but seems not to understand the significance of the question and the answer. He thinks Val is playing a childish game: 'Sticking names on each other' (*BF*, 281). Val is implying, of course, that the names identify Pen as a Welshman, and indeed, with their references to the Puritan martyr John Penry and the warrior-bard Aneirin, go some way towards defining his inheritance, as do Lance-Corporal Lewis's names in *In Parenthesis*. Val and Pen are close to each other in their passion for a political solution to the suffering of the Welsh working class in the 1930s, but Pen would abolish the past in order to create a new world, and Val would link past and present in order to make a new Wales, saving civilization by beginning with the particular. In the event, neither succeeds in achieving his aims, but both live on after their deaths as influences on others, and so do succeed in a way.

It is probably inevitable that at times Humphreys appears to manipulate myth. Examples of this, I feel, are Eddie Meredith and Gwydion, types of the magician, who use their power over others unscrupulously to advance themselves. Gwydion, in particular, uses his Welshness to exploit Wales through his position in television. He is so fundamentally disloyal that he is actually quite predictable. Humphreys is subtler when he shows characters discovering them-selves through myth. Peredur is an obvious example: his quest is that of a man who grows into knowledge of where he comes from and who he is. When we first meet him, Peredur is, in Maxine's words, 'not part of anything' (*NW*, 22). Returning to Wales for a job interview, he looks out of the college window at the sea, and reflects: 'I was a place before I became a person. Everything I looked at was part of an inheritance. Even the air I breathed was refurbished with myth and magic' (*BA*, 30). His story unfolds what is implied here: in becoming a person he has to know his place, and to know it as his inheritance.

It is with the aim of helping all his boys to achieve this that Cilydd gives them their names:

> They are names I gave them each in turn and the boys should know how they relate to something greater than themselves. The names should support them to live through a new age when all the appropriate commandments will be weakened because the myths that sustained them are fading away. (*BA*, 303)

Knowing how to relate to something greater than the self is a function of myth, and it is knowledge that relates to power, which is one of Humphreys's central themes. His characters have power, or seek power, in various forms: political power to change or influence the world; social position; moral force; sexual power. Amy Parry is driven by her fear of poverty to seek a power that raises her above it.

From her childhood as an adopted orphan in an impoverished home in rural Wales, through her friendship with Enid Prydderch and her betrothal to Val Gwyn, both of them idealists and Welsh nationalists, to marriage to Cilydd and involvement with Pen Lewis, and espousal of British Labour politics in 1945, and eventually to becoming the lady of Brangor Hall, Amy Parry is at the centre of the first five novels in the sequence. But if her story involves the acquisition of power, and the compromises and what others see as the betrayals by which she obtains it, Amy herself is also a power. It is in this respect, I think, that she is a symbol. In a sense she is a symbol of Wales, though this statement has to be qualified if one is not to give a wrong impression of the kind of novelist Humphreys is. Amy is a symbol because she is a source of life. Hence she is perceived by others as a princess, 'a warrior queen' (*OS*, 203), the queen of the land. Cilydd tells her: 'A Celtic goddess was always a mother . . . And a politician too. They were the real rulers of the old world' (*OS*, 199). Others tend to see her according to their needs, however. After she has brought the Red Dragon flag which is raised on the roof of the town council offices, Val sees her as 'the future. Her image is stamped on my heart' (*BF*, 18). Later he describes her as 'a very powerful symbol' (*BF*, 119). Nathan Harris perceives her as 'one of those choice, one of those rare beings able to restore the poetry that belongs by right to living' (*SOE*, 53). This is true. It is also profoundly ironical. Amy herself says: 'There's no poetry in me' (*FB*, 249). Moreover, unlike Enid, she has no understanding of Cilydd as a poet, and in consequence she has a distorted idea of him as a man. But Amy, through their perceptions of her, is a cause of poetry in others. Men (and women), Val, Cilydd, Pen, Hans Benck, the Jewish artist who is a refugee from Hitler's Europe, and others, all identify her with their life purposes. Cilydd says he cannot live without her, and he does not (although his suicide can also be ascribed to other causes). As an ideal and as a force of nature Amy is what other men and women desire, and it is in this sense that she may be described as a symbol of Wales.

It is ironic, of course, that she, who is identified with Wales, turns away from the Welsh nationalist cause. Yet, at the end of the sequence, she remains a source of hope. *Bonds of Attachment* ends with Peredur kissing her 'thin' hand (she has cancer). It is an ambiguous gesture, which may imply his assent to her plans for him to take over Brangor Hall and turn it into 'a centre of excellence and culture renaissance' (*BA*, 357), and, therefore, his acceptance of this as a fit role for his 'father's son'. This in itself may imply the opposite of hope, since the recurring idea of the big house as a 'centre' in the novels has suggested a kind of ghettoization: the retreat of Welsh culture and language from the country as a whole to a privileged enclave. Peredur kisses Amy's hand, however, as a courtier would kiss the hand of a queen, and as a son who acknowledges his mother with affection. Thus, at the end of the sequence of novels, Peredur has not only found his father, he has also learnt to accept his mother. As a Welshman, he is ready to draw upon both vital sources.

Both history and myth are involved in the theme of power in 'Land of the Living'. Humphreys's Wales is full of characters playing parts modelled on both. Among the most important roles is that of Arthur. Arthur, in fact, appears in two opposed forms. He is the Welsh Arthur, of which Llywelyn ap Gruffydd ('The Last Prince') is a type: a man such as Val Gwyn dedicated to the protection of Wales, and prepared to sacrifice his life in its defence. The other Arthur, a product of Geoffrey of Monmouth's fertile imagination, is the type that played a leading part in the Tudor myth, by which Wales came to lose the possibility of real political independence in performing a subservient role in the British Empire. As the principal modern representative of this type, David Lloyd George plays a significant part in 'Land of the Living'. Indeed, his presence may be said to haunt the sequence, as an idol in the minds of his admirers, as an inspiration for those ready to betray or exploit Wales in pursuit of their ambitions to become actors on the world (or London) stage, as an example to be avoided by those loyal to Wales. While Val Gwyn is seen by his followers as a type of the Welsh Arthur, Cilydd, in one of his mythological roles, is Myrddin, Arthur's friend, the magician driven mad by loss.

Before turning to a discussion of Cilydd, and while still dwelling on myth, it cannot be emphasized enough that Humphreys is a novelist concerned above all with lived experience. It is not for nothing that he has called the sequence 'Land of the Living', while his words about the making of *Outside the House of Baal* apply equally to it: 'That quality of the stream of living which separates the novel from the monumental marble of well-written history had to be a central element.'[11] His linguistic and formal originality as a novelist stems from his combination of a kind of Joycean 'objectivity', which relies heavily upon the construction of visual and filmic scenes, and the mythical method and other elements analogous to modernist experiment in music and painting, with a solid socially realistic rendering of men and women as members of a historical community. Talk of social realism will be misleading, however, if Humphreys's fundamental concern for the spiritual is ignored. In a talk quoted above which he gave in 1953 he spoke of Tolstoy and Dostoevsky as writers who 'looked upon themselves and upon all mankind as souls thirsting equally for salvation'.[12] Although it would be wrong to hold the mature novelist to account for everything the young writer said, it is surely true to say that the value Emyr Humphreys places upon the individual soul has not diminished. One of the ways in which this is depicted in the novels is by a method close to the Joycean epiphany. Humphreys's highly visual scenes depict moments of choice, in which what we 'see' is not all there is. The scenes or episodes occur in time, and the characters are inheritors of a past, and are faced in the present with choices that will affect the future. The main characters, moreover, have depths which are never fully revealed, partly because the characters themselves lack complete self-knowledge, and partly because Humphreys respects the essential mystery of human personality. He is a religious novelist for whom the idea of divine judgement is a reality. He is not, however, an omniscient author who presumes to the elevation of God's-eye view. Writing within a tradition of religious idealism, he describes characters who are judged by their own ideals or by the ideals handed down to them. This accounts for the quality of light which is peculiar to the novels. The light of day defines his vividly pictorial or cinematic scenes, but in addition, as these are moments of choice, another light – the light of the ideal – is present. One of his highest achievements is an art that is well described in the talk cited above:

> Each situation is not merely an event to be described, or even to be carefully and honestly interpreted: at the heart of each significant situation there is a mystery – like the universe in the grain of sand – which the artist must touch or at least approach: and the mark of his power will be a glow and a flourish about his work that indicates the sureness of his aim.[13]

This kind of illumination applies particularly to Amy Parry, Enid Prydderch and Val Gwyn. Cilydd and Peredur are 'darker'. The portrait of Cilydd is vulnerable to the criticism that it is too 'dark', because his 'failure' is overdetermined. That is to say, the question arises of why we are offered so many different reasons for his suicide. Does he kill himself because Amy leaves him? Or because he is ashamed of his homosexual attraction to Ken Lazarus? Or because he feels he has failed as a poet? Or because he believes Wales is dying, and sees himself as the last of the tribe? The question is worth asking, but not in order to single out one of the reasons as the decisive one. The fascination of the portrayal of Cilydd is that it focuses attention on the manifold pressures to which the Welsh poet in the twentieth century is subjected. It is also a means by which Humphreys sounds the depths of the modern predicament, through the particular situation of the Welsh poet. In other words, Cilydd, for all his particularity as a Welshman and a Welsh poet, indeed because of it, has something of the universality of a Hamlet, who is nonetheless European man for being Danish.

The parallel with Hamlet should not be taken too far, although it can be taken farther. Cilydd shares with the Danish prince the condition of being between worlds, in more than one sense. To begin with, he is a product of traditional Nonconformist Wales, represented by Glanrafon, home of the family presided over by his grandmother, the formidable Mrs Lloyd. The depiction of Glanrafon is one of the outstanding achievements of the sequence. Looked at from a distance, it is tempting to see Glanrafon as an ideal representation of old Wales: the strong, principled old woman, whose conviction of mankind's sinfulness is the foundation of her Nonconformist religion; the Stores; the farms; the brothers with their different occupations; Nanw, Cilydd's sister, who is bound to her 'place'; neighbours who frequent the Stores, such as Robert Thomas. The temptation to idealize Glanrafon is integral to the themes of the novel. Sali Prydderch says Enid 'idolised the place. She always talked about Glanrafon as if it were the earthly paradise' (*AH*, 15). Tasker Thomas describes it as 'salt of the earth', explaining:

> It's not the shop . . . It's what lies behind it. The economic base as our Marxian friends would say. There you have the earth and there you have the salt that gives the old Glanrafon family its savour. Two farms, Ponciau and Glanrafon. All maintained by family units and their

dependents and all equal in the eyes of the Lord. Now there is the true soil of civilisation. (*SOE*, 59)

In a significant phrase, he describes it as 'the poet's cradle'. 'Poetry', he says, 'needs roots in a community if it is to flower over a consistent period of time and not fizzle out like a firework or a nine days' wonder.' Tasker repeats this view in the next novel in the sequence, *An Absolute Hero*, but when he calls Glanrafon 'the poet's cradle' Cilydd replies: 'Or his prison' (*AH*, 66). Cilydd and Nanw, in their different ways, both experience their bonds to the place as a kind of bondage. That both ultimately commit suicide can be ascribed in part to the repressive effects of Mrs Lloyd's regime on their sexuality, and, more generally, to the fact that they find no new channel for the potent energies locked up in the old way of life. Glanrafon offers Cilydd as the model of a poet his Uncle Gwilym, whom he sees as 'self-important, over-sensitive, interfering, a bundle of prejudice, a rag-bag of illusions, the fag-end of an exhausted culture pattern and worst of all . . . a terrible portent of what I shall end up being myself' (*SOE*, 67). Talking to Amy, he remembers being able to 'communicate to no one except myself. Imagine a youth driven into himself and letting it seep out in convoluted tortured dollops of obscure poetry' (*AH*, 83). Rather than constituting a judgement upon Glanrafon, the fates of Cilydd and Nanw indicate the need for a tradition to renew itself, if what is true for one place and one time is to be true for another. This is a very different view from that which Welsh writers in English have frequently brought to bear on Nonconformity – Caradoc Evans offers grotesque and entertaining examples – in which it is caricatured as being inherently cruel and hypocritical and a breeding ground of sexual pathology.

As he breaks out of his 'prison' Cilydd loosens the pattern of his inheritance and experiences the chaos of modernity. He needs others to stabilize his life and give it structure, and he finds support in Enid and a leader in Val Gwyn. Constitutionally unsure of himself, and tormented by a sense of inadequacy, he adopts a divided way of life, working as a solicitor and, especially after the deaths of his first wife and friend, becoming more private as a poet. Enid has understood him as a poet and has encouraged him to write drama, on the grounds that 'the tradition needs expanding in order to contend with the complexities of new ways of living. Poetry can digest life best at the crisis point. And the crisis point has to occur in any dramatic form' (*BF*, 65). But Cilydd is no Saunders Lewis, and although we do hear of him writing drama, his poetic fragments quoted in the novels suggest an essentially lyric gift.

The chief of these is 'The hawk descends / With burning eyes / And where he strikes / The singing dies.' This becomes the poem with which he is identified in the public mind, and it recurs as a kind of refrain in different contexts throughout the novels, sometimes ironically, as when the 'elder statesman-like' Sir Joseph Macsen Morgan recites it 'with a resonant intonation' (*NW*, 151). In this instance, it forms part of the repertoire of one of Humphreys's influential windbags and wire-pullers, who have what he sees as the fatal gift of eloquence, which is a substitute for real action in Wales. The verse, in fact, is a fearful expression of menace, and a prophecy of Cilydd's silence. Like his other bird poems, it is associated with death. Peredur, discussing their father's poetry with his brother, Bedwyr, who thinks it 'a bit old-fashioned', says of Cilydd's 'apparent obsession with birds': 'They weren't just birds. They were people. He was trying to say something about people. Things he couldn't say out-right and directly because he was a member of what was still a very closely knit community' (*NW*, 118). Peredur is surely right in thinking the bird poems have human significance. Birds are traditionally symbols of the soul and of freedom, and in my view Humphreys uses Cilydd's obsession to express what is referred to at the beginning of *Open Secrets* as 'another spirit trapped somewhere in the depth of his material being' (*OS*, 1). Hefin Mather represents Cilydd as 'a figure straddled across an ideological abyss' (*BA*, 197). His specific reference is to 'the socialist vision and the processes of national regeneration in Wales', but the metaphor applies to Cilydd in other ways too. In respect of his art, it points to the conflict in his mind between an idea of artistic freedom and his need to fulfil the traditional role of the Welsh poet to celebrate and criticize his people. If he is to be taken at his own valuation as a failure, it is because he is unable consistently to transpose 'traditional motifs into modern formations' (*BA*, 102).

Near the end of his life, isolated from his wife, alienated from a large part of his community, and feeling that the Welsh culture is dying, Cilydd sees himself as 'the internal exile' (*BA*, 297). To Welsh nationalists of a later generation, such as Hefin Mather, he appears differently. Mather says to Peredur that his father and his friends 'revived the national spirit by returning to the source: the essential poetic vision' (*BA*, 194). So Cilydd lives on, influencing another generation; he is not only Peredur's father, but a vital part of the Welsh inheritance Peredur is seeking. Cilydd himself, though, had suffered the ultimate tragedy of the Welsh poet: internal exile.

Divided in his social roles, Cilydd is divided psychologically too. He is strongly influenced by his Nonconformist inheritance, but in reacting against it he espouses a kind of paganism. Through his worship of nature he is attracted to the 'Otherworld. Where there is no sickness. No pain. No loss. No betrayal' (*BF*, 370). This is a theme explored by a number of 'marginal' writers who draw upon Celtic myth – John Cowper Powys and Edward Thomas, for example – and it expresses, among other things, the inward-looking and backward-yearning condition of the isolated writer. Feeling 'a basic incapacity inside me. To connect with what I should connect with. To find what I should express' (*BF*, 371), Cilydd says, touching Enid's skin: 'This will cure my sickness. This is my salvation' (*BF*, 376). Later, with Amy, sex becomes for him a substitute for religion: 'When you stretch your waist I can picture a centre of grace as well as a centre of gravity' (*AH*, 86). In this respect, as in others, Cilydd is representative in his particularity. It is characteristic of other modern religious men without a religion, such as D. H. Lawrence and Alun Lewis, that sexuality or romance becomes the 'centre' of their universe.

Cilydd's homosexual attraction to Ken Lazarus echoes the homo-eroticism of First World War poetry. As the sequence unfolds we learn that, as Cilydd says, the war 'lies deep down inside me' (*SOE*, 17). He wants to place an image in the school memorial window to the pupils killed in the war. It is an image that he has seen in reality: 'A boy stripped to the waist. Little more than a boy. A sacrificial figure lashed to the wheel of a gun-carriage. Field punishment number one. In cruciform. Can you imagine a more powerful image?' (*OS*, 20). It is 'an image he had to impose on the society to which he belonged'. Cilydd sees Ken Lazarus, literally and symbolically, in the light of the window:

> The boy is beautiful. I first saw this when the school choir sang Pergolesi's Stabat Mater. The light from the stained glass window of the school memorial for the Fallen of the First War, fell on his face and gave it the innocent immortality of an Italian renaissance painting. The music

issues from his rounded mouth and the shaft of light glitters on his golden curls and domed forehead. It puts me in mind of the love I bore those whom the gods loved and took. (*BA*, 291)

Seeing Ken and other boys bathing, Cilydd says: 'Their naked figures restore the world to the unsullied innocence that must have been its original intention' (*BA*, 292). Ken, he writes, 'understood perfectly that the practice of art was a way of imposing discipline, order, significant form on the ungovernable torrents of subterranean passion' (*BA*, 292). Humphreys is at his most Joycean in these passages. The image of Ken's shyness adding 'to his attraction like the plumage of a rare bird' is reminiscent of Joyce's description of the girl wading in the sea in *A Portrait of the Artist as a Young Man*. It is more than a verbal echo, for Humphreys, like Joyce, shows the growth of the image of beauty in the mind, and how religion and romantic idealism and sexual desire play a part in its formation. In Cilydd's case, the idea of primal innocence in the Garden, with its source in the religion of Glanrafon, haunts his imagination. We are enabled to see something of the complex formation of the meaning of Ken Lazarus for Cilydd, but he sees the image only, 'the unsullied innocence', and does not acknowledge *his* 'ungovernable torrents of subterranean passion'. While Cilydd is highly self-conscious he seems, as he himself admits, unable to connect with the passions in his depths.

The poems ascribed to Cilydd do not provide intimate revelations of his personality or philosophy, as is the case with Taliessin in John Cowper Powys's *Porius*. They are revelatory, nevertheless, in their very fragmentariness. As the Americans work on the construction of the hydrogen bomb, Cilydd reflects: 'Fissile material was no longer poetic material because this degree of fragmentation undermined all previous known forms of coherent poetry' (*BA*, 306). Now, towards the end of his life (he dies in 1952), he is possessed by the feeling of powerlessness which has, in fact, dogged him all his life. 'There was a time', he says to Amy,

'when we believed we had some power to influence the way things were going. We could save Wales if we put effort into it. A little more effort and we could save the world. If anything, that would be easier. We believed that what we said and what we did would make a difference. So naive and childish it all seems now. I can't even save this little patch from desecration. I've no influence over anything. I'll end up an outcast even in my own country.' (*OS*, 257)

In this period, he is writing a poem 'about Merlin in his glass prison', as Amy tells Hans (*OS*, 230).

Cilydd, with bitter irony, informs the English Colonel Ricks that Myrddin 'was a good deal more than a wizard. He went mad in the woods.' He goes on to tell the colonel that Myrddin was driven mad by war, which 'forced him as it were outside the human race' (*NW*, 251). That Cilydd has identified himself with Myrddin is an ominous sign of his state of mind. In what is taken to be his suicide note, Cilydd writes: 'I have seen the black sail . . . The son of purity will not come . . . The hero lies under a sea of glass' (*NW*, 310). These are fragments of his Myrddin poem, with images of death, and the magician's imprisonment in his Otherworld realm (the 'sea of glass'), and the failure of the heroic ideal. The despair is clear enough; as Ken Lazarus says: 'He died of despair' (*NW*, 352). Ken remembers 'a poem called *The Black Sail*' (of which the note is presumably a fragment). 'It was full of the idea of death. His own end was the end of a culture. He was the last of a defeated tribe. He saw his corpse washed up on a shore of time' (*NW*, 253).

While the identification with the imprisoned Myrddin portends Cilydd's death, it also contains seeds of hope. He himself has emphasized that it was in his state of madness that Myrddin 'acquired the gift of prophecy' (*NW* 251). Myrddin, moreover, 'goes on talking from the grave'.

> His body is corrupted in the usual way, but his consciousness still has a voice and the heroes search for his tomb in order to consult the oracle about their own behaviour, their courses of action, their decisions. So that the loser in the end turns out to be the only guide to the true winner. (*NW*, 252)

As this stands, in *National Winner*, it may seem too schematic. As the pattern is worked out in living in the sequence, though, it is much less so. Peredur actively searches for his father's tomb, and is consciously in quest of his inheritance. But Bedwyr and Gwydion too, although far less interested in their father, and certainly not consciously wanting to consult him as 'the oracle', realize different possibilities of the inheritance he has bequeathed to them. Cilydd's voice lives on in his poetry, with ironic and ambiguous effects. It is probably in the nature of all poetry with sufficient life for it to be useful in different ways to readers with different needs. In W. H. Auden's crude but effective formulation: 'The words of a dead man are modified in the guts of the living.'[14] In the context of Cilydd's frustrated aspirations, it is particularly important that Hefin Mather asks Peredur: 'You know that your father was a national poet of real importance' (*BA*, 38). Mather places Cilydd in what Humphreys has called 'The Taliesin Tradition', in which poets are voices of resistance, defenders of Welsh identity: 'He was essentially a shape-shifter: a Gwion Bach on the long flight to illumination and rebirth.' By this image, Cilydd's obsession with birds is transformed into the imaginative flight he felt he had failed to make. In a sense, the truth of Ken Lazarus's words is borne out: 'He despaired too soon' (*NW*, 352).

This is a tempting judgement to make, but as Humphreys shows through his treatment of characters as 'souls', we are not in a position to make absolute judgements on other people's lives. It is in this respect that I find M. Wynn Thomas's phrase 'the creative spirit of uncertainty'[15] so suggestive. Humphreys shows us lives in time, in which the meaning of individual lives is not bounded by death, since they have shaping effects on those who come after them, as they have been influenced by those who came before. Given the complexity of life with all its bonds of attachment, in weighing motives and ultimate meanings, anything but 'the creative spirit of uncertainty' is crude. The history of which Emyr Humphreys writes is not finished; the ideas and ideals and powers that clash in his fiction continue to struggle for the determination of Welsh identity. In the sequence, as in real life, Wales is imagined through its poets, and poetry is a source of renewal. Thus, visiting Glanrafon, now 'The Glanrafon Arms', Peredur wonders what he would have to tell the new owners to convey the importance of his father as a poet to them:

> What doctoral chair was reserved for the justification of fragments? I would have to tell them that he had in mind the celebration of one particular landscape throughout the aeon of its being and the mystical relationship nurtured in time between the genius of the place and the genius of the people? A huge ambition encompassed in a modesty of means because it would have been a continuation and extension of a poetic tradition which had itself been sustained for centuries by talents as skilled and anonymous as the medieval cathedral builders. (*BA*, 78)

Is this the ambition Cilydd had nurtured? This is not really what the novels have shown. What we have been made aware of is his tense situation as a man between two worlds: his inner divisions, including his need for 'self-expression' and his resistance to it, because it is associated with the bourgeois concept of 'freedom' that alienates a poet from his community. But, tragically, Cilydd becomes alienated in any case. As a young man he reflected: 'The dislocated imagination indulges in choices which are no choice at all – a condition made worse by being bilingual. To have always two tongues you need two faces' (*BA*, 266). The 'two tongues', English and Welsh, present him with irreconcilable choices. He asks himself why he has 'to say "no" to selfish passions that could transform pedestrian lines with their incandescence' (*BA*, 273). He cannot reconcile this desire with his destiny as a Welsh poet, or, more poignantly, he cannot find the poetic means to reconcile it. Cilydd is depicted by Humphreys as a man under intolerable strain *because* he is a poet unable to resolve psychological splits that arise out of his predicament as a Welshman. It is the author's choice to do so, of course. He could have chosen to create the figure of a modern Welsh poet who makes a whole art in dark times. As Gerwyn Wiliams has indicated, the novels are echo chambers of allusions to Welsh writing: 'There is a kind of hidden stratum of reference to Welsh literary texts and literary figures running throughout the novels.'[16] The references create a structure that one might expect to sustain the idea of the modern Welsh poet in the novels. But the fictional Cilydd, by contrast with actual poets such as Gwenallt and Saunders Lewis (and Emyr Humphreys himself), collapses under the conflicts and strains endemic to the predicament of Welsh identity in the twentieth century, and in consequence his fate and his 'fragments' help to reveal that predicament in depth. However, although he despairs, not only is the situation not hopeless, but, paradoxically, Cilydd helps to sustain the hope with which others carry on the struggle.

Peredur himself is not completely certain that he has understood his father's ambition correctly, as the question marks and conditional 'would have' in the passage above indicate. The vision, however, is Peredur's developing perception of the relationship between the landscape and the people, which he is building on his interpretation of his father's ambition. It is in this way that an individual existence, though concluded in time and shaped by choices which no other human being can judge, survives as a creative force that acts upon other lives.

4

Alun Lewis: A Study in Poetic Courage

Alun Lewis mocked himself when, in 1943, he wrote, in a poem from India:

> I curled up in the darkness like a dog
> And being a romantic stubbed my eyes
> Upon the wheeling spoke shave of the stars.[1]

But, while Lewis made fun of himself for 'being a romantic', it is evident that he was strongly influenced by poets who could be described, broadly, as romantic (or even Romantic) – John Keats, W. B. Yeats, Edward Thomas, Rainer Maria Rilke and D. H. Lawrence – and that his sense of being connected to the cosmos (which he here makes light of), or disconnection from it, is an integral part of his Romantic inheritance. Lewis was in India as a soldier; he was serving as an officer with the South Wales Borderers, and his war, since his enlistment in 1940, had been one of physical training and intense mental and emotional activity, which he expressed in his poems and short stories, but no battle experience. Nor was he to have any experience of combat, since he died in an accident in Burma shortly before his battalion was due to go into action against the Japanese. In this chapter, I shall begin by looking quite briefly at the conflict within Lewis between his humanism and official responsibilities as an officer, and his isolation and loneliness, since the subject has been dealt with fully by Lewis's biographer, John Pikoulis, and other critics; my main aims are to consider Lewis as a poet in the Romantic tradition, a poet whose concerns were essentially religious,[2] and to define what I take to be his poetic courage.

John Pikoulis, in his biography of Lewis, makes the point that when, in 1926, Lewis was sent away from his home in the Mid Glamorgan coal-mining village of Cwmaman, to Cowbridge Grammar School, 'he had, in effect, been rendered isolate'.[3] Pikoulis shows, however, that a certain isolation, within his community, had characterized Lewis's life from the beginning, since his parents, as teachers, were somewhat set apart from their neighbours, and his mother had not insisted on her children attending Sunday school or chapel, which, as Lewis's own poems show, was a focal point in the village. Moreover, Lewis's father was Welsh-speaking, but Lewis himself received an English education. He was therefore distanced from the Welsh language and Welsh religion, with the result that, like other English-language writers from modern Wales, he developed ambiguous feelings towards his native community. On the one hand it seemed to him narrow and rigid. On the other it represented an idea of social warmth and of 'The People', an idea that he romanticized because he was partially excluded from the reality.

Lewis's populism was bound up with his sense of himself as a teacher. This was manifested in the venture of the Caseg Broadsheets – poems with wood-engravings, in the tradition of seventeenth- and eighteenth-century chapbooks, on which Lewis worked, with Brenda Chamberlain and John Petts, from November 1941 to June 1942.[4] About these Lewis wrote to Chamberlain that he had 'two urgent needs': 'one, to write for, the other, to educate, *The People*' (*Life*, 130). His draft prospectus, headed 'for the people of Wales', is especially revealing of his populist idealism centred on Wales, and how it related to the war:

> Welsh cities are being destroyed. Welsh boys are soldiering in other lands. Wales is proving herself by her blood and her faith, as so many peoples the world over are doing.
>
> The Caseg Broadsheets want to express that faith, to prove that it is a living, creative spirit, the spirit that has informed the land and its people for hundreds of years. (*Life*, 277)

Lewis goes on to say that the Broadsheets consist 'of poems by Welsh poets from Aneirin and Taliesin a thousand years ago to Williams Parry and the Welsh poets living today', and 'will include, it is hoped, poems by Dylan Thomas, Vernon Watkins, Glyn Jones, Keidrich Rhys, A. G. Prys-Jones, Huw Menai and Alun Lewis'. The draft prospectus is written in a public language, which confidently affirms the existence of a thousand-year-old Welsh poetic tradition, links Welsh-language and English-language poets together as though both groups were equally part of it, and co-opts the 'blood and faith' of Wales, 'the living, creative spirit informing the land and its people', to the prosecution of the present war. The contradictions inherent in this become vividly apparent if one imagines the reaction to it of Emyr Humphreys's fictional Welsh poet, John Cilydd More, or of any actual Welsh poet who was a nationalist and a pacifist.

There is no doubt, however, that Lewis, who was a democrat and a socialist, is sincere in what he says; he believed that the war against Hitler had to be fought and won, and in the name of a superior 'faith', which initially integrated his commitment to Wales into his service with the British army. It is when one looks at his actual writings about Wales that a more complicated picture emerges.

The poem 'A Welsh Night', for example, looks fairly straight-forward in its celebration of 'the hand-pressed human warmth / Of families', but its conclusion is ambiguous.

> Hearing the clock strike midnight by the river
> This village buried deeper than the corn
> Bows its blind head beneath the angelic planes,
> And cherishing all known and suffered harm
> It wears the darkness like a shroud or shawl. (*CP*, 100)

Imagery of darkness so pervades Lewis's poetry that it virtually con-stitutes a poetic language in itself, one that is rich in different, and frequently ambiguous, meanings. In this instance, the shawl suggests maternal protectiveness, and the shroud death, while 'buried deeper than the corn' intimates both. 'Cherishing' harm, moreover, bal-ances comforting nurture with incubated ills, while 'the angelic planes' suggest a disembodied evil – powers of the air – in contrast to the blindly rooted village. Darkness thus carries the contrary meanings, as it often does in Romantic poetry, signifying that which would protect but may also suffocate, and death that is feared, but also longed for as bringer of peace.

'A Welsh Night' is also typical of Lewis's writings about Wales in associating religion with the people and the land. Here, Garth mountain 'Lies grey as a sermon of patience / For the threadbare congregations of the anxious'. The lines evoke a landscape saturated with chapel religion, and, as in Lewis's famous 'The Mountain over Aberdare', with its 'Grey Hebron in a rigid cramp', the sentiment belongs to a structure of feeling about the life-denying character of

Nonconformity, which is common in English-language Welsh writing, and present in English writers such as D. H. Lawrence and Ted Hughes. In 'The Mountain over Aberdare', however, the lines

> that white frock that floats down the dark alley
> Looks just like Christ; and in the lane
> The clink of coins among the gamblers
> Suggests the thirty pieces of silver. (*CP*, 87)

strike a different note. A more familiar idea would be that of a community betrayed by the economic and political forces that caused the Depression, but Lewis's imagery suggests rather an inner betrayal, which the poet, to whom the 'white frock' 'Looks just like Christ', is also conscious of in himself. This incipient sense of betrayal is especially significant in relation to the guilt Lewis was to feel in his later encounter with India.

Lewis was a man who periodically suffered from terrible depressions, in which he turned ferociously upon himself. In 1937, for instance, he wrote to a friend: 'I've lived too introspectively, and I feel just as though I've been feeding on myself until I've eaten myself up' (*Life*, 62). Later letters, written in more desperate circumstances, tell the same story. In 1943 he wrote to Freda Aykroyd about the 'trouble' that 'becomes a force in me, disrupting and corroding, & I've got a real fight then. It's always manifested itself in an intense awareness of the *waste* that I'm causing or suffering' (*Life*, 243–4). This sense of being lived by a destructive force is, as it were, the negative side of Lewis's vitalism, his affirmation of 'Life'; it is also related to the feeling of being 'possessed' that he sometimes expresses in writing about poetic inspiration, and his awareness of the attendant risk of insanity[5] – again an experience that was part of his Romantic heritage.

In a letter to his wife Gweno in December 1943 Lewis wrote: 'I am aware always of forces more powerful than myself. They are the determinants: it's always been a hard fight for me to keep my self as an individual integrated against these forces.'[6] It was a fight which he won temporarily through love, which for Lewis meant more than the relationship with another person on which it was founded. As he wrote in 'War Wedding V, *The Marriage Bed*':

> The fragile universe of self
> In all its fine integrity

Becomes a cosmic curve, a thrust
Of natural fertility;
And Gods who shivered in the dust
Have found their lost divinity. (*CP*, 65)

This divinizing of human love, by which the lover, connected to
nature through the beloved, becomes a force within the universe, is
strongly reminiscent of D. H. Lawrence, whose thought and imagery
were among the most potent influences on Lewis. One may wonder
whether both men, in the critical circumstances of their lives, having
practically turned marriage into a religion, did not put too much
pressure upon human frailty.

It is easy to see that Lewis was a poet of internal conflict, and
tempting to describe this as *his* war. As he wrote to Gweno in a later
letter in December 1943:

My main reason for living is to write and I've got a very strong feeling
that I could have done the job better in the ranks. But I'm not interested
in pips and crowns, and all my efforts are bent otherwise and at present
inwards where all the battle is. (*LTMW*, 415)

Obviously, Lewis's subject was not that of combatant poets, such as
Wilfred Owen and Keith Douglas. But it is only a little less obvious,
perhaps, that their battles also were partly 'inwards'. In words that
would become famous, Lewis declared to Gweno, in a letter from
India, that he was 'more and more engrossed with the *single* poetic
theme of Life and Death, for there doesn't seem to be any question
more directly relevant than this one of what survives of all the
beloved' (*LTMW*, 326). The words are redolent of Lewis's religious
sensibility, but, making due allowances for different emphases of
other poetic minds, it is hard to see what else would engross a
soldier-poet in wartime, whether like Lewis and Edward Thomas he
wrote his poems outside the battle zone (in so far as anywhere could
be described as that during the Second World War), or whether like
Owen and Douglas he wrote in periods of respite from actual
combat.

Lewis took the title for his second book of poems, *Ha! Ha!
Among the Trumpets*, from the Book of Job. He said that he chose
the title 'sarcastic-like'.[7] But sarcasm, except at the expense of 'the
officermind and its artificial assumptions' (*LTMW*, 291), did not go

very deep with Lewis. He struck a more characteristic note when, early in the war, he wrote to Robert Graves of 'the simple, cosmic loneliness that is as natural to a man today as to the old Ecclesiast'.[8] The sense of a living biblical perspective was greatly reinforced for Lewis by what he found among the people and in the land of India, where he was powerfully drawn to Buddhist and Hindu wayside shrines and rituals. Writing to Gweno two months before his death, for instance, he describes his reaction at hearing 'the villagers at their orisons': 'I wished to be away among them and of them, for in the hypercivilised world you and I belong to I've never been able to accept or discover a religion as simple and natural as I need' (*LTMW*, 419). The need of the man standing apart from the Indian villagers to be 'among them and of them' recalls Lewis's distant, and longingly idealized, relationship to his original Welsh community, and to 'the Welsh People' invoked by the Caseg Broadsheets; it also reflects the relation in which he stood, as an officer, to the Welsh 'boys' he was leading; and in each case the need to be 'among them and of them' was, inevitably, frustrated. It is equally true, however, that if Lewis had had a lesser sense of connection to his own land and people he would not have come to feel in India, as acutely as he did, the plight of 'the landless soldier lost in war' ('The Mahratta Ghats', *CP*, 131).

There is no reason to doubt Lewis's sincerity when, in a letter from India in November 1943, he told his parents: 'I regret my lack of Welsh very deeply: I really will learn it when I come home again', and went on to say, 'When I come back I shall always tackle my writing through Welsh life and ways of thought: it's my only way.' But it is hard not to see this as a reaction to the isolation and self-consciousness that India forced upon him, or, rather, accentuated. The man who in the same letter writes of getting 'to grips with the details of life as I haven't yet done; the law, the police, the insurance, the hospitals, the employment exchanges, the slums',[9] is the same man who, at the shrine of a 'little granite Buddha', has asked a question and *felt the refusal*. A wall of darkness, hard, resistant, smooth-surfaced'.[10] He is also the man who has lost faith in the civilization which, as a soldier of an army of occupation in India, he represents. Earlier in the war he had written in a journal: 'Some writers starting among the people climb a Jacob's ladder into loneliness and introspection . . . They have gone wrong. They must come back to Tolstoi, to the art which works through a vast human sympathy, through the community of human beings . . . We must go into Life.'[11] Now, he felt that the 'problem' of the British in India was 'too vast for us. I wish I had come here as a doctor, teacher, social worker: anything but a soldier. It's not nice being a soldier in India' (*LTMW*, 394). With its cool understatement, this is all the more effective in showing the predicament of Lewis, with his Tolstoyan sympathies, as a soldier in India. And as a writer, too: no wonder the man who was a poet and teacher with a highly developed social conscience should have turned back to 'the community of human beings' in Wales.

Lewis was in some ways very much a man of the thirties, who shared with the Auden generation, who had been too young to fight in the First World War, the need to put himself to a test.[12] In India it was the test of 'cosmic loneliness'. Aloneness, however, had always been one pole of Lewis's experience. He had sought it by the sea and among the mountains of Wales – a condition that could be equated with the solitude beloved of the Romantic poets. It was a significant moment when Lewis wrote to Gweno from Longmoor in January 1941 asking her to buy the Penguin edition of Richard Jefferies's *The Story of My Heart*. 'I read it in the train on Tuesday', Lewis says. 'It's the nearest expression of my religion that I've read' (*LTMW*, 93). In his sometimes rhapsodic spiritual autobiography, Jefferies described how he 'stood bare-headed before the sun, in the presence of the earth and air, in the presence of the immense forces of the universe', the literal 'bare-headed' being also a metaphor for Jefferies's iconoclastic dismissal of the entire human thought-world. Edward Thomas had been profoundly influenced by Jefferies's nature mysticism, and it was not entirely a positive influence as we see in, for example, Thomas's treatment of the 'mystic' David Morgan in *The Happy-Go-Lucky Morgans,* a man who dies because in seeking 'the One' he breaks his ties to the human world. Morgan's desire for aloneness was Thomas's, as it was also Jefferies's (though both men sought solitary communion with nature rather than 'the One'). It was Alun Lewis's desire, too; he was spiritually akin to Jefferies and Thomas, although he was quick to add to his comment on Jefferies, 'Except that I think more of others than he does'.[13]

Solitary communion with nature is one thing; isolation is another, and Lewis experienced it as self-imprisonment, in states of severe depression and tortuous introspection. This was partly what drew him to Edward Thomas, who had suffered from similar states. Lewis in his aloneness could be rapt or despairing, and he frequently dramatized in his writings the tension between solitude or loneliness and companionable involvement with others at work or play. Even in 'All Day It Has Rained' he alternates between the 'we' of experience shared with his fellow soldiers, and perceiving and remembering as 'I', the sensitive individual who feels close to Edward Thomas, who 'brooded long / On death and beauty – till a bullet stopped his song' (*CP*, 23).

Writing about his first book of poems, *Raiders' Dawn*, Lewis said that for him 'like Edward Thomas the war has become an integral part of his life experience, not a violent thought-slaying wound as it was to Owen' (*Life*, 115). Life experience is the key to Lewis's poems, and it should be understood not only in relation to Thomas's personal 'voice', but also to the thought of Rainer Maria Rilke, which deeply influenced Lewis. Rilke, in *Letters to a Young Poet*, urged patience upon the poet and said: 'the point is, to live everything. *Live* the questions now. Perhaps you will then gradually, without noticing it, live along some distant day into the answer.'[14] Rilke urged the necessity of experience:

> We must assume our existence as *broadly* as we in any way can; everything, even the unheard-of, must be possible in it. That is at bottom the only courage that is demanded of us: to have courage for the most strange, the most singular and the most inexplicable that we may encounter.[15]

Rilke used a number of terms that came to have a talismanic significance for Lewis. These included patience, simplicity, experience, strangeness and courage. The passage quoted above continues with Rilke saying that mankind has been cowardly in crowding out 'the experiences that are called "visions", the whole so-called "spirit-world", death, all those things that are so closely akin to us'. Lewis, even more than Rilke, had reason to develop a daily intimacy with death, and like Rilke he became fascinated by the 'spirit-world'.[16]

Rilke's idea of courage has a special relevance for my present argument. Rilke sees it as integral to the poet's inner depth, and willingness to experience that which is strange, and necessity of waiting, humbly and patiently, 'To let each impression and each germ of feeling come to completion wholly in itself, in the dark, in the inexpressible, the unconscious'.[17] The dark, in this sense, is a kind of germinative darkness, essential to the creative process. This helps to explain Lewis's use of organic metaphors which connect the mind to the world. Understood thus, darkness has a healing quality, as in 'the dark imagination' of Lewis's 'After Dunkirk' (*CP*, 40); it is both in the poet, as his faculty of creative imagination, and outside, in the circumambient unknown. Unlikely as it may have seemed to other people, such as the instructor at Karachi who accused Lewis of being 'the most selfish man' he had ever met, because 'You think the war exists for you to write books about it' (*LTMW*, 397), Lewis was 'living the artist's life' in Rilke's sense, even as he was 'sloping arms or doing a fifteen mile route march' (*Life*, 107).

On one occasion Lewis wrote to Gweno: 'I cherish the power to think and feel above all; even when it's agony to think' (*LTMW*, 226). This is indeed what the letters and poems and stories show: that Lewis's whole effort as a human being (not as a writer only, for he equated writing with life experience) required great psychological and spiritual courage. The demands that his writing made on his spirit and mind can be gauged from his description of struggling over several nights to write a poem:

> I was enticed, seduced and destroyed by the long octopus arms and hungry hard mouth of a shapeless poem that will never be written. It seized me with soft little thrills as I entered the tent, and each night till long after midnight, I've wrestled vainly with it in the long battle of thoughts and words. When I did at last go to bed I felt spiritually bewildered and unnerved, as though the thoughts had battered and exhausted me. And I knew last night, that I couldn't *live* with the thoughts that encircled this particular poem . . . (*LTMW*, 335)

Lewis's imagery here could be regarded as a sign of sexual frustration. It would be truer, I think, to see it as a manifestation of the fact that Lewis wrote from the whole of himself, body and spirit. More coolly and more schematically, his surrogate in 'Prologue: The Grinder' says:

> I've used my strength in striving for the vision,
> And *with* the vision – like old Jacob's stress;
> And I have worked to outline with precision
> Existence in its native nakedness. (*CP*, 21)

In the far greater stress of his life 'within the darkness / Of India' ('To Rilke', *CP*, 125), the striving with an angel has become wrestling with an octopus, creature of the deep sea, of chaos.

The struggle is one that Lewis was aware could kill him. This was something he knew about himself and I do not think anything is to be gained by a wisdom after the event that describes him in terms of a 'death wish', any more than we learn anything about Edward Thomas by taking the last line of his poem 'Old Man', 'Only an avenue, dark, nameless, without end', and interpreting his life as a quest for the darkness of death. Such psychological readings take up a position outside the poet's existential situation, the 'darkness' in which he or she lives and writes, which is also the darkness in which the reader lives. There is a temptation to simplify Lewis by interpreting his work in terms of his 'end' – the death in mysterious circumstances, which has widely been supposed to have been suicide. My view is that the meaning of his work is in the questions that he lived, not only questions specific to his time and circumstances, but metaphysical and social questions which still concern us today. The meaning is not to be found in his death, any more than the meaning of Edward Thomas's life and work is to be found in 'the bullet' that 'stopped his song'. Lewis saw India as his 'test' as a man, but it was also the test of the values of western civilization. In 'Midnight in India' he compared West and East:

> Here is no mined and cratered deep
> As in the fenced-off landscapes of the West
> Within the Eastern wilderness
> The human war is lost. (*CP*, 162)

As I read Lewis, the 'point' of his work is not in that despairing, 'The human war is lost', but in the dramatic exploration of 'the human war' that his writing as a whole constitutes.

Lewis was in some ways a confessional writer, as the letter about his struggle with the poem reveals. Before leaving for India, he had written, in 'On Embarkation', a personal confession summarizing his experience of the past twenty years:

> A girl's affections or a new job lost,
> A lie that burns the soft stuff in the brain,
> Lust unconfessed, a scholarship let go
> Or gained too easily, without much point –
> Each hurt a search for those old country gods
> A man takes with him in his native tongue

Finding a friendly word for all things strange,
The firm authentic truth of roof and rain.
And on the cliff's green brink where nothing stirs,
Unless the wind should stir it, I perceive
A child grow shapely in the loins I love. (*CP*, 116)

This is a poignant moment, for several reasons. There is the way in which the contingent autobiographical details disclose their underlying significance as 'a search for those old country gods'. There is the contrast between the idealized 'firm authentic truth of roof and rain' and the actual complexity of Lewis's life in Wales, as revealed in the preceding autobiographical passage, or in a poem such as 'The Mountain over Aberdare'. There is also the fact that one would suppose 'those old country gods' to inhabit the 'native tongue' that Lewis's father spoke, but he did not. And now, at this moment, and in this place, at the edge of Cardiganshire where Lewis faces 'the green Atlantic', he also confronts the imagined future, which he sees as a continuity that will live beyond him, in the child his wife carries. This was not to be, however. The passage suggests a continuous tradition such as that which Lewis had celebrated in his draft prospectus for the Caseg Broadsheets: 'the spirit that has informed the land and its people for hundreds of years'. But his words disclose another reality, which is that of the poet's longing for a 'truth' he does not have, and will not have.

For Lewis, it was poetry rather than the war that was the life-or-death struggle. But his inner battle was, of course, connected to the outer war, which shaped his experience for three years, and which forced him to ask ultimate questions. The latter required considerable moral courage. As he wrote to Gweno:

> Death is a great mystery, who can ignore him? But I don't *seek* him, oh no – only I would like to 'place' him . . . isn't Death a stranger that one 'takes'? So much is strange in all things – the essential virtue in such strangeness is courage – to test, and endure and abide by what so slowly and surely emerges. (*LTMW*, 354)

Again, the key terms are Rilke's, which Lewis has made his own. One is aware here of Lewis's idea of 'patience, which in Latin means suffering or enduring, and implies having faith' (*LTMW*, 198), which recalls Rilke's idea of waiting 'to let each impression and each germ of feeling come to completion wholly in itself, in the dark'. Rilke's life of leisure, one would suppose, was a good deal more conducive to patient waiting than Lewis's life of army fatigues and discipline and frictional contact with 'the officermind', and one can only wonder at his determined and persistent self-opening to inner depths in the circumstances in which he found himself. The language he uses is that of 'vision', because his quest is metaphysical. He seeks ultimate meaning: in the cause for which he is fighting, in marriage, in 'the *single* poetic theme of Life and Death'.

Initially, life was his supreme value. This was not an abstraction. Julian Maclaren-Ross said of him: 'Lewis had a deep tenderness towards life itself', by which Maclaren-Ross meant 'small things – animals, children', and 'his Welsh village, his wife'.[18] Lewis's love was for particular identities within 'the whole of Wales', which in 'In Hospital: Poona (1)' he embraced 'within the parish of my care' (*CP*, 140). But like D. H. Lawrence, who, as I have already said, profoundly influenced his vitalism, Lewis also apprehended life as a dynamic force. Sometimes this was a force which he felt lived through him, without his ability to control it – on one occasion, writing to Gweno from India, he described himself as 'just some animation the world has set flowing and compelled to develop into and out of itself' (*LTMW*, 396). Sometimes it was a force which he felt he himself represented. In 'Lines on a Tudor Mansion', for example, he says of himself and his fellow soldiers: 'We are of Life' and likens them to 'the soft silk flash of the swifts / Which do not care for the houses of the wealthy / But have instead their own instinctive life'. How will they be remembered?

> Only the fleeting sunlight in the forest,
> And dragonflies' blue flicker in quiet pools
> Will perpetuate our vision
>
> Who die young. (*CP*, 34)

The soldier-poet here dramatizes his shared predicament. He speaks of transience, but of a vital fleetingness that is, paradoxically, perpetuated: not only by things that die, but by a vision of life.

One may set beside this poem a passage from a letter which he wrote to Gweno from camp at Longmoor in 1941. He tells her that, looking at his face in the water of a stream, he has asked 'Why have

I been so abominably miserable this week and now?' The answer came from 'my voice . . . in my head'.

> It said: 'Not because of myself am I unhappy. I must know that. For I have solved my own problems. I have found myself which I have always always known could only be by finding the woman with whom I have always, in my dreaming and miseries loved and loved and for a long time could not find. Now I have found you and I myself know the course that leads to harbour.' Why am I unhappy then? Well, because I am unhappy for the world; because the world is full of war and ambition and cruelty, and the defeat of goodness and the victory of the brute. And I am in the toil and turmoil of trying to overthrow that evil dispensation and recover its soul for the world. (*LTMW*, 130)

The reported episode ends with Lewis spitting over the parapet of the bridge into the water, 'to break my face'; an action which shows a self-mocking awareness of the romantic narcissist, but takes nothing away from the seriousness of his reflections.

It is characteristic of Lewis that he expresses his ideals in high terms which link him to the world, whose 'soul' it is his purpose 'to recover'. This is virtually an expression of religious faith in his reasons for fighting, and it shows how much he had to lose should anything occur to undermine it. Consequently it is poignant for the reader to recall the letter when, in India, Lewis came to look into another river, and to write 'The Jungle'.

This poem begins, mysteriously, with an image of 'the stagnant pool' holding 'Autumn rotting like an unfrocked priest'. It is not too literal-minded, I think, to ask 'which priest?' Surely Lewis means himself, and we may infer a burden of personal guilt,[19] but also the sense of failure of the man whose mission was to recover its soul for the world. 'The Jungle' is a poem of loss of faith, possibly in the ideal of a single love upon which, earlier, Lewis has founded his life, and certainly in western civilization, which it is his function to defend. Underlying this failure is renunciation of the world which Lewis, in accordance with eastern religions, has made. As Jacqueline Banerjee says:

> The call to seek 'less and less of world', as he put it in 'Karanje Village', was bound to be bewildering to a man with strong humanist values and deep personal attachments, and all the more perplexing when these values and attachments were such an important source of strength to him.[20]

In 'The Jungle' he seems to be recalling his own earlier poem, 'Lines on a Tudor Mansion'. Now,

> we who dream beside this jungle pool
> Prefer the instinctive rightness of the poised
> Pied kingfisher deep darting for a fish
> To all the banal rectitude of states,
> The dew-bright diamonds on a viper's back
> To the slow poison of a meaning lost
> And the vituperations of the just. (*CP*, 156)

He remembers 'Instinctive truths and elemental love'; but these now exist in the past tense, recalling 'their own instinctive life, / The flight and rhythm of the blood', which, in the earlier poem, the soldiers, in Lawrencian fashion, are said to 'have'. But 'The Jungle' is a poem of lost meaning, of corrupted faith; and while in the letter in which Lewis described viewing his face in a stream he had projected a whole image, in this poem the image is drowned.

In his diagnostic overview of social ills in 'The Jungle' Lewis shows what he has learnt from W. H. Auden. He too sums up what Auden in 'September 1, 1939' called 'a low dishonest decade'.

> The weekly bribe we paid the man in black,
> The day shift sinking from the sun,
> The blinding arc of rivets blown through steel,
> The patient queues, headlines and slogans flung
> Across a frightened continent, the town
> Sullen and out of work, the little home
> Semi-detached, suburban, transient
> As fever or the anger of the old,
> The best ones on some specious pretext gone. (*CP*, 155–6)

The detail of the third line is as graphically visual as Stanley Spencer's *Shipbuilding on the Clyde* and the whole passage recalls the contemporary cinema, as Graham Greene's novels and Auden's poems did, while the position from which Lewis looks down on his society, as he had done in 'The Mountain over Aberdare', also recalls Auden in being a critical as well as pictorial overview. This is social poetry; but it is not the primary focus of 'The Jungle', which is interior: 'the black spot', in which Lewis, as in 'On Embarkation', has a summary vision of his own life, personal detail augmenting 'The tangled wrack of motives drifting down / An oceanic tide of Wrong'. This remorseless invocation of waste and wreckage concludes:

> And though the state has enemies we know
> The greater enmity within ourselves. (*CP*, 156)

'We', he says, but the emphasis in 'The Jungle' is on 'aloneness, swinging slowly / Down the cold orbit of an older world / Than any they predicted in the schools'. This is the world as it appears on the far side of 'the humming cultures of the West'; and here, the high ideal of the poet born in that culture, the priestly function in which he conceives of himself as restorer to the world of its soul, is seen as a corrupted, drowned image.

It is hard not to think of 'The Jungle' as being like the poem encircled with thoughts Lewis felt he could not live with. But 'The Jungle' was not his last poem, and in any case the idea that it is a suicidal confession sells both Lewis and the poem short. He knew what he was talking about when he described his depressions as 'Mr Death'. Knowing that about himself was an aspect of his courage – the moral and spiritual courage with which he explored the contradictions in his situation as a soldier-poet, and a Welshman who had a sense of what a community was, a socialist and a democrat who found himself, in India, representing a 'tinpot civilization' (*LTMW*, 423); an idealist who felt acutely the betrayal of an ideal. Nor is this to forget that the soldier-poet has a peculiarly intimate relationship with death, which is not his alone but 'Everyman's darkness', as he calls it in 'Encirclement' (*CP*, 105).

The image of 'the black spot' belongs to Lewis's 'dark' language. This is a metaphorical language rich in ambiguity and one that shows several powerful influences working on his susceptible poetic imagination. One of these, again, is W. H. Auden, who, in his poems of the 1930s, conflated psychological and social analyses. Thus Auden diagnosed 'England, this country of ours where nobody is well'.[21] A favourite trope of his early poems is that of himself and his friends as 'agents', but agents with a difference, spies who carry the disease of a bourgeois society that will help to destroy it from within. Lewis develops his own version of this imagery – in 'the dark cancer in my vitals / Of impotent impatience' in 'The Soldier' (*CP*, 24), for example, where it is the disease of the soldier-poet, and in 'We bear the dark inherited disease / Bred in the itching warmness of your hand' in 'Home Thoughts from Abroad' (*CP*, 139), where the soldiers of an occupying army represent a corrupt, materialistic civilization. The latter is one of Lewis's poems in which the darkness is both internal and external: the soldiers 'feel the darkness twitch / With death among the orange trees', and 'bear the dark inherited disease'.

Clearly, in Lewis the dark disease is also a metaphor for his depression, and in this respect it links with Edward Thomas's use of a similar image. It is hardly necessary to dwell on the reference of Lewis's dark imagery to death, which was all around him in Britain at war, and in India, as well as an object of personal apprehension and fascination. One of the ways in which he sees death, as other soldier-poets have done, is in terms of female seduction and sexual fulfilment. Thus, in 'Burma Casualty', the dark which promises release from pain, the 'beautiful singing sexless angel', recalls 'sweet sister death' of David Jones's *In Parenthesis*.[22] Both Lewis and Jones could be described as 'muse poets', sensitive to the 'phases' of the female archetype as mother, lover, and the figure which links the peace of death with return to the earth envisaged as a maternal womb. Given Lewis's marked religious and formal differences from Jones, a stronger case could be made for associating Lewis with Robert Graves in this respect.[23]

'Everyman's darkness' has an echo in the conclusion to Lewis's story 'The Earth is a Syllable', where the dying soldier 'was in the night, in the common ground of humanity, and he wasn't alone now'.[24] This may be contrasted with a different use of darkness in another story, 'Ward "O" 3(b)', in which Weston felt 'some small salient gained when for many reasons the men whom he was with were losing ground along the whole front of the darkness that there is'.[25] What is important to note about both instances, I think, is that they relate to *common* experience. It is worth repeating that in exploring death Lewis was not expressing a private 'death-wish', but responding to a situation in which he, along with every other man and woman, was living with fear and loss – experiences that many others, too, internalized. He was set apart from others not by his preoccupation with death, but by his willingness to risk exploring its emotional and thematic aspects in depth.

This is partly what I mean by his poetic courage. I have referred at times to moral and spiritual courage, and this is included in my meaning but does not exhaust it, for I am also referring to a vital

principle within the writing itself. Courage involves facing aloneness, as Edward Thomas in, for example, 'Lights Out', chose 'To go
into the unknown / I must enter, and leave, alone'.[26] The forest
meant to Thomas something similar to what the jungle meant to
Lewis: death as mystery, which the poet must approach alone.
Fundamental to my idea of poetic courage is John Keats's 'Negative
Capability', which he described in a letter to his brothers dated 22
December 1817. It was a quality Keats believed 'Shakespeare
possessed so enormously': 'that is when a man is capable of being in
uncertainties, Mysteries, doubts, without any irritable reaching after
fact and reason'. Keats himself amply demonstrated this quality, of
course – in 'Ode to a Nightingale', for example, where he both
confesses and confronts his death-longing. 'Darkling, I listen', he
says, being literally in 'embalmed darkness', but also in the dark of
'Mysteries, uncertainties', to which he has opened his mind. The
poem itself is an exploration; the poet does not know where it will
lead, what it will make him say, or say through him.

Edward Thomas frequently displays a similar quality. In poems
such as 'The Unknown Bird', for instance, he occupies a liminal
situation between the known and the unknown, venturing upon an
experience whose outcome, or meaning, he does not know in advance.
Lewis also occupied a 'frontier' – 'this last / Cold shore of thought I
guard' of 'The Sentry' (*CP*, 28), for example. He described his
position in 'Encirclement' as 'this abandoned frontier / Where many
visions falter / And youth and health are taken'. It is here that he
strives to find 'The elusive answer of love' (*CP*, 105). The underlying
sense of the liminal situation in Thomas's and Lewis's poems is that
life itself is a mystery – a mystery to which religions respond but
which they do not explain. As in Lewis's 'Westminster Abbey',

> Something profounder than the litany
> Moves in the dark beneath the restless steps
> Of this pale swirl of human flux. (*CP*, 101)

As well as Keats's Negative Capability, another great Romantic statement of poetry as a form of spiritual risk is Rilke's 'To Hölderlin':

> O restless spirit, most restless of all! How smugly
> the others all live in their well-heated poems, and linger
> long and with interest in narrow comparisons.[27]

This restless venture beyond the familiar world with its 'well-heated poems' was one that Lewis undertook: a spiritual quest, through poems whose outcome is not predetermined. Another exemplar of this quality was D. H. Lawrence, especially in such wonderful poems, written when he was a dying man, as 'Shadows', 'The Ship of Death' and 'Bavarian Gentians', in which the flower becomes 'torch-flower of the blue-smoking darkness' to lead Lawrence 'to the sightless realm where darkness is awake upon the dark'.[28] The Lawrence poem is a good example of the fecundity of the 'dark' imagery and its possibilities of intelligence and invention – imagery to think and feel and see by – imagery with its sources in the unconscious, which becomes a means of expression and exploration. Lewis is at best this kind of poet, instead of one for whom the language of darkness is a lazy expression of what the poet does not want to think about or see, or an automatic response to mystery.

It is not my intention to make a qualitative comparison between Lewis and the great poets who influenced him, and with whom he had close affinities, such as Edward Thomas, Rilke and Lawrence. My aim, rather, is to describe his poetry in terms of the poetic courage that seems to belong to a particular Romantic tradition. It is tempting to say that this is an intrinsically *agnostic* quality, since it is manifested in face of uncertainty and the unknown. It would be wrong, however, to claim that the writing of poetry founded upon an assured faith does not require courage. Quite apart from the leap required in any act of faith, we may consider the example of Henry Vaughan in *Silex Scintillans*, which are poems of deep religious faith, but also effectively re-vision traditional Christianity in the circumstances of the Civil War of the seventeenth century. Vaughan was conscious of living and writing behind the lines of enemy territory, in which his church had been closed and his task was to recreate its truth in the language of his poems. This example helps us to see that poetic courage, at whatever period in history it is manifested, always declares itself in new vision or re-vision or re-creation, as distinct from the expression of familiar assumptions. It is also, often, written in enemy territory, if not literally then in the sense that the poet does not stand securely on the safe ground of what people expect, or want, to hear.

Keats's courage was to be in 'uncertainties, Mysteries, doubts', Rilke's courage to live the questions. Lewis followed them both, struggling with poems encircled by thoughts he felt he could not live with, in his effort to understand the darkness that surrounded him, and the darkness that he knew within. This was, in the main, his way. He sought meaning in experience, even the experience of death, rather than confining himself to the safe territory of the familiar and the known.

5

John Cowper Powys: 'Figure of the Marches'[1]

In middle age, John Cowper Powys recalled the vow he had made as
a boy at Sherborne Preparatory School to become a poet:

> I remember well one night going out under the stars through the new
> yard of Acreman House to visit the urinal; and as I gazed upward, dazed
> from reading Bulwer Lytton, at that time a new discovery to me, making
> a vow to those flickering, glittering points of white light and to the starlit
> roof of the latrine towards which I was directing my steps, that what I
> would be, when I grew up, was a poet.[2]

Powys goes on to say that 'the transporting ecstasy' he felt 'must
have been of an unusual violence, else I could hardly remember it, as
I do now, after nearly half a century'. But this, surely, is disin-
genuous. What we have here is not simply a memory, but a recollection shaped according to retrospective wisdom.

Powys is well aware of the significance of what he is showing us,
because in *Autobiography* he is not just remembering experience,
but formulating a vision of himself based on his 'life illusions', the
dominant one of which was that he 'was, or at least would
eventually be, a magician' (*A*, 24). This idea is closely bound up with
his concepts of poetry and imagination. While he thought of himself
as a magician when he was a child, it is the man who has constructed
'the magical view of life' (*A*, 626), and written imaginative and
philosophical works that justify it.

In this passage, then, Powys is constructing a scene for us. He
shows us the bookish boy he was, under the spell of the historical
and 'occult' novelist Bulwer Lytton, and situated between urinal and
stars as he makes his vow to be a poet. But when he wrote this Powys
had already become a poet; he was the author of several volumes of
verse, but he had shown far more *poetic* originality in constructing
the mythological landscapes of his novels, especially *Wolf Solent*
and *A Glastonbury Romance*.[3] In his novels he had developed a

strain from nineteenth-century fiction, such as Bulwer Lytton's, but had transformed it into something rich and strange, with an admixture of modern psychology and ancient myth. Powys's novels are better described by the word he used for some of them: 'romances'. They are books in which the poet and storyteller is working through fictional forms to explore regions of human experience that are essentially religious. Broadly speaking, this region lies between the excremental and celestial realms, symbolized in this passage by the latrine and the stars. In more orthodox terms, the region is that between matter and spirit. Powys, however, was not an orthodox thinker, and although his concern was with fundamental dualisms,[4] such as matter and spirit, man and woman, life and death, his aim was to expand the bounds of the human, rather than confine it within traditional concepts.

In this chapter I shall explore what it means to describe Powys as a poet who embodied his vision, most fully and successfully, in the form of prose romance. In examining his function as a poet in this respect I shall also consider its relationship to his idea of himself as a magician, and the part played in the Powysian imagination by his idea of Wales and of himself as 'aboriginal' Welsh. Emyr Humphreys has said that when Offa's Dyke was built it made Wales 'a cultural fortress, that became both a crucible of myth and a cauldron of rebirth'.[5] John Cowper Powys described 'mythologizing of one's own identity and its projection upon reality' as 'this way of life and this way alone that makes the essence of every writer's imaginative world'.[6] Powys found the main materials and creative principles with which he constructed his own mythological identity in the Welsh crucible and the Welsh cauldron.

Powys's fascination with Wales had its roots in his father's pride in the Powys family's descent 'from the ancient Welsh Princes of Powysland' (A, 26). John Cowper maintained that their lineage was indeed 'from an old Welsh family long ago established in the town of Ludlow in Shropshire in what were formerly called the Welsh "Marches"' (A, 26). I am not here concerned primarily with biographical facts, but with Powys as a figure of the 'Marches' in a different sense; my focus is upon Powys's imaginative construction of a sense of Welshness, and his use of it in his novels.

As a young lecturer in England before the turn of the century, Powys, feeling embattled and insecure, identified Wales as the place where he could seek 'refuge' (A, 336). From this period, 'Welshness' was Powys's response to his personal crisis, and his sense of Wales accorded with his idea of imagination, which was the faculty with which he combated his difficulties: 'Probably the oldest wisdom in Wales was that wisest and most ancient of all wisdom; namely that it is within the power of the will and the imagination to destroy and recreate the world' (*A*, 26). From this time, then, when Powys 'suddenly acquired a passion for everything Welsh' (*A*, 334), his real interest was in 'the oldest wisdom', for which he found hints in the scholarship of Sir John Rhŷs and also in Matthew Arnold's *On the Study of Celtic Literature*, rather than in modern Wales. This was still the case thirty years later, when, in 1935, having returned to England from America in the previous year, Powys settled in Corwen in north Wales. He was to write that, here, 'the thing that most stirred my own imagination about the land of my fathers' was 'the obliteration of the last four centuries!'[7] This, of course, was an obliteration in his mind, aided by the landscape of north Wales and the survival there of a traditional Welsh society; an obliteration which cleared the ground for Powys to construct his own landscape of myth. Much earlier, when he first sailed to America, in December 1904, he had a vague sense of himself going to reveal an 'oracle', 'like Taliessin in some new incarnation' (*A*, 440). Vague it may have been then, but Powys's identification with Taliessin,[8] the boy transformed into the fabulous poet 'in that immortality-giving Cauldron of Ceridwen' (*A*, 335), went very deep.

Powys's romance of Wales bears the marks of Matthew Arnold's influence and is vulnerable to the same criticism that sees Arnold exploiting Wales in the interests of England. Arnold, following in the footsteps of Ernest Renan in *Poetry of the Celtic Races*, emphasizes 'Celtic' spirituality at the expense of practicality. Arnold's whole vision of Wales is contained in the scene at the beginning of the *Study*, in which he looks eastward from Llandudno, towards the 'Saxon hive' of Liverpool, and then westward, towards 'mystic Anglesey'. On this side he sees

Wales – Wales, where the past still lives, where every place has its tradition, every name its poetry, and where the people, the genuine people, still knows this past, this tradition, this poetry and lives with it, and clings to it; while, alas, the prosperous Saxon on the other side, the invader from Liverpool and Birkenhead, has long ago forgotten his.[9]

Arnold has a political agenda, which may be summed up as the exploitation of Welsh spiritual and cultural resources to alleviate the philistinism of prosperous Saxons, while denying Wales and the Welsh language the right to an independent existence, based on an autonomous culture with its own political institutions, in the present. Arnold's construction of the Welsh as a 'poetic' people, whose contribution should be to benefit England, was influential, not least in Wales, when Powys was a young man. As Emyr Humphreys succinctly remarks: 'In the Welsh wonderland, this unlikely brew "Celtic Magic" became the elixir of Assimilation.'[10]

Powys's libertarian politics were quite different from Arnold's, and Powys revered the Welsh people and the Welsh language and culture, and acquired a reading knowledge of Welsh. Nevertheless, he effectively identified Wales with the past, and his idea of Wales as a personal refuge is a version, given a peculiar slant, of the Celtic 'defeat-tradition'.[11] This in part – but only in part – accounts for his preoccupation with Brân the Blessed as a 'corpse god': The Head of Brân, which represents a kind of survival in death, and victory won from defeat.[12]

Herbert Williams mildly observes 'something in [Powys's] assiduous analysis of the Welsh character that many might find patronizing and irritating'.[13] Ned Thomas, writing about *Obstinate Cymric*, expresses exasperation: 'Does any nation deserve to have inflicted on it the zanier projection of the romantic imagination?'[14] Thomas links Powys's concern with 'the Aboriginal Welsh' to turn-of-the-century 'confusion in the discussion of "race" and "culture"' and says Powys 'never seems to have got beyond those confusions of his youth'.[15] In one way, this is fair comment: Powys's 'romance of race', as he called it in *Autobiography* (161), looks back to Renan and Arnold and a confused racial ideology that lasted well into the twentieth century. Powys, it has to be said, drew enthusiastically on highly dubious scholarship, another example being the diffusionist theory behind H. J. Massingham's *Downland Man* (1926), which enabled Powys to cultivate his myth of an original 'Non-Aryan' bloodless culture – a Golden Age culture – as though it were based on historical fact.

It might be observed in Powys's defence that imaginative writers commonly rely on contemporary 'scientific' theories that become discredited. More to the point, I think, is the imaginative use Powys makes of the theories. In this view, Powys's primitivism has affinities both with that of Romantic poets, such as William Blake, and that of modernists, such as W. B. Yeats and James Joyce. At the heart of Powys's primitivism is magic, which is a form of transformative imaginative power.[16] Powys opposes 'the magical view of life' to every sort of materialistic determinism. It should also be said that Powys is fundamentally a writer with a comic vision, which includes himself and his pretensions to Welshness, as witnessed by such self-descriptions as 'a fairy-tale Welshman' (*A*, 469), 'a tatterdemalion Taliessin' (*A*, 626) and 'an imaginative charlatan' (*A*, 335). Although in many ways an eccentric modernist, Powys recalls Yeats and other self-transforming twentieth-century writers both in his interest in magic, and in his half-serious, half-playful invention for himself of a role and a persona with magical propensities.

Another objection to Powys's use of Wales in his writings is Roland Mathias's criticism of *Owen Glendower* on the grounds that Powys 'trifles' with Welsh history.[17] 'It is a pity', Mathias writes, in his first essay on the subject, 'that John Cowper Powys, for all his gifts, should have decided to tackle a subject so intrinsically concerned with the nature and the making of a *Prince*, and yet to circumvent history, against all credibility, with a formula of his own.'[18] I acknowledge that, when I first wrote about Powys,[19] I was under the influence of this view. My position now is that Mathias's argument, in its own terms, is incontrovertible; but it does not alter the fact that *Owen Glendower* is an immensely entertaining work of fiction, rich in character and psychological interest, and 'poetic' in its embodiments of conscious life in a mythological landscape. Mathias also comments that 'a number of the minor characters' are in *Owen Glendower*, 'it would seem, to indulge their author's sexual fantasies'.[20] But this is to overlook an aspect of the book that is essentially Powysian, its treatment of sexual relationships as the main source of conflict and enchantment in human affairs. Powys invites the Mathias criticism as it were by calling *Owen Glendower* 'an historical novel' and appending a historical 'Argument' to it.

The question centres on different ideas of 'history', Powys being concerned with an idea of continuity in human experience, to which he applies his modern psychology, while Mathias is a historian with a scrupulous regard for historical veracity. We should be alerted to Powys's different spirit by the opening words of the novel: 'Don Quixote might well have recognised in the gaunt piebald horse that carried young Rhisiart down that winding track towards the river Dee a true cousin of Rosinante's.'[21] In invoking Cervantes, Powys immediately places his 'historical novel' in the great European tradition of romantic comedy, which deals with human ideals and illusions, rather than socio-political reality.

In respect of the whole question of Powys's use or misuse of his Welsh materials it now seems to me that Joe Boulter is near the mark when he argues that Powys 'celebrates Welshness and yet deconstructs it'.[22] Powys was hostile to all nationalisms;[23] the spirit he found in Wales represented a possibility of universal liberation, not an idea of Welsh nationhood. This is, nevertheless, not a complete justification of the element of Arnoldian romanticism in Powys's exploitation of Wales for imaginative resources that he did not find in his English background. A reductive perspective would see Powys, the 'figure of the Marches', as marginalized in a social sense; an English upper-middle-class gentleman who chose to 'de-class' himself, and, having rejected his father's evangelical Christianity and the career in the Church that was traditionally expected of him, became an itinerant lecturer, and invented a religious role for himself as magician and poet. Moreover, in divesting himself of English social expectations he reconstructed himself as a Welsh mythological figure, playing the part of 'restorer of the hidden planetary secrets of these mystical introverts of the world' (*A*, 335) in America, before eventually seeking refuge in a Wales that he had made over in his own image. This is not how I see Powys, because I take seriously the resistance of the magical view of life to all such reductions; it has, nevertheless, to be acknowledged as *a* perspective. Moreover, I do see the transition from Powys's 'Wessex Romances' to his 'Welsh Romances' as necessitated by the exhaustion of nostalgic childhood memories on which the former draw, and by the much greater difficulty he would have had in England in obliterating the past four centuries.

Having confessed in *Autobiography* that 'my dominant life-illusion was that I was, or at least would eventually be, a magician', Powys asks, rhetorically, 'what is a magician if not one who converts God's "reality" into his own "reality", God's world into his own world, and God's nature into his own nature?' (*A*, 25). The hesitation implied by the question is salutary, for Powys has a tendency in his discursive writing to emphasize the power of magic over 'reality', whereas his more subtle treatment of the subject, in his romances, dramatizes the conflict between imaginative power and external realities, such as suffering, that are not easily transformed. A temperate statement of his view occurs in *Mortal Strife* where he says: 'Of course the soul of a man is never entirely free; but . . . there is a margin. In this margin the soul of a man *is* free.'[24] 'Margin', as I shall later show, is a profoundly significant word for Powys.

Powys was a democrat, even a populist, in the sense that Walt Whitman, who profoundly influenced him, could be said to be. In consequence his thinking about magic has none of the élitist connotations that attached to occult studies and societies, in the period from the later nineteenth century when an interest in magic was widespread among writers and thinkers who were reacting against Victorian materialism and scientific rationalism. 'The mind is the great magician',[25] Powys wrote; and again, in *Mortal Strife*, 'the soul of man, that supreme magician'.[26] Similar to Yeats in his interest in magic, Powys is defending a belief in the soul:

> What is wrong with so many clever people today is the fatal distrust lodged in their minds – and lodged there by a superstitious awe in the presence of transitory scientific theories – of the power in their own souls. What we need – and the key to it lies in ourselves – is a bold return to the *magical* view of life. (*A*, 626)

'We are still potential magicians', he goes on to say, 'as long as we have faith in the power within us to create and to destroy.'

True to his inheritance from the Romantic poets, Powys connects 'the power within' to the child. The child's 'sorcery' is the 'power of finding the infinitely great in the materially small', which Powys calls '*the ecstasy of the unbounded*' (*A*, 2). His philosophy emphasizes the capacity of the individual soul to recover this ecstasy, through solitary communion with nature; and the quest for ecstasy, by the individual alone with nature, or through relationships between men and women, is a central motif of his romances. The desire to return to origins is strong in Powys, where origins are both the child within the adult and the natural matrix – perceived in a key image as the primary sea of being – from which life first arose. Hence the central significance of the figure of Taliessin for him. Taliessin is indeed 'Primary chief bard' for Powys,[27] who calls him 'our greatest poet previous to Shakespeare',[28] and although in *Porius* Powys conflates the historical bard with the fabulous figure, it is clear that he is mainly interested in the latter, as a vehicle for his own idea of imagination. Thus Taliessin is *'an undying child'*,[29] the Gwion Bach who became privy to the secrets of Ceridwen, the Great Mother, and was reborn of her, as Taliessin, the poet with an infinite capacity for becoming other. He is an elemental being who is able to become everything, projecting his spirit into all forms of organic and inorganic life.

G. Wilson Knight wisely warns against 'attending to separate pieces of Powys's explicit thinking in his philosophical books or similar strains in certain persons of his narratives, without giving our primary attention to those narratives as wholes'.[30] I accept this as a salutary reminder that Powys is primarily a storyteller, and the 'truth' of his stories inheres in the whole narrative, not in any extractable theme or even in the poetry of his mythological landscapes. Powys himself, however, defined a story as 'the struggle of a soul, conscious or half conscious, with the obstacles that hinder its living growth, that obstruct the lilt of its pulse and joggle to left or right its integral continuity' (*A*, 46). Moreover, the poetic dimension of his romances is grounded mainly on the relation between the souls of his characters and their natural landscapes, and on the symbolic or dramatic treatment of dualisms, such as night and day, life and death, and man and woman. For this reason, while I recognize the danger of doing violence to the intricate weave of Powys's narrative fabric, I think it well worth exploring what Powys's art owes to his reading of the poets. Before doing so, however, I must add another caveat.

Powys, as he recognized, was the most bookish of writers. He once said that he had 'lived through three great literary dictatorships' – that of Dostoevsky and Nietzsche, that of Anatole France and Thomas Hardy, and that of Proust and Joyce.[31] If he had made a similar statement later, he could have added names to this list – Hemingway, for example, to whose style he seems to refer in a passage in *Porius*.[32] Powys lived a long life, and at each stage of it he was responsive to contemporary writing, as well as a voracious reader of the literature of the past. Thus, just as Powys as a boy responded to Bulwer Lytton, and to Walter Scott and Harrison Ainsworth, so he later opened himself to the influence of Walter Pater, Thomas Hardy, Fyodor Dostoevsky, James Joyce, Dorothy M. Richardson and others. Influence, however, is not quite the right word, at least as far as Powys's mature fiction, from *Wolf Solent* to

Porius, is concerned, for, as I have shown elsewhere in examining his debt to Hardy, Powys transforms influences into the fabric of his own vision.[33] Something similar has to be said about the poets who influenced him in depth. In each case, like Taliessin of the many incarnations, Powys transformed himself into the other, but remained fully himself.

Among English poets, Powys's greatest debts were to Wordsworth, Blake, Keats and Arnold, and to Shakespeare as constructed by the Romantic imagination. In perceiving Shakespeare as having the power of *'becoming'* 'all his hapless and desperate and eloquent characters',[34] Powys is following Coleridge,[35] and Keats's 'Negative Capability'. Again, though, Powys gives the idea an individual twist, claiming not only that he had 'the magic power of *becoming women*' that he found in Shakespeare and Dostoevsky, but that, when possessed by 'the old Druidic spirit, the spirit of Taliessin of the many incarnations', he 'could become inanimate objects' (*A*, 528). Powys sees Shakespeare not only as Protean, moreover, but as dramatist of the 'clashing discord of multitudinous life-illusions'.[36] The dramatic basis of Powys's own art may be said to be Shakespearean in that he sets his characters' ideas and self-images at odds with one another.

In Blake, Powys seems to have responded most keenly to *The Marriage of Heaven and Hell*. Blake's 'that All deities reside in the human breast' is a key article of Powys's belief.[37] Indeed, he widens it: 'As William Blake says, everything comes out of the human mind.'[38] It is a belief that coincides with his conviction of the power of life-illusions, and defines the quality of his scepticism, with which he subverts totalizing ideas of 'reality' by depicting a multiverse which is the production of myriad minds. Powys is attracted also to the idea of the marriage of opposites or contraries. 'Life', he says in *In Spite of*, 'works by opposites and by contradictions. At the heart of everything good and great there is, as William Blake taught, a marriage of heaven and hell.'[39] In the sense defined by Alwyn Rees and Brinley Rees in *Celtic Heritage*, the 'marriage' may be said to be the subject of Powys's romances:

> 'The wall of Paradise,' says Nicholas of Cusa, 'is built of contraries, nor is there any way to enter but for one who has overcome the highest spirit of reason who guards the gate.' It is a function of mythology to confound this guardian spirit of reason so that finite man may glimpse

the infinity which lies beyond the confines of the cosmos. Coincidences of opposites and of other irreconcilables give a shock to the understanding and transport the spirit to the gateway of the Other World.[40]

This view of the function of mythology helps to explain why, as I shall later show, Powys needed to create an Otherworld landscape for his romances. It also indicates the connection between the Blakean idea and Powys's use of Grail Quest motifs drawn largely from Welsh mythological and literary sources. Mr Evans, like Powys heavily dependent upon the scholarship of Sir John Rhŷs, is interpreter of these in *A Glastonbury Romance*, where he describes Glastonbury as '*yr Echwyd*, the land of Annwn, the land of twilight and death', the land in which the Fisher Kings 'sought for the knot of the opposites . . . for the bride-bed of the contradictions'.[41] The marriage of opposites, however, is one that Powys shows his heroes approaching and yet withdrawing from, as in the case of Porius, who determines 'to accept without protest the whole destiny of ease and unease, comprehensibility and incomprehensibility as these entangled opposites presented themselves in ever new and ever more complicated combinations' (*P*, 827).

Acceptance or rejection of 'entangled opposites' is bound up with the idea of suicide, which is a recurring motif in Powys's fiction. Suicide, in one form or another, tempts characters who want to escape from the dualism of life and death, whether to end their torments or 'to gain more life'. The latter is the case with John Geard in *A Glastonbury Romance*, who, in drowning himself, may be seen, in terms introduced into the novel by Mr Evans, to enter Merlin's 'Esplumeoir', which Evans glosses as 'some mystic Fourth Dimension, or Nirvanic apotheosis, into which the magician deliberately sank, or rose; thus committing a sort of inspired suicide, a mysterious dying in order to live more fully'.[42] For Geard, as for Blake at the end of *The Marriage of Heaven and Hell*, 'every thing that lives is Holy'. What Powys is doing, I think, in exploring the theme of suicide is both expressing a 'dark' tendency within his own nature and imagining forms of life-and-death acceptance, or a metaphysical ground in which death, too, is 'holy'.

As well as Negative Capability, Powys valued Keats's paganism, his 'poetry of earth'.[43] 'Paganism', Powys maintains in his study of Keats, 'springs in an absolutely *organic* manner out of the unregenerate earth.' He calls it 'what Christianity itself was, before the Fall', and 'the Golden Age from which all religions start and towards which they all make their pilgrimage'. Paganism 'is the true religion of the earth, because it worships not the earth, but the poetry of the earth'.[44] Powys himself aspired to write such poetry, as we see from his early collections of verse. These, as he realized, were imitative. It was, nevertheless, his desire to write a poetry of earth that led him to write romances.

In his function as a poet of earth Powys was following Wordsworth as well as Keats. Powys called himself 'a congenital Wordsworthian'.[45] The words of Wordsworth that he repeats most often, and that become integral to his own vision, are 'The pleasure which there is in life itself', from 'Michael'. Powys calls this a 'cult of sensations', and finds it in many other writers too. He describes it, further, as a 'liberating art of living entirely by physical sensation'.[46] His most significant use of the Wordsworth quotation as far as his own art is concerned occurs in his study of Dorothy M. Richardson, where he describes her as being 'intent on Life Itself, in its mysteriously flowing stream'.[47] This, indeed, is what Powys himself is 'intent on', as he develops an art that is acutely sensitive to consciousness of sensations, and sensations of consciousness, in his individual characters and, through them, in the stream of life down the generations.

Goethe and Matthew Arnold both contributed significantly to Powys's sense of the 'secrets of life that Aryan science has destroyed',[48] especially the secret of 'the ancient femininity of the earth itself, that immortal goddess-creature' (*P*, 487). Powys was deeply impressed by Goethe's 'superhuman understanding of that mysterious creativeness in the heart of Nature which he himself calls [in *Faust*] the Mothers'.[49] Goethe intimates, Powys says, 'that Nature, in a manner totally beyond our comprehension, possesses a consciousness of her own, a consciousness not less but *more* than human'.[50] There is a direct link between Goethe's idea of 'the Mothers' and the feminine element in Celtic mythology, which was one of the main things that attracted Powys to *The Mabinogion* and other Welsh mythological stories.[51] The link is palpable in Powys's treatment of Arnold's attraction to what he saw as the 'antique' materials which the medieval storyteller of *The Mabinogion* uses without fully understanding their 'secret':

> he is like a peasant building his hut on the site of Halicarnassus or Ephesus; he builds, but what he builds of is full of materials of which he

knows not the history, or knows by a glimmering tradition merely – stones 'not of this building', but of an older architecture, greater, cunninger, more majestical.[52]

It is obvious that such a view would greatly appeal to Powys, since it accords with his own idea of Welsh 'aboriginals'; and Powys proceeds to translate it into his own terms, by describing Arnold's response as 'some kind of navel-string nostalgia – a yearning to revert to our pre-natal condition within the body of our mother'.

> And if the maternal womb of us all, as the drift of speculation seems to point, was nothing less than the shell-strewn *windrow* between sea and shore, may we not regard this worship of water and stone, this atavistic 'religion' *un*-touched by morality, as a longing for that untroubled *bios-akinesis*, that blessed existence without motion or thought, which was interrupted when we were born?[53]

Thus, Powys finds, in *The Mabinogion*, recession into the depths, the cosmogonic source, the watery matrix in which all life was born. In terms of one of his favourite metaphors, which he develops here, 'the maternal womb' was the '*windrow* between sea and shore'. The landscapes of *The Mabinogion* are in any case 'liminal' or 'March' locations, where the supernatural erupts into the natural scene, and the Otherworld exists alongside this world. Powys gives this imaginative domain a twist of his own, developing its feminine associations in line with his thinking about what Myrddin Wyllt in *Porius* calls 'our mother the earth' (*P*, 287) and making it, like the maternal womb, not just a 'refuge', but a place ripe with potentiality.

In terms of Powysian metaphor, 'this magical windrow at the sea's edge . . . seems to become more and more significant as an embodiment of our whole relation to the supernatural'.[54] In fact, this is what happens in Powys's art of romance-writing as it develops from *Wood and Stone* (1915) to the maturity of his middle period, between *Wolf Solent* (1929) and *Porius* (1951): his fictional landscapes become 'windrows', or liminal situations – margins or boundaries or thresholds – in which he embodies 'our whole relation to the supernatural', which he understands, in pagan terms, as 'the poetry of the earth'. Before exploring these landscapes further, however, it is first necessary to say something about Powys's idea of romance and how it relates to his concept of continuity.

'What is romance?' Powys asks, appropriately in an essay on Emily Brontë, to whose spirit he dedicated *Rodmoor*, his second romance. His answer lays emphasis upon the importance of 'background', and he says the characters 'must be penetrated through and through by the scenery which surrounds them and by the traditions, old and dark and superstitious and malign, of some particular spot upon the earth's surface'. 'Romance implies, above everything else,' Powys says,

> a long association with the human feelings of many generations. It implies an appeal to that background of our minds which is stirred to reciprocity by suggestions dealing with those old, dark, mysterious memories which belong, not so much to us as individuals, as to us as links in a great chain.[55]

Fittingly, there is a remarkable continuity in Powys's thinking about continuity, and his hero Dud No-man, the 'historical' novelist in *Maiden Castle*, holds essentially the same view: 'It was this stream of life flowing down the ages, with its magical overtones and undertones, that he had come to seek in a thousand chance-given groupings of things and people.' Dud admits that 'he was no historian in a scientific sense'. 'History to him was life *at one remove*, life purged and winnowed of its grosser impact!'[56] It is one thing, however, to affirm the existence of 'the poetry of the life of generations' (as Powys calls this continuous life-stream elsewhere),[57] and quite another to express it convincingly in modern novels, in an age that knows the fragmentation of traditions.

'Midway' is the first word of the opening chapter of Powys's first romance, *Wood and Stone* (1915). It locates Leo's Hill, 'between Glastonbury and Bridport, at the point where the eastern plains of Somersetshire merge into the western valleys of Dorsetshire'.[58] The midway setting plays a part in the theme of 'the two opposed Mythologies – the one drawing its strength from the impulse to Power, and the other from the impulse to Sacrifice' with which *Wood and Stone* is concerned.[59] The use of a 'March' or borderland location as the site of warring contraries and the 'penetration' of characters by scenery serve as fairly rudimentary devices in this romance, compared to Powys's later development of them.

In Powys's third novel, *After My Fashion* (completed in 1920, but not published until 1980), the hero is a poet, Richard Storm, who, returning to England from France after the First World War, senses 'the continuity of the generations' in his ancestral Sussex. He feels 'something essential' in England, 'something that belonged both to the earth and the race', and determines to write poetry that would express 'some definite vision of things'.[60] Powys further describes what Storm feels to be 'the very secret of his native soil' as 'the evocation of a strange marginal purlieu, lying midway between the loneliness of solitary human beings and the loneliness of inanimate things'.[61] This may be glossed by passages in Powys's expository writings. It is 'that psychic-sensuous margin of life which is the most precious thing in the world', as Powys calls it in *Autobiography* (493), where he also describes himself as 'the medium' for 'the *marginal sensations* of the human race itself' (*A*, 294). The margins are 'those obscure regions of animal-life and plant-life that lie at the background of all human consciousness', about which he writes in *The Meaning of Culture*, describing 'the mystery of the inexhaustible margin . . . the flowing stream of those simple not-to-be possessed elemental things that make up the background of all human life'.[62] It corresponds to John Geard's belief 'that there was a borderland of the miraculous round everything that existed and that "everything that lived was holy"'.[63]

Richard Storm fails in his attempt to create a poetry that will evoke 'the marginal purlieus', as Powys himself failed to embody his vision fully in his verse. Powys is much more successful, though, in his Wessex Romances. In *Wolf Solent* he develops a character 'penetrated' by scenery, a character with an inner landscape, which he calls his 'mythology', which corresponds to elements of the external West Country scene, 'the umbrageous threshold of Somerset, the first leafy estuary of that ocean of greenness out of which rose, like the phallus of an unknown god, the mystical hill of Glastonbury!'[64] Powys continues to use this device linking human consciousness to the sacred earth in the other Wessex Romances, and strengthens it by increasing use of Welsh mythology to intensify the 'borderland' locations. In *Weymouth Sands*, where Welsh mythology is much less in evidence, Sylvanus Cobbold is described as 'always dwelling in a mystical borderland of his own'.[65] The relative absence of Welsh mythology from this novel may be explained by the fact that for Powys 'the marginal sea' (*A*, 152) at Weymouth was, from childhood, his own magical threshold. For this reason, it is one of the least strained of Powys's 'Wessex Romances' as far as the introduction of a mythological dimension is concerned. A *Glastonbury Romance* and, especially, *Maiden Castle* reinforce their uses of myth by the introduction of a good deal of explicit scholarship, drawn from Sir John Rhŷs and other students of the Grail Quest. The major change in Powys's fiction that ensued upon his move to Wales was that he was able to draw upon Welsh mythology (especially from *The Mabinogion* as translated by Lady Charlotte Guest, in which she included the tale of Taliesin), much more fully and, in a way, more 'naturally', for both his landscapes and characters.

In Welsh mythology Powys found 'the shadowy purlieus of that queer no-man's-land or border-limbo between the human and the sub-human, the queer underworld which was also an overworld, that the ancient Britons called Caer Sidi'.[66] It is significant that in describing *Pedeir Keinc y Mabinogi* he might be describing his own Welsh romances.

> The ever-mysterious prose-epic of Wales . . . is literally haunted by all manner of magical *mixings* up – I can use no other expression – of life and death and death with life; so that on all sides we grow aware of half-alive things and of half-dead things, of life vanishing as the death-mists rise or fall, of birth appearing even from the lap of death.[67]

To understand how Powys works as a poet through the form of the romance in *Owen Glendower* and *Porius,* it is necessary to realize that he is drawing on a tradition of storytelling far older than that of any 'historical' novelist. In a way, he is close to the medieval Arthurian romances, which Proinsias Mac Cana describes as being set 'in a realm where nature has primacy and where sacred and profane are constantly fused'. Mac Cana's words about these romances, with their 'imaginative freedom', their 'sense of the meeting and blending of the contemporary world with the primeval world when historical limitations of time and space were still without meaning',[68] can be applied to Powys's 'Welsh Romances'. We may cautiously apply to Powys the definition of 'the story-teller (*cyfarwydd*)' given in *Celtic Heritage*, as 'originally a seer and a teacher who guided the souls of his hearers through the world of "mystery"'.[69] Understood in these terms, Powys can be linked to other modern writers and artists who have adopted the role of shaman, 'whose function is to establish contact with the Otherworld'.[70]

Understanding Powys in archaic terms, whether as medieval storyteller or shaman, is something that he himself encouraged, as in his humorous self-description as 'a born-Camp-Fire or a Cave-Fire Story-Teller with a gift for narrating or even of chanting my interminable story'.[71] The problem with this view, however, is that it overlooks the modernity of Powys: both the personal and cultural crisis that led him to identify himself with the 'aboriginal' Welsh, and the literary sophistication of his romances. I have already indicated something of the crisis which led him to adopt the role of Taliessin – and the story of his self-torment and deracination as a modern man from his family's traditional religious and social world is vividly recounted in *Autobiography*. His career as an *English* novelist, moreover, may be seen as the progressive exhaustion of childhood memory and its partial replacement with Welsh mythology, and it is hard to see where he could have taken this method after *Maiden Castle,* in which one of the major characters identifies himself with Urien (Brân), except to a Wales that Powys could treat in his own mythological terms.

The literary sophistication of *Owen Glendower* may be seen in part in Powys's treatment of consciousness, uses of the mind and will, and emotional and sexual experience, which obviously interest him far more than political and military matters. His primary concern is 'the *mythology of escape*', the *hiraeth*, which he identifies with Owen, and the Welsh people and 'the very geography of the land', the ' "longing" that the world which *is* should be transformed into Annwn – the world which is *not* – and yet was and shall be!'[72] *The Mabinogion* is a significant presence in the novel through characters' knowledge of its stories and identification of themselves or others with figures or incidents in the stories. Robin Wood goes as far as to claim that 'the basic structure' of *Owen Glendower* is 'shaped by the mythology' of *The Mabinogion*.[73] I am not entirely persuaded that Powys's method is as systematic as this would suggest. I do think, however, that the mythology is more essential, more integral, to this romance than its historical circumstances are. Indeed, through his major characters, Owen and Broch-o'-Meifod, and through the poets among his cast of characters, Powys identifies Wales itself as a March land, or border between this world and the Otherworld.

Porius, set in north Wales in the Dark Ages, is the romance in which Powys exercises his imaginative freedom most fully. He is able to do this in part because of the documentary blank of his historical setting – albeit a blank Powys fills with the ideas and beliefs formative of western civilization. At the same time as this liberates him to make full use of ideas and myths drawn from the past, it also enables him to construct a more convincing parallel with the present, in a world at mid-century still reeling from the war against Hitler, than was the case in *Owen Glendower*. 'As the old gods were departing then, so the old gods are departing now. And as the future was dark with the terrifying possibilities of human disaster then, so, today, are we confronted by the possibility of catastrophic world-events . . .' (*P*, xix).

Powys was religious, as he defines religion in *A Philosophy of Solitude*: 'a feeling of wonder, of awe, of fearful joy, of ecstatic and rapturous contemplation, in the presence of the mystery behind what we call Nature'.[74] As Powys perceived the pilgrimage of Dorothy M. Richardson's Miriam as 'a sort of Quest of the Holy Graal', so his characters too, and especially those who most resemble him, are seekers after 'the divine object of the ecstatic contemplative life'.[75] *Porius* is concerned not only with conflict between different religions, but with the war between different versions of Christianity. It is an anarchistic and libertarian response to tyranny, which, in Blakean fashion, links political tyranny – Hitlerism – with authoritarian religious ideas. Powys's use of *The Mabinogion* in his romance is integral to his religious aims. Here, the author of the Welsh 'ever-mysterious prose-epic' is a character, the Henog, and figures central to Welsh mythology, Myrddin Wyllt and Taliessin, fulfil important roles, so that Powys is constructing his own vision parallel to the Welsh tales, as well as using them as materials, thus justifying Morine Krissdottir's claim that *Porius* is 'a twentieth century *Mabinogion*'.[76]

Myrddin Wyllt is referred to as both 'sub-human' and 'this Christian magician' (*P*, 99). The contradiction is only apparent, as may be seen by referring to Powys's essay 'The Bible as Literature' in *The Pleasures of Literature,* where he speaks of 'the psychological evolution of Christ's Kingdom'. There, he asks: 'How can we do justice to the divine anarchism that emanates from this Person until, as He suggests himself, we prefer to blaspheme against Him rather than against the Spirit?'[77] Elsewhere, Powys further defined the evolution of the Christian spirit when he described 'the "Aquarian" principle of the *equality of all souls*' as 'the most fantastic metamorphosis ever recorded in any religious cult'.[78] From the time of his youth when Powys espoused Keats's poetry of earth, the whole drive of his resolution has been 'upon a whole-sale *transference of reverence* from Science, Religion, Universality, Deity, Sanctity, Holiness, and so forth, to the forms of life that are immediately around me'; to 'every manifestation of the natural and the organic'.[79] It is the fanatical Christians in *Porius* who condemn nature and human nature as evil, and seek to enslave everyone to the Church. It is the 'sub-human' Myrddin, whose multiple identity slips 'back into the elements' (*P*, 65), whose magic liberates everything they condemn. This is shown most dramatically in a scene paralleling Gwydion's transformation of the flower-maiden, Blodeuwedd, created by his magic, into an owl for her faithlessness in 'Math Son of Mathonwy'. But in Powys's scene Myrddin, 'defender of lost souls', in liberating Teleri, releases 'all the under layers of earth-life', and does so by 'a magic that declared itself able to destroy all powers that ruled by force' and in 'defiance of the dark intention of a second primary world-ruler, one to whom everything connected with the pleasure of sex was totally and entirely evil' (*P*, 796–7). Myrddin's magic, therefore, is a power that opposes all worldly power including that of orthodox religion.

Myrddin embodies the truth expressed by Pelagius in the novel, that 'Man's imagination and not God's will is what creates' (*P*, 152). He is, indeed, Powys's supreme embodiment of the power of imagination, a power which springs from nature, and his equality with all souls, and his renunciation of his power as a god. He is, therefore, in Powys's scheme of things, most fully man, his soul suspended 'between worm-life and god-life'[80] – a figure of the March. Drom, by contrast, is '*anti-man*'. His kiss 'enslaved the person kissed to the person kissing'. 'It was the kiss of rounded identity, of perfect balance, of the reconciliation of all opposites' (*P*, 658). From his contact with Myrddin, Porius, the eponymous hero of the romance, thought

> that it was possible to enlarge a person's identity till it embraced other identities, till it could escape at will *into others*, till it could even discover that all the while beneath the obstinate opacity of itself, it was on the verge of becoming these others. (*P*, 66)

But there is no merging with others on Myrddin's part; instead, he respects the loneliness of every soul. In this he is like Powys who, as I have said, approaches 'the reconciliation of all opposites', or the marriage of heaven and hell, in his novels, and draws back, recognizing the singularity of each soul, and that it is from 'the necessity of opposites', not their reconciliation, that all pleasure and all creativity spring.

In accordance with Powys's essentially comic vision, the Henog, author of *The Mabinogion*, represents the comic principle, which is the acceptance of life's 'incomprehensibility' (*P*, 818). He shares this view with the figure who speaks for enjoying and accepting life in 'divine *Nescience*' in *Owen Glendower*, Sir John Oldcastle, 'original' of Shakespeare's Falstaff, and one of the means by which Powys places his novel in the tradition of Shakespearean comedy.[81] *Porius*, with its magical transformations, is strange, but not eccentric. On the contrary, in H. W. Fawkner's fine phrase, Powys 'belongs to the circle of life itself'.[82] *Porius* is a book in a great European tradition, in more than one sense. It incorporates elements of Greek tragedy, but is a comedy in the spirit of Aristophanes, with 'the "aboriginal levity" ' with which 'the mother of the muses insists on the recognition of a vein of pure grotesquerie and simple gargoylishness in some of Nature's most natural creations'.[83] Its thought-worlds encompass, among others, Heraclitus and Plato and Boethius, Jewish Rabbinical teachings, Mithraism, and versions of orthodox and heterodox Christianity. It brings together Celtic and Greek and Roman and Nordic mythology, and an ancient religious strain from Berber Africa, for which Powys found hints in the writings of H. J. Massingham and H. J. Fleure; and its preoccupation with 'non-Aryan' values is a riposte to Nazi racial mythology.

That it is a sophisticated literary work with elements of a 'Cave-Fire' story aligns *Porius* with *Finnegans Wake*. The affinity is not based upon Powys's use of language, but upon his mixings and minglings of myth, which serve a similar purpose to Joyce's linguistic devices. Like Joyce, Powys uses imagination 'to indicate the un-unified, refreshingly pluralistic, un-imprisoned anarchy concealed beneath the hypocritical broad-cloth of Law and Order'.[84] The poems of Taliessin in *Porius,* the 'undying child', with 'an almost babyish abandonment to pure unadulterated sensation' (*P*, 423), teach the same lesson. The secret of his philosophy 'had the power of rendering all matter sacred and pleasure-giving to the individual soul' (*P*, 425), and his poetry proclaims 'The beginning forever of the Peace paradisic' (*P,* 428).

Emyr Humphreys has said that Powys

> became so well-versed and so absorbed in the mythological origins of the
> landscape and history of Wales that he was able to use them as keys to a
> cosmogony of his own. The strength of his understanding allowed him a
> control over dynamic forces reminiscent of those possessed by the family
> of Don in the Mabinogi.[85]

This pays handsome tribute to Powys's imaginative powers as a
'magician'. It is all the more generous in coming from a novelist
whose idea and use of 'the Taliesin tradition' were very different
from Powys's. Powys's magic found ample scope in the March lands
of Welsh mythology, but he did not deploy it in the service of an idea
of Welsh national identity. Powys's Otherworld, which is a transformation of the supernatural realm which he found in Welsh
mythology, became the most complete vehicle for his poetry of
earth. In this fictional landscape he was able to tell stories of the
liberation of the mind through an enlarged awareness of its creative
power and to celebrate chaos, 'divine anarchism', and 'the feminine
element in the heart' of Christianity, 'an element that would in the
end resolve everything back into nature' (P, 673).

~ 6 ~

David Jones and the Question of Arthur

In this place of questioning where you must ask the question and the answer questions you

(The Roman Quarry)

David Jones has said, in the Preface to *The Anathemata*: 'making a work is not thinking thoughts but accomplishing an actual journey' (*Ana*, 33). In his own writings, the journey is a kind of initiation, for writer and for reader. It is a journey analogous to the Grail Quest, but one in which the answer to the question is a question. Ultimately the question is about the nature of existence, and central to it is the question posed at the end of *The Anathemata*: 'But the fate of death?'

The lesson of any initiation, according to David Jones, is 'the great wisdom that the iceberg of existence is vaster, by many times in its hidden bulk, than what appears on the midday ocean'.[1] The metaphor reminds us that Jones's imagination was remarkably inclusive: he was an artist and writer who, in Stanley Spencer's words about making a painting, gathered all in.[2] Gathering in does not imply passive holding of materials, but their acquisition and imaginative transformation. In considering Jones's use of a central figure, such as Arthur, we must, therefore, remember both the inclusiveness and the process of metamorphosis. He expressed this dual nature of the work of art succinctly in writing about his painting *Vexilla Regis*: 'So many confluent ideas are involved in a single image.'[3]

As confluence characterized Jones's making and thinking, so he saw connections and analogies between poetry or art, myth and religion. In his view, each is inclusive. Thus, in the Preface to *The Anathemata* he wrote: 'The arts abhor any loppings off of meanings or emptyings out, any lessening of the totality of connotation, any loss of recession and thickness through' (*Ana*, 24). It was in these terms that he described myth as well as poetry:

To conserve, to develop, to bring together, to make significant for the present what the past holds, without dilution or any deleting, but rather by understanding and transubstantiating the material, this is the function of genuine myth, neither pedantic nor popularizing, not indifferent to scholarship, nor antiquarian, but saying always: 'of these thou hast given me have I lost none'. (*E & A*, 243)

It is probably not too much to claim that in Jones's thinking poetry and myth are functions of religion: the Christian religion with 'its historic ability to absorb, integrate, develop, fulfil' (*E & A*, 203). All are forms of making: religion absolutely, through God's creation of the universe and the redemptive act of Christ's death on the Cross; poetry and myth, partaking of the benefits of the divine creative acts, are involved in the search for 'formal goodness' even in existence at its worst, 'in a life singularly inimical, hateful, to us' in the trenches of the First World War (*IP*, xiii).

More often than the iceberg metaphor, David Jones uses figures drawn from geology for the inclusiveness of poetry or myth. Of uses of the tradition of Arthur, for example, he says: 'all the time we should feel, along with the contemporary twist, application, or what you will, the whole weight of what lies hidden – the many strata of it' (*E & A*, 234). Catholicism is his model of that which contains all. Like Julian of Norwich's hazel nut: 'That which the whole world cannot contain, is contained.'[4] Catholicism is universal, and syncretic; it does not know heathenism as opposition, but as prefiguration. Jones's desire is to affirm a universal redemption:

> What is pleaded in the Mass is precisely the argosy or voyage of the Redeemer, consisting of his entire sufferings and his death, his conquest of hades, his resurrection and his return in triumph to heaven. It is this that is offered to the Trinity (Cf. 'Myself to myself' as in the *Havamal* is said of Odin) on behalf of us argonauts and of the whole argosy of mankind, and, in some sense, of all sentient being, and, perhaps, of insentient too. (*Ana*, 106)

As, in the words of his friend Saunders Lewis, the Mass '*makes sense* of everything', so Jones's work, within its human and personal limitations, means, like the title of *The Anathemata*, 'as much as it can be made to mean, or can evoke or suggest' (*Ana*, 28).

As for many artists and poets, especially those within the Romantic tradition, the things 'given' to David Jones as a child were among the most precious to him. Primary among these were his mother and father, and what might be called, in a geological metaphor, the parent materials. These included, on his father's side, the land and culture of Wales; and on his mother's (she was the daughter of a mast- and block-maker of Rotherhithe and of Italian extraction on her mother's side), London, the Thames, ships and the sea, the Mediterranean world. In line with the view that the parent materials were the major shaping influence on Jones, it might seem possible for me to short-circuit my present argument by saying that, for him, the figure of Arthur was based upon his Welsh father, James Jones. This would, in fact, contain an important truth; but it would also be far too simple.

In discussing the importance of the figure of Arthur for Jones we have to give due consideration to the significance for him of a book dealing with King Arthur's knights, one of 'a children's pink paper-covered series called Books for the Bairns' (*Ana*, 41), which, before he could read, David would pay his sister a penny to read to him. It is reasonable to speculate that his first hearing the story told in his sister's voice helps in part to account for the tenderness of Jones's Arthur figure, for the reference to Aneirin Lewis sleeping 'in Arthur's lap' (*IP*, 155), for instance, although this also echoes the idea of Falstaff sleeping 'in Arthur's bosom' in *Henry V*. In any event, it may have influenced Jones's later feminization of Arthur. Complex though his poetry becomes, it continues to echo a sister's voice and the voices of mother and father: 'the womb-songs and the songs the fathers told – the songs of origin – the real songs'.[5] These gathered later knowledge to them, but went on sounding under his reading of the Romances and of Malory. They also affected his apprehension of a thought-world opened by his reading of scholars and historians, such as Jessie L. Weston and Christopher Dawson. The open secret of David Jones's genius is love. There was as it were a stream of primal, innocent feeling that continued to flow through his mature treatment of cherished themes. Coleridge's words about the child continuing to live in the man are particularly apposite to his case:

> To carry on the feelings of Childhood into the powers of Manhood, to combine the Child's sense of wonder and novelty with the Appearances which every day for perhaps forty years had rendered familiar . . . this is the character and privilege of Genius, and one of the marks which distinguish Genius from Talents.[6]

The painted inscription with which he dedicates *The Anathemata*, which reads (in English translation from the Latin) 'To my parents and their forebears and to all the native people of the bright island of Britain' (*Ana*, 48), is an instance of the *pietas* that pervades all his work, in the form of a stream of feeling that joins love and gratitude towards his parents to his love for the whole Island and its heritage.[7]

As an adult student of Arthurian myth Jones became familiar with the sequence unearthed by research and conjecture: 'Bear – Goddess – God of the soil – God of weapons – Romano-British general – Christian King' (*E & A*, 233). With an eloquence recalling Walter Pater invoking the Mona Lisa, Jones the scholar-poet was able to write:

> The Bear of the Island is inestimably old, its visage reflects millenniums of change. It knows sex-transmogrification, as it knows ploughshares can become swords, as it knows the waters of baptism can find a valid subject in the most elemental of creatures, as it knows that totems can be susceptible to chrismal acts. (*E & A*, 233)[8]

First, however, long before he was able to speculate about Arthur's ancient lineage, at an age when the boy was still being read to by his sister, he saw a bear in the street, and did a drawing of it 'from the window' (*DG*, 24). *Dancing Bear* remained David Jones's favourite drawing. Not surprisingly, for in its sensitive rendering of the animal it expresses that sense of kinship with all creatures that informs his greatest art and writing.

The brown bear which the boy depicted is powerful, but muzzled. In a sense it has been overcome, subdued by human force and cunning, but without becoming less than a bear. When Jones writes about Arthur as tribal totem, 'The Bear of the Island', it is hard for one familiar with the drawing not to feel it as a shaping influence upon the figure. The more so in that Arthur is defeated, but in the Chestertonian sense that 'nothing succeeds like failure'. The passage in his letters in which this reference occurs is worth quoting at length. Jones is talking about R. H. Hodgkin's *History of the Anglo-Saxons*:

> He is unable to be anything but a bit superior about the Welsh; it comes out in the oddest ways. But at *least* he admits that with the loss of the Island to the 'steady, prudent etc. Teutons, they in their hills wove, as he

would say, a web of magic and imagination round the story of their defeat, which in turn gave to the world the Arthurian cycle. Which is indeed worth the loss of many islands and continents, seeing that nothing succeeds like failure, as Chesterton might say.[9]

It is hardly to be supposed that a Welsh nationalist, such as Jones's friend Saunders Lewis, would see 'the story of their defeat' in this light. What this does reveal, however, is Jones's essentially protective view of Wales – protective of Wales, and protective also in the sense that the Welsh 'web of magic and imagination' holds in keeping all that he values, and provides a model for his paintings and writings on Welsh themes.

The actual location of *In Parenthesis* is, of course, the Western Front. But the poem introduces us, as we follow the initiation of the soldiers into the world of the trenches, into a mythical domain.[10] This, indeed, is real, in the sense defined by Jones when, in *The Anathemata*, he says of Troy Novant, 'the myth proposes for our acceptance a truth more real than the historic facts alone discover' (*Ana*, 124). Or, as he says succinctly in *Epoch and Artist*, art 'deals with realities and the real is sacred and religious' (158). The reality into which we are initiated in *In Parenthesis* is, as I have shown in a previous chapter, that of 'the genuine tradition of the Island of Britain'. This takes the form of an ancient cultural unity which the soldiers recreate among themselves. The trenches are accordingly 'a place of enchantment' – 'perhaps best described in Malory, book iv, chapter 15 – that landscape spoke "with a grimly voice"' (*IP*, x–xi). As a threshold or liminal situation, under the influence of 'magic', the Front or Forward Zone is, in terms that Jones would develop later, a border 'where matter marches with spirit' (*E & A*, 86), or where matter and spirit are rent asunder, the shells 'dung-making Holy Ghost temples' (*IP*, 43).

In this dual realm horrors occur, but there are also intervals of enchanted peace, as in this passage about a sentry on night watch:

> And the rain slacks at the wind veer
> > and she half breaks her cloud cover.
> He puts up a sufficient light dead over the Neb; and in its
> moments hanging, star-still, shedding a singular filament of
> peace, for these fantastic undulations.
> He angled rigid; head and shoulders free; his body's inclination

> at the extreme thrust of the sap head; outward toward
> them, like the calm breasts of her, silent above the cutwater,
> foremost toward them
> and outmost of us, and
> brother-keeper, and ward-watcher;
> his mess-mates sleeping like long-barrow sleepers, their
> dark arms at reach.
> Spell-sleepers, thrown about anyhow under the night. *(IP, 51)*

So begins the passage in which the Arthur figure enters most fully into *In Parenthesis*, calling forth the author's notes about 'the persistent Celtic theme of armed sleepers under the mounds', which Jones calls 'this abiding myth of our people' (198–9). Speaking of the Arthur of Romance literature Jones says:

> But there is evidence shining through considerable obscurity of a native identification far more solemn and significant than the Romancers dreamed of, and belonging to true, immemorial religion . . . an Arthur the Protector of the Land, the Leader, the Saviour, the Lord of Order carrying a raid into the place of Chaos. *(IP, 200–1)*

Before commenting on the passage about the sentry, I wish to observe that First World War poets gave new meaning to Keats's idea of 'the poetry of earth'. I am thinking of Wilfred Owen's 'Futility', for instance:

> Was it for this the clay grew tall?
> – O what made fatuous sunbeams toil
> To break earth's sleep at all?[11]

And Owen's 'Strange Meeting', influenced by Keats and Shelley, as well as the classical and Dantesque theme of the journey to the underworld, but giving a new meaning – a meaning that speaks 'with a grimly voice' – to an encounter between the living and the dead in a subterranean location. There is also Isaac Rosenberg's 'Dead Man's Dump':

> Burnt black by strange decay,
> Their sinister faces lie
> The lid over each eye,

> The grass and coloured clay
> More motion have than they,
> Joined to the great sunk silences.[12]

Examples drawn from these and other poets could be multiplied. For the war made men newly intimate with the earth. They lived in earthen caves and labyrinths; earth buried them, alive or dead. The intimacy made them horribly aware of their own clay and its vulnerability; it also kindled in them a sense of kinship with other creatures, such as rats and mules, and with trees and other plants, whose sap resembled blood and was mixed with their blood. As another soldier-poet, Saunders Lewis, wrote, with specific reference to *In Parenthesis*:

> private soldier and Mother Earth belong to each other with an intimacy that not even the shepherd can know. He befouls her, he digs her, he sleeps on her, he lies on her in action and inaction, wounded and unwounded, alive, dying and dead. She is Matrona, Modron, Tellus, the Mother . . .[13]

In Parenthesis is earth poetry in this spirit. Saunders Lewis goes on to quote the following passage:

>   . . . mother earth
> she's kind:
> Pray her hide you in her deeps
> she's only refuge against
> this ferocious pursuer
> terribly questing.
> Maiden of the digged places
>   let our cry come unto thee.
> *Mam*, moder, mother of me
> Mother of Christ under the tree . . . (*IP*, 176–7)

In Parenthesis shows how the strongest emotions take a religious form and seek a religious response, as here, where the terrified soldier literally digs into the nurturing and sustaining earth for protection, at the same time invoking the process by which the Mother of Christ subsumes both the personal mother and the primitive figure of Mother Earth. The poem depicts men 'wombed of earth, their rubber-sheets for caul' (75–6); men such as John Ball who 'pressed his body to the earth and the white chalk womb to mother him' (154); terrified men who, in the passage quoted above, 'curroodle mother earth / she's kind'.

Whether the soldier who would write *In Parenthesis* saw the meaning in this imagery at the time of experiencing the needs that gave rise to it, we do not know. What we do know is the post-war vision of a Catholic poet and artist. He had read Sir James Frazer's *The Golden Bough* and was familiar with Jessie L. Weston's interpretation of the Waste Land (which had influenced T. S. Eliot's poem of that title, which Jones greatly admired). Remembering the war ('remembering' is a weak word – the whole of his subsequent life was pervaded by it), he sought 'formal goodness' in what had been 'a life singularly inimical, hateful', and found meaning in the idea of life springing from sacrificial death. This was, of course, the 'sense' that Catholicism made of 'everything'; it was also (as he learnt from Frazer and Jessie L. Weston and others) the reality of 'true, immemorial religion'.

This is the idea that bestows significance on the imagery of earth as mother, as both grave and cave. As place of death, the trenches are also, in a sense, the place of rebirth. It is the imagery that intimates this – a largely pagan imagery drawn (especially in the last part) mainly from Frazer and existing in uneasy tension with the Christian perspective. A profoundly religious imaginative idea is at work here. It involves the materiality of the body in relation to the redemption of natural processes through 'Mother of Christ under the tree', and the projection of an as yet shadowy androgynous Arthur. I doubt that the theology of this idea is worked out in *In Parenthesis*, or, perhaps, was ever worked out by Jones in a way that would pass the test of orthodox theologians. It might be more accurate to call it a desire than an idea, a desire to find religious meaning in the carnage of war. At any event, the idea (or desire) transforms poetry of earth, and gives a special potency to the 'sleepers', such as Arthur and Cronus: 'this abiding myth of our people'.

Returning to the passage about the sentry, we observe a feminine influence over the scene – in 'she' (the moon), in the Very light 'hanging, star-still, shedding a singular filament of peace'. It is an influence hinting at the presence of the Mother of God and simultaneously giving the scene a cosmic dimension which comprehends earth and stars. The sentry, too, is feminized, under the image of a ship's figurehead, 'outward toward them, like the calm breasts of her, silent above the cutwater'. Among confluent motifs in the passage we are aware of the sleepers under the mounds (we do indeed see 'that the tumbled undulations and recesses, the static sentries, and the leaning arms that were the Forward Zone, called up this abiding myth of our people'); Celtic enchantment ('Spell-sleepers'); the sentry as 'Protector of the Land'. The Arthurian associations are implicit; the scene, however, occurs in a landscape where we are shown 'corkscrew-picket-iron half submerged, as dark excalibur, by perverse incantation twisted' (50). The Arthur of *In Parenthesis* is also the Arthur of the poem ascribed to Taliesin, *Preiddeu Annwn* ('The Harrowing of Hades'), which describes Arthur's Otherworld voyage, when 'he and his men went, like Our Blessed Lord, to harrow hell' (*IP*, 200). The figure with its multiple functions is also a shaping principle in the poem, helping to realize its 'formal goodness'. It is as if Jones in writing *In Parenthesis* follows 'the Lord of Order carrying a raid into the place of Chaos'.

We enter the depths of Island myth here, coming into contact with the immemorial Protector, the Sleeping Lord, of which Plutarch wrote, in the first century AD, providing an image that William Blake took up, at the beginning of the nineteenth century, and which David Jones now recalls: 'An Island in which Cronus is imprisoned with Briareous keeping guard over him as he sleeps; for as they put it, sleep is the bond of Cronus' (*IP*, 198). We may also observe the curious effect by which the trench landscape, with its 'tumbled undulations and recesses' *becomes* the landscape of the British Isles with its prehistoric earthworks; becomes, indeed, a *speaking* image of what Jones would later call (invoking a traditional name) 'Brut's Albion'. The image of 'armed sleepers under the mounds' suggests defeat (imprisonment), but, more importantly, it implies latent potency. Here, Western Front, Waste Land, island of the dead, combine to form a single visionary location. Instead of being only a prison for the defeated, it is a place of imaginative possibility, revival, redemption, new life.

The Arthur who emerges from *In Parenthesis* has female as well as male associations. He is identified as the genius of the Island, as a figure symbolizing spiritual and cultural renewal. As a sleeper underground, he may be conceived as part of the very land, and as a germinative principle. But he is Arcturus too, and therefore a cosmic power.[14] As the different elements constituting the figure flow together, we are aware of an androgynous Arthur, who symbolizes wholeness.[15]

Cultural and personal beginnings are confluent influences upon David Jones's shaping of 'the Bear of the Island'. His feeling for the actual bear he drew as a boy comes together with his knowledge of the cave-dwelling bear, which Paul Shepard and Barry Sanders describe in *The Sacred Paw*, their book about 'The Bear in Nature, Myth, and Literature', as 'an ancient sacred presence since the beginning of European culture'. Its many meanings, according to Shepard and Sanders, 'fit in with the idea of the parent-creator'. As such, the bear has played a formative part in the construction of human culture.

> The bear has for thousands of years been the master of souls, bodies, and minds in transition. The syllable from which comes 'bear' also produces 'basket', 'amphora', and, perhaps most important of all, 'metaphor', meaning literally to 'carry over'. Metaphor is the bear's carrying of his poetic and transfiguring messages between the human and the spiritual domain.[16]

The bear is also, among other things, 'the guardian of the under-world' and 'giver of life'.

The bear in fact is a life source, and very like Arthur, 'The Bear of the Island'. Master of 'souls, bodies, and minds in transition', the bear is a liminal figure and, therefore, appropriate for David Jones, poet of the borderland or March, to use as a carrier of compre-hensive meanings. Jones is drawn repeatedly to the Front, to the *limes*, not only the walls of the Roman world, but the place where, like the sentry guarding the temporary order the soldiers have made, he looks out upon chaos. The liminal 'site' of David Jones's writings is cultural and political; it is also the condition of human life. 'Man is a "borderer", he is the sole inhabitant of a tract of country where matter marches with spirit' (*E & A*, 86). It is characteristic of his 'incarnational' imagination that the religious truth which he here affirms should have been embodied for him in particular landscapes.

The Arthurian Marches in David Jones's writings after *In Parenthesis* are identified with Wales, and especially with the parts of south Wales he knew best, the Black Mountains and the country of the oldest and most magical *Mabinogion* stories, the 'Land of Enchantment'.

Ah! *Gwlad y Hud*, and where the *lledrith* binds and looses, even there,
where west-land slowly drains to west-sea and hills like insubstantial
vapours float – is this by some dissolving word or by straight erosion?

Are they Goidel marks for Pretani monolith or do the *mamau* with the
adze of night incise the standing stones?

Does the riding queen recede from the pursuer or does the unbridled
pursuit recede from the still queen?

In this place of questioning where you must ask the question and the
answer questions you

where race sleeps on dreaming race and under-myth and over-myth,
like the leaf-layered forest-floor, are the uncertain crust, which there has
firm hold, but here the mildewed tod-roots trip you at the fungus-tread.[17]

This is not a 'finished' passage, but, for that reason, it has a special
interest. For here we see materials that David Jones would reuse and
clarify in 'The Hunt' mixed with materials from the confused combat
in Mametz Wood at the end of *In Parenthesis* – known and literary,
enchanted Welsh landscape merging with (or emerging from) war
landscape, and both rich with ancient history, legend and myth.

These later Arthurian landscapes are 'the march-lands of matter
and spirit, time and not-time' (*E & A*, 202). In one sense, they
represent a retreat, a contraction, as 'the genuine tradition of the
Island of Britain' is identified with Wales, and excludes England,
except as a threatening *imperium*, and domain of post-Reformation
secularism and utilitarianism. We can see the effects of this falling
back upon Wales as sacred place in *The Anathemata*:

> West horse-hills?
> Volcae-remnants' crag-*carneddau*?
> Moel of the Mothers?
> the many *colles Arthuri*?

> All the efficacious asylums
> *in Wallia vel in Marchia Walliae*,
>   *ogofau* of, that cavern for
>   Cronos, Owain, Arthur.
> *Terra Walliae!*
>   Buarth Meibion Arthur!
>   Enclosure of the Children of Troy! (*Ana*, 55)

David Jones is not a poet of 'West horse-hills'. (It is perhaps not
irrelevant for me to record that when I visited him towards the end of

his life, he had a postcard of the Uffington White Horse prominently displayed in his room. Certainly he did have a strong feeling for ancient English landscapes, in the north and the south as well as in East Anglia; but these were not, in the main, his magical landscapes. Significantly, his writings show little interest in the Glastonbury and Cornish Arthurian sources, compared with the Welsh materials.)[18] He is a poet of Wales as sacred 'enclosure', shrine, 'asylum'.[19] This has a bearing on the form as well as the content of his later writings and paintings – the crowding details, the containing lines, as in *Y Cyfarchiad i Fair* and 'The Tutelar of the Place', a painting and a writing which have, as 'webs of magic', an equivalence. There is in his work at times a barely held tension, which brings home to us the resonant ambiguity of the word 'asylums', which he certainly intended. He experienced trauma, in war and in mental break-downs. As man and maker, he lived and worked at the frontier between order and chaos, stability and loss of balance. He knew that his Tribune's words, 'Only the neurotic / look to their begin-nings' applied to himself.[20] Indeed, it was an example of his acute intelligence that, rather than simply suffering the consequences of being the kind of artist he was, in an unpropitious time, he knew the forces opposed to him, and understood the critical view ('neurosis') of his own art.

Jones frequently invoked 'the tradition of matriarchy, a thing of pre-Celtic provenance working up through the Aryan patriarchy' (*E & A*, 48). Following Christopher Dawson in *The Age of the Gods*, he saw 'duality, a dichotomy perhaps, in the Celtic thing. The warrior-aristocracy had its sky-gods but beneath it were peoples of earlier cultures, different in physical and psychological make-up, for whom the Mother Goddess and various chthonic deities were tutelar' (*DG*, 57). Was it a dichotomy, a division built into the human species, or had there been an imposition of warrior values upon 'traditions more "cosmic" – less wholly warlike, more magical, from the archaic peoples' – 'pre-Celtic "wisdom" ' (*DG*, 126–7), as John Cowper Powys thought? This was, I think, a question David Jones never fully answered. It was an easier question for Powys, who could entertain ideas of a matriarchal Golden Age that could in some sense be restored. But Jones had been a soldier – he always remained a soldier – and was a Catholic, with a strong sense of human sinfulness; he was not, like Powys, a pagan. Rather than resolving the dilemma, he faced it, making Arthur a composite figure, with elements of Mother Goddess *and* sky-god, instead of a Golden Age ideal. In all his poems he was a war poet – he knew that 'ploughshares can become swords'; he was not surprised by 'the frequent phenomena of agricultural deities becoming war deities noted by students of mythology' (*E & A*, 233). That was twentieth-century experience, as well as ancient myth.

Is it possible, though, that Arthur can be both warrior and 'female goddess of fruition'?

> What was he called – was his womb-name Cronus or had he another – was he always the stern Maristuran. How did they ask for the wheat-yield? Was the nomen's ending he or she? What did he answer to, lord or ma'am – was he breaker or creatrix?[21]

So asks the voice in *The Roman Quarry*. It is a peculiarly personal question, perhaps, asked by a man instinct with kindness, who had been a soldier, wounded and dealing wounds. It is certainly a question about the nature of human existence. And in one sense, perhaps, it was not such a baffling question for David Jones, since he was familiar with the medieval idea of paradoxical gender. As he wrote in *The Anathemata*:

> Sophia's child that calls him master
> he her groom that is his mother. (*Ana*, 235)

In a note he comments on 'the Mother of God who represents Wisdom. She was quickened by the Spirit and the bringer-forth of the Logos-made-Flesh. Or, to use a mythologer's terms, she is both bride and mother of the cult-hero' (*Ana*, 234).[22] In a letter, he remarked: 'I suppose all my stuff has on the whole been central round the Queen of Heaven and cult hero – son and spouse.'[23]

In the light of the religious paradox, it is not difficult to understand Arthur as a type of Christ, one who combines male and female principles. More difficult to answer is the place of war – specifically modern mechanized war – in the religious scheme of things. In my view David Jones asked the question, and provided us (and himself) with answers that are questions.[24]

The contradictory elements of the Arthur figure – if that is what they are – make for its greater inclusiveness as a life symbol. As it tends towards wholeness, so it enables a poetry that combines the cosmic or elemental, rooted in particular places and things, with myth and religion.

> And is his bed wide
> > is his bed deep on the folded strata
> is his bed long
> > where is his bed and
> > where has he lain him
> from north of Llanfair-ym-Muallt
> > (a name of double *gladius*-piercings)
> south to the carboniferous vaultings of Gwyr
> > (where in the sea-slope chamber
> they shovelled aside the shards & breccia
> > the domestic litter and man-squalor
> of gnawed marrowbones and hearth-ash
> with utile shovels fashioned of clavicle-bones
> > of warm-felled great fauna . . .)[25]

The comprehensiveness of this figure, as it continues to unfold in 'The Sleeping Lord', makes it comparable to Blake's Albion. As Blake wrote, in *Jerusalem*, 'All things Begin & End in Albion's Ancient Druid Rocky Shore', so Jones's Lord, 'the young *nobilis* / the first of the sleepers of / Pritenia', is identified with the materiality of the land, with geological parent materials; his 'bed' is the rock itself. Jones quotes Blake on Arthur (in his 'Descriptive Catalogue') in a note in *In Parenthesis*:

> . . . Arthur was the name for the Constellation of Arcturus, or Boötes the Keeper of the North Pole. And all the fables of Arthur and his round table; of the warlike naked Britons; of Merlin; of Arthur's Conquest of the whole world; of his death or sleep, and promise to return again; of the Druid monuments or temples; of the pavement of Watling-street; of London Stone; of the Caverns in Cornwall, Wales, Derbyshire and Scotland; of the Giants of Ireland and Britain; of the elemental beings called by us by the general name of Fairies; of those three who escaped, namely Beauty, Strength, and Ugliness. (*IP*, 199)

The real imaginative affinites between Blake and Jones (as distinct from their different metaphysical and political beliefs) can be seen in the marriage Blake effects between native myth and actual British place-names and ground ('the pavement of Watling-street', 'London Stone', 'the Caverns in Cornwall', and so on). A further connection is evidenced by Blake's *retreat* from the powers of the world, and channelling of sacred power into the local and the particular, as shown in a line from *Jerusalem*: 'And Albion fled inward among the currents of his rivers.' Blake spoke of 'Arthur's Conquest of the whole world'. His concern, however, was with spiritual or imaginative power, rather than imperial conquest; and his concentration on the Island is actually a defence against the latter, in its contemporary forms of war, industry and scientific materialism. Broadly speaking, the same is true of Jones's falling back upon Wales and upon Arthur as the embodiment of latent sacred power.

A reader of *The Anathemata* will recognize 'the first of the sleepers of / Pritenia' as William Buckland's 'Red Lady', the prehistoric skeleton that was later discovered to be that of a young man, 'buried with rites', in the Paviland cave, 'in a cerement of powdered red oxide of iron, signifying life' (*Ana*, 76). It does not matter, however, if we are unaware of this case of gender confusion – female potency is amply presented, in association with the Sleeping Lord, through Marian references, such as 'Llanfair-ym-Muallt' ('Mary's church in Buellt') and 'double *gladius*-piercings' (recalling 'the passage in the gospel of the *gladius* that would pierce the heart of the God-bearer').

This is 'incarnational' poetry.[26] Like all David Jones's work, it is grounded upon his faith in the divine creation, and the entry of the eternal into time. From a Protestant point of view, the image-making might appear idolatrous. It does not present a prior concern with image, however; it is based, rather, on Christopher Dawson's idea of history, in which religion is the animating idea behind culture, so that all cultural products, including language and landscape, are informed by the religious idea.[27] In poetic terms, the incarnational metaphysic marries an informing spiritual presence to rock-solid materiality. Through place-names, Welshness in this passage is incarnate in the land, thus creating an extraordinary intimacy – flesh of flesh – between language (the repository of prehistory and history) and terrain. Geology and culture, flesh and spirit, time and not-time 'march together'.

The passage continues with an invocation of 'the life-signa'. On this sacred border, these (which represent sacrament) work together with use ('utile shovels'). Poetry, myth and religion find fulfilment in the embodied idea of the Sleeping Lord. Like priest and like poet, the figure 'intends life'.

But – 'the fate of death?' This is the question on which, as René Hague says, 'the whole of the poet's faith' depends.[28] But what kind of question is that anyway, except one to which any of our answers questions us? David Jones had seen more actual death than most people ever will, and he lived with the question with which death starkly confronts us. His faith gives an answer, which questions all human assumptions, turns the world inside out, and suggests that only myth is real. Everywhere is the Otherworld; all places are 'March-lands', though it usually takes crisis or trauma for one to recognize it. That, and not illusion, is the real significance of enchantment, as the ancient Welsh storytellers and poets knew. David Jones experienced recurring states of crisis, which, whatever their circumstantial causes, faced him with the question of ultimate meaning, which depends upon the fate of death. As we follow the evolution of the figure of Arthur through his writings, we see it becoming his most comprehensive symbol – made out of parent materials, uniting past and present, child and man, male and female, embodying his thinking about culture and religion, incorporating his muse:

> Could we remove the Gothic attire, the figure beneath would be very other than that of 'a fair lady and thereto lusty and young'. Rather we should see displayed the ageless, powerful, vaticinal, mistress of magic, daubed with ochre, in the shift of divination, at the gate of the labyrinth – the spell-binder of some earlier society, where, though *Teste David cum Sibylla*, it was the latter who had most to say. (*E & A*, 235)

It would be easy to conclude with a general statement to the effect that, for Jones, Arthur as a type of Christ, symbolized the belief that human life depends upon the sacrificial death upon the Cross – itself prefigured in 'true, immemorial religion' from the foundation of the world. But that would be to turn the journey that is an initiation into a map. It would be to miss the experience of wholeness, tense with contradictions, that the figure of Arthur in David Jones's writings offers. Our exploration of 'the iceberg of existence' leaves us with a sense of the unfathomable depth of the waters. Or, to put it in another way, what we are finally left with after an initiation into David Jones's imaginative world is, as well as the aesthetic pleasure of the journey, a sense of possibility:

you never know *what* may be
                            – not hereabouts.
No wiseman's son *born* do know
                            not in these whoreson March-lands
of this Welshry.[29]

7

'God is Who Questions Me':
A Portrait of Roland Mathias[1]

The publication in 1996 of *A Field at Vallorcines*, a new book of poems by Roland Mathias, was a remarkable event. It was remarkable not only because the book appeared eleven years after he had suffered a severe stroke, and showed the will and determination which had helped him to recover sufficiently to complete the poems it contained, but also because of its continuity with his earlier work. Here, for example, is the harsh inner 'weather', corresponding to a bleak season and a hard place, familiar from earlier poems:

> A fortnight has gone since her death.
> February hangs browned at the edge
> Like the snowdrop's sheath.
> If there is life still, low in the old drudge
> Garden, its crying virtue belongs
> With the ground wind, with the weary pokings
> At door-jambs, the shuddered gravel
> Dry-soled, back and fore, bleak with conscience left behind. ('Tŷ Clyd')[2]

This is unmistakably by the poet who had written, in 'Craswall', many years before, 'nightingales / Struggle with thorn-trees for the gate of Wales':[3] a poet with a strong lyrical impulse, for whom a harsh music is appropriate to mental and emotional conflict, to a Christian conscience subject to God's questioning, and to Welsh landscapes imbued with the values of the Nonconformist tradition.

The poem from which these lines come, 'Tŷ Clyd', is about the house where Roland Mathias's parents had lived in Brecon. True to his sense of community, in describing the house he remembers, also, people outside the family: the builder, the man who held the deeds, and 'The rich draper, Arafnah Thomas called / To be minister'. It is in the main an accessible poem, which carries forward the quality of the opening lines, which admirably portray the bleak period following his mother's death, at the same time as they convey, as though it formed the very garden she tended, the tough religious 'ground' on which she had founded her life. Later in the poem, however, we encounter these lines: 'two storeys of deed / Slapped on word'. I have to confess that on first reading them I had no idea what they meant. Unusually, though, Mathias supplies notes to the poems in this book. The note on these lines tells us that they describe 'the conflict between my mother's independent, uncompromising pacifism with its rejection of organized "established" religion and my father's position as a Congregational minister, formerly an army chaplain'.[4] As in finding the answer to a difficult crossword puzzle question, the answer made me feel I should have seen it at once. But, indeed, this is highly compacted, indirect writing.

What is the reason for it? In my view, the religious impulse to confession is strong in Roland Mathias. But equally strong is his resistance to what might be regarded as 'merely' personal confession, or the use of personal details for egotistic purposes. My aim in this chapter is to place Mathias's poetry in the context of his biography, and thus to portray the Puritan as poet, and the Anglo-Welsh writer acutely aware of responsibilities, and unwilling to claim for himself any rights.

Roland Glyn Mathias was born at Ffynnon Fawr, a farmhouse near Talybont-on-Usk, Breconshire, in 1915. The farm belonged to his maternal grandfather who had worked in a small way as a builder before moving from Cardiff to the farm in an attempt to improve his health. Roland's other grandfather, David Mathias, was from Carmarthenshire, and, Roland tells us, 'had emerged as one of those men of practical bent who, whether as carpenter, builder or wheelwright, could undertake any or all of the tasks found for them by their neighbours in a poor and undernourished rural area'.[5] For generations, his ancestors had been squatters. Roland Mathias has described his Welsh-speaking father, who was a minister, as 'heir to much that the Nonconformist tradition had made possible',[6] and his mother, who was from Crickhowell, as 'a monoglot English speaker, who inherited that faint disparagement and secret hostility which was characteristic of areas which had lost the Welsh language'.[7] For Mathias the poet, the parental differences in language and culture were to prove a source of creative tension, while the fact that his father was an army chaplain and his mother a strong pacifist was to affect his moral outlook. The tensions existed, however, within an overall unity, based upon a shared Christianity. Mathias remained closely attached to his parents, and has sought in his work as a whole to reconcile the cultural differences of his dual inheritance. From his family and ancestry he acquired an attachment to the land, an awareness of poverty and a respect for the practical skills that help to alleviate it and secure the community. He gained, too, a staunch loyalty to the Nonconformist tradition. As he has written of the same quality in Vernon Watkins, that loyalty has 'an obstinate face as well as a rare and shining one'.[8]

Roland Mathias left Wales with his parents at the age of four and did not return to live and work in Wales until 1948. It is evident, however, that he often returned in imagination to Ffynnon Fawr, which was eventually abandoned at the edge of the valley flooded by Newport Water Board reservoir. In that place, as he was to show in 'The Flooded Valley', he rediscovered ancestral bonds:

> Am I not Kedward, Prosser, Morgan, whose long stones
> Name me despairingly and set me chains?

It was to this place and these people, too, that he envisaged an ultimate homecoming:

> swear to me now in my weakness,
>   swear
> To me poor you will plant a stone more in this tightening field
> And name there your latest dead, alas your unweaned
>   feeblest child. (*BB*, 50)

The strong sense of personal inadequacy in face of his ancestry, which marks much of his poetry and is, in fact, a product of the loyalty which underlies all his work, also appears in a fictional form in his short story 'Ffynnon Fawr'. There, Rendel Morgan, who had left the farmhouse as a child to emigrate with his parents to Australia, returns alone to spend a haunted night in the derelict house. He finds that his dead father is 'yet alive in the hulk of Ffynnon Fawr, still speaking for him as he had always done'. Rendel fails the challenge to his 'mastery' of mechanical skills which in fact blocks his access to a different reality, a true sense of identity. He is 'too timid for Ffynnon Fawr, too timid to make a future where the generations cried out on him in their sleep',[9] and retreats back into exile.

The painful emotions of the poem and the story belong to the modern Welsh experience of exile, which, as Mathias has said when writing of T. Harri Jones, is not 'a fact solely of geography', but 'also a complex and agonised condition of the heart'.[10] The emotions have, too, the distinctive self-lacerating edge which Mathias hones on his Puritan conscience. The potency of Ffynnon Fawr as an image for him may be gauged from what he has said in an autobiographical essay about being 'outside' the Wales in which he came back to live:

> If the house I cannot enter now seems smaller and my inheritance of it a matter of document and notation rather than living relationship, the cause is age and the deprivations of death, not a diminution of my desire to enter and know it. I am sorry in my heart to be shut out, but glad that memory gives me strength to go on knocking. Memory and guilt.[11]

The idea of Wales as a house evidently owes something to particular houses, Ffynnon Fawr and others, in which Mathias first heard the Welsh language spoken and felt a sense of belonging to Wales, and also, perhaps, to a biblical image and Waldo Williams's use of it: 'Beth yw gwladgarwch? Cadw tŷ / Mewn cwmwl tystion' ('Patriotism, what's that? Keeping house / In a cloud of witnesses').[12] The ruin standing before a waste of waters is also a type – not to say the cause – of the setting of a number of Mathias's finest poems, in which the poet alone with his memories faces the chaotic element which erodes all that he is and all that he values, and symbolizes his absolute dependence for salvation upon a power that is not his own.

From 1920 the Mathiases led a 'wandering life', and Roland was educated at British army schools in Germany and England, and, from 1925 to 1933, at Caterham School, Surrey. From 1933 to 1938 he was at Jesus College, Oxford, where he both achieved distinction as a student of history and won college colours for hockey and rugby. His ability at sport and his wide interest in the arts were later to distinguish his career as a teacher. Now he was earning the academic success which was originally made possible by the Nonconformist belief in education and the self-sacrifice of poorer family members for the sake of his father and, ultimately, himself. At the same time, he was experiencing the relative cultural deracination to which social mobility had led, but also, in visits to Wales, coming closer to his mother's people and his father's, and grounding his ideals upon the qualities they had retained. He received in Wales 'an unsurpassed quality of welcome, untainted by any feelings of jealousy or injustice, unaffected by the derogations of privilege, from uncles, aunts and cousins who would have thought it odd to be described as anything other than common people'.[13] In the Rhondda in particular, he felt 'the texture that was tight enough for community'. The later description of the feeling interestingly unites, in a word, the qualities which, as teacher and poet, he most values – as if there were indeed a correlation between poetic 'texture' and the texture of the community to which the poet belongs, and which he praises. But the student and young teacher, who had found in his kin a people to celebrate, knew himself separated from them by more than geographical distance. He had also yet to develop the poetic means by which he could pay his debt to them.

Mathias's first teaching appointment was at St Helen's, Lancashire, from 1938 to 1941. In the latter year he served a term in prison as a conscientious objector. Relating the strong conviction which he held 'for religious reasons' to his mother's influence, he also came to see it as 'one step back to Wales',[14] to the anti-militarism of nineteenth-century Nonconformists. For the time being, however, his working life lay in England, where he taught at a number of schools until 1948. In that year he returned to Wales as headmaster of the grammar school at Pembroke Dock. His first commercially published book of poems, *Break in Harvest*, had appeared the previous year. His next book of poems, *The Roses of Tretower* (1952), and a book of short stories, *The Eleven Men of Eppynt* (1956), were both published by Dock Leaves Press.

The magazine *Dock Leaves*, published by the same press, originated from a literary group which Roland Mathias formed at Pembroke Dock in 1949. Initially edited by Raymond Garlick, who renamed it *The Anglo-Welsh Review* in 1957, the magazine was the first major literary undertaking involving two men who, as editors, scholars and critics, were to do much to establish the tradition of Anglo-Welsh literature. The collaboration of Mathias and Garlick, which began as a local initiative with the founding of *Dock Leaves*, may be said to have culminated in a national event, with the publication in 1984 of their jointly edited *Anglo-Welsh Poetry 1480–1980*. The modesty characteristic of both men should not belie the fact that this book made a bold and ambitious claim, extending the territory for Anglo-Welsh poetry far beyond that of the commoner view that it is only a modern phenomenon.

There can be no doubt that the establishment of the Anglo-Welsh literary tradition, by a handful of writers and against initial and in some instances continuing inertia and even hostility on the part of the Welsh educational establishment and media, has been a heroic effort. Not that Roland Mathias would see his part in it as that; but so it has been. Before 1948, however, it must have often seemed to him that he would have no part to play in Wales. The fact that he was able to make a significant contribution owed much to his work as a historian, and was directly due to his profession as a teacher.

At Oxford he had developed his gift for meticulous study of historical records and his mastery of detail. These are scholarly arts which both serve the imagination and empower the moral passion for doing justice to issues and individuals. Together, imagination and moral passion constitute the historical sense. This sense is evident both in Mathias's purely historical work, such as *Whitsun Riot* (1963) and in his contributions to *Pembrokeshire County History*, vol. III, and in his literary history, such as *Anglo-Welsh Literature: An Illustrated History* (1986). He has said that when he began teaching in England, he achieved a kind of return to Wales 'by way of history'.[15] He meant by this that his historical researches into recusancy in Herefordshire and Monmouthshire gave him an intellectual and emotional foothold in border areas which he then felt were as far into Wales as he had a right to venture. This is a typically modest way of regarding his contribution, as poet and historian, to exploration of the 'border'. Sam Adams does Mathias more justice when he says of his fascination with Archenfield ('the old Welsh region of Ergyng'): 'The March, the border between England and Wales, the shifting border between English and Welsh, is more to him than an intellectual preoccupation. It reflects his perception of his own position, on the edge of things, viewing them with engrossed detachment.'[16]

Wherever he is in Wales, Mathias evidently takes the 'border' with him, in this sense. In 'Porth Cwyfan', for example, he says: 'I can call nothing my own.' Yet he knows the place; he remembers Cwyfan, 'when the finer / Passions ruled, convergent answers belled / Weather-like towards God'; recalling Cwyfan and Beuno, he wonders whether it will be possible now to 'bond men to single / Living'. With his historical knowledge, he knows Roger Parry, too, whose tombstone is in the graveyard. But still he sees himself as a tourist, and, meeting a man from Lancashire with his wife and child, asks himself: 'But how is my tripright sounder, / Save that I know Roger Parry and he does not?' (*BB*, 119–20). The implication seems to be that historical knowledge alone is not sufficient for a person to claim to belong to Wales. But it is not only knowledge Mathias has, but a passion and a commitment to the land and the people and their history which would be rare anywhere. Even the Mathias long resident in Wales, however, cannot eradicate exile from his heart and mind. That is itself a matter of his historical perspective, of course. And, as he writes in 'Memling', 'The history we choose speaks largely of ourselves' (*BB*, 142).

One thread running through all Mathias's intellectual activities is his belief that in learning about the world it is necessary and desirable to begin by understanding where, in place and time, one is. Another thread is his sense of responsibility to the community. Thus, as a teacher he was concerned with the school as a community, which he believed should be of a size to allow individuals to see that their actions affect the group of which they are part, and so help them to develop a sense of responsibility. It is a Christian ideal,[17] and its model is the neighbourhood focused upon the Nonconformist chapel, in which concern for the individual soul and concern for the community are closely related. The same religious tradition shaping the teacher has shaped his criticism and his idea of the poet's function, too. In his major book of critical essays, *A Ride Through the Wood*, Mathias describes the Welsh inheritance of 'Puritan seriousness' as 'seriousness about the purpose of living, about the need for tradition and the understanding of it, about the future of the community as well as the individual'.[18] He opposes the attitude of Welsh poets writing as members of their community to a romantic individualism concerned with the separated ego. What he apparently does not take into account is the danger of the opposition becoming too absolute. There is, after all, as I have emphasized in this book, a side of English Romanticism that reminds us of our bonds with one another and the need to love and care for the Earth. It also needs to be borne in mind that some modern Welsh writers, like writers in other places, know the meaning of isolation. The opposition is useful, however, as a delineation of an area of choice, and of social and ideological tensions, in which Anglo-Welsh writing exists.

Mathias is a moral critic, concerned with what a writer is saying, with what he is (his major criticism concentrates on male authors), with what his inheritance has made him, and with what he has made of it. He is incisive in laying bare substitutes for religious truth, doctrines of beauty or art or nature which in his view are confused, and cause confusion. At the same time he shows considerable psychological understanding, and writes with learning and heuristic sensitivity, patiently illuminating complex and densely textured imaginative worlds and intellectual systems. This is especially true of his work on David Jones, on Vernon Watkins and on Henry Vaughan. If Mathias occasionally probes motives with a too ministerial mind, his combination of moral passion with concern for the integrity of the writer and of the work is rare in contemporary criticism.

From 1958 to 1968, Roland Mathias again lived and worked in England, as a headmaster at schools in Derbyshire and Birmingham. He continued to shoulder extra-mural responsibilities in the fields of his various interests, which included drama as well as sport. His third book of poems, *The Flooded Valley*, was published in 1960, and in the following year he became editor of *The Anglo-Welsh Review*, a position he held until 1976. Of his editorship he has fairly said that:

> while turning out editorial after editorial urging greater understanding between the English-speakers and Welsh-speakers of Wales, I sought to create another kind of unity, by making *The Anglo-Welsh Review* a vehicle for a greater part of the authorial output of Wales by having reviewed books in and from other disciplines which seemed not incompatible with a central interest in the Arts.[19]

From his editorials alone one could derive an image in depth of Wales as seen by a mind alert for signs of unity, as he ranges between contemporary issues and the distant past, applying a spirit of reconciliation to questions of Welsh identity and fulfilling an essential function of community as he memorializes the known and unknown Welsh writers in both languages who died in those years. As well as maintaining an excellent record of encouraging new writers, *The Anglo-Welsh Review* under Roland Mathias continued the work of drawing attention to important earlier writing in the neglected field of Anglo-Welsh literature, a function which he has also fulfilled with the several collections of stories, essays and poems he has edited or jointly edited.

Following his retirement from teaching in order to become a full-time writer in 1969, Mathias settled in Brecon. Subsequently he has published four books of poetry: *Absalom in the Tree* (1971), *Snipe's Castle* (1979), *Burning Brambles* (1983) and *A Field at Vallorcines* (1996). That the last-named contains work as good as his best may be seen from the conclusion of the title poem:

> The run down the gorge to the frontier, the silent place
>
> We peered at this morning with so little
> In mind, will be full of jerks and slowings
> Like the blind climb up. But the station has grace. It has borne
>
> The faces of doubt, the comings and goings
> Of millions. We shall stand there solid in
> The goodly counsel with which a world back we set out.[20]

The writing is at once fluent and textured, with a subtle verbal music, and the meaning is carried by the description of the place, embedded in the references – 'grace', 'goodly counsel', 'faces of doubt' – that give a local habitation to the religious tradition which the poem affirms.

In the same period Roland Mathias has published *The Hollowed-Out Elder Stalk: John Cowper Powys as Poet*, and, as well as the critical books referred to above, a considerable body of other literary and cultural criticism. True to his principle of service to the community, he continued as chairman or committee member to play a full part in organizing and administering the structures that support Anglo-Welsh literary life, and in encouraging other writers. Always his aim has been to work towards building 'a Wales in English which is not England and which is in touch with the living heart of a Wales that beats in Welsh'.[21] Mathias the poet has satirized Mathias the committee man, 'alive and jack in office, / Shrewd among the plunderers' (*BB*, 96). But those who have worked with him, or are aware of his work as a founder member of Yr Academi Gymreig (English Language Section), or his chairmanship of the Literature Committee of the Welsh Arts Council, 1976–9, for example, know that he is motivated by a sense of justice and a sense of responsibility. He has given to other writers and to the literary community a large measure of his creative energy, just as he did as a teacher to his pupils and staff.

In 1985, on the occasion when he received an honorary doctorate from the University of Georgetown, he was described as a man who has, 'through all his work, affirmed the value of literature to the life of a nation and its people and has laboured, with extraordinary commitment, to make that value felt'. Mathias belongs to what he has defined as 'the second movement' of Anglo-Welsh writing, which includes Emyr Humphreys, David Jones, Gwyn Williams and R. S. Thomas. Compared with the movement away from Wales of writers of 'the first flowering', this was:

> a movement much less popular, much more erudite, much less immediately successful or desirous of being so, one which, in emphasising heritage and tradition, was already conscious of the damage to the Welsh way of life which so much exploitation and popularisation had caused. It was, in brief, less self-absorbed, reverting to the older Welsh tradition in which the poet had a duty to his community as well as to his muse.[22]

These are stirring words; but, it may be asked, is so much emphasis upon 'duty' and 'responsibility' on the part of a poet altogether a good thing for his poetry? Roland Mathias has described himself as 'a wordsman',[23] but also as 'a poet with the brake on',[24] to counter-act his sentimentality. What he is capable of achieving when the brake is off may be seen in his Pembrokeshire sequence, 'Tide-Reach', which was included in his selected poems, *Burning Brambles*. It was, no doubt, partly a consequence of this sequence being written for music that helped to make it his most lucid and powerful celebration of Wales. The following lines from the tenth movement, 'Laus Deo', are to my mind among the most memorable lines among all Anglo-Welsh poetry:

> It is one engrossing work, this frail
> Commerce of souls in a corner,
> Its coming and going, and the mark
> Of the temporal on it. It is one
> Coherent work, this Wales
> And the seaway of Wales, its Maker
> As careful of strength as
> Of weakness, its quirk and cognomen
> And trumpet allowed for
> The whole peninsula's length.
> It is one affirmative work, this Wales
> And the seaway of Wales. (*BB*, 163)

Naturally, the Puritan poet emphasizes that Wales is a 'work'. In this instance, the freedom to be affirmative must surely have resulted from the public nature of the collaboration with a musician, which liberated the poet from his concern with his own shortcomings.

One result of the Puritan conscience is the self-condemnation which, especially in Mathias's earlier poems, creates areas of disturbance and often tortures language and syntax when his personal 'I' appears. This impedes the masterful delight in word music and rhythmic flow which is released when he looks away from himself, as he does with marvellous effect in the poem just quoted, or in 'Freshwater West':

> Over, break white and wash swiftly
> Around this rock where earlier
> Suds sand hiding swish and uncover.
> Press, press on the slope of glass
> Sliding over, over. White and pass
> Me, wish peace and deliver
> From hope, all you byegones, hush
> And recover. Break ground and foam
> Over and over . . . (*BB*, 52)

Another result of what is, literally, fear of self is that powerful, contained emotion is a feature of his poetry first and last.

It is possible to make too much of the difficulty of the poems, especially in view of the fact that difficulty is a necessary part of modern poetry that tackles the complexity of life and the predicament of the religious poet in a secular age. There are passages that are clear and direct in many of Mathias's poems, and whole poems, such as 'An Age', that represent his lyrical gift at its finest:

> The blue singleness of summer was in that air
> And the bushes hazed after the light
> Though it was September gone.
> Is it blackberrying, sun
> And juice in the hand, or a flight
> Of birds shearing over the ferry that holds me there?
>
> The envelope has let an age escape to the sea
> And I am old, but not so
> Old as Mabon taken from between

His mother and the wall. When
I was young I saw the sun go
Purple on my thumb and birds stand shoaling in the estuary. (*BB*, 63)

The immediate accessibility of this is due not to simplicity of means
or content, but to its lyrical movement, emotional impact and
development of imagery. The reference to Mabon will tax the wits of
any reader who is unfamiliar with Welsh mythology, and the
concentration of meaning is demanding; 'the blue singleness of
summer' and the child's identification of 'blackberrying, sun / And
juice in the hand', together with the man's recapture of the moment
within the passage of time, are the result of remarkable poetic
organization and imagistic compression. The natural flight of time
and the visionary moment that transcends or transfigures it are a
recurring theme of Mathias's poetry, and 'An Age' is its most joyful
embodiment, as 'A Last Respect' is its most profound and most
moving expression. But to claim that he often writes with directness
and clarity would be to substitute another half-truth for the notion
that he is invariably opaque.

Except in poems such as 'For Warren Davies, Two Years Dead', in
which he speaks for and commemorates a particular individual,
Roland Mathias rarely speaks with the confidence in communal
feeling or shared belief that one might expect from his prose
accounts of the role of the poet in Wales. Even in 'A Last Respect',
when a heightened, visionary moment at his father's funeral offers
him an opportunity to affirm a shared faith, he speaks questioningly,
defensively:

Who are you to say that my father, wily
And old in the faith, had not in that windflash abandoned
His fallen minister's face? (*BB*, 81)

The defence may seem to be against worldly scepticism, but it is
really against the presumption of rhetoric. Mathias is a poet in love
with language, and with poetic texture and form, who fears that
they may 'say' more than he, a scrupulously honest man, can assent
to, or may say what he feels and believes, but with an indulgence that
invalidates it.

When occlusion occurs in work of his poetic maturity, which he
achieved in the 1950s, it results from his struggle to dramatize the

difficult relationship between himself and his subject, and is often a necessary part of the poem. But the demands of his poetry should not be allowed to obscure either his splendidly vigorous poetic monologues, whether in his own person or that of a historical figure, such as Henry Vaughan, Absalom, or Sir Gelli Meyrick, or the emotional directness and force of poems such as 'The Flooded Valley', 'A Letter', and 'Departure in Middle Age', of which this is the second stanza:

> But I cannot go back, plump up the pillow and shape
> My sickness like courage. I have spent the night in a shiver:
> Usk water passing now was a chatter under the Fan
> When the first cold came on. They are all dead, all,
> Or scattered, father, mother, my pinafore friends,
> And the playground's echoes have not waited for my return.
> Exile is the parcel I carry, and you know this,
> Clouds, when you drop your pretences and the hills clear. (*BB*, 85)

In the first stanza of the poem, the poet has described himself as 'cold / And strange to myself'; this is the 'sickness' of the second verse, and it is a characteristic state of the poet. The primary cause of this is stated in 'God Is':

> God is who questions me
> Of my tranquillity. (*BB*, 98)

Accordingly, there is little tranquillity in Roland Mathias's poetry, and his Christianity, as far as he personally is concerned, manifests itself principally as a conviction of sin. While R. S. Thomas in his later poems espouses a mysticism centred partly upon love of nature and partly upon the ways in which God hides himself, and eludes our definitions of him, Mathias is a moralist concerned with what God asks of him personally and of humankind in general. His love of nature and of place shines through his poetry, but he is both more grudging with the consolations of nature or affirmative vision and more morally demanding than R. S. Thomas. There are more difficult poets than Mathias who have found a wide readership, and I suspect that it is the radically disquieting focus of his attention, together with its mediation by Welsh history and places, that is the main cause of his relative neglect. After all, there has probably never been another time like the present when a preoccupation with human sinfulness was less likely to attract readers. The seriousness makes embarrassing demands, even though Mathias, in common with most important modern religious poets, uses biblical metaphors and images drawn from nature – fountain, dust, light, and so on – instead of dogmatic or technical terms. However, he does also use words such as 'covenant' and 'justification' which ground his religious vision firmly upon the Nonconformist tradition.

Light is thrown on Mathias's Puritanism by his essay on Emyr Humphreys's earlier novels, included in *A Ride Through the Wood*, in which he says the following of Humphreys:

> His writing and its preoccupations are the result of Wales's heritage of the last three centuries: they begin in that Puritan seriousness about the purpose of living, about the need for tradition and the understanding of it, about the future of the community as well as the individual, that has almost no place in the writing of contemporary English novelists . . .[25]

These words apply almost equally to his own work; they also help to explain, incidentally, why neither he nor Humphreys has had his due outside Wales.

Mathias writes well about people, especially those who could not write or speak for themselves. As he says in 'For Warren Davies, Two Years Dead': 'You rarely wrote. I am your remembrancer.' Addressing his late grandfather in 'Expiation', he writes:

> But to deny
> The dead a voice is to falter
> In justice.[26]

Nothing could show more clearly that he is not concerned only with memory and loss. His consciousness of time colours much of his poetry with an elegiac mood, and his settings and metaphors based on an eroding coastline, as in 'For an Unmarked Grave' and 'A Letter from Gwyther Street', produce some of his most evocative and haunting lines. But he is not primarily an elegist in the sense that Thomas Hardy was, because, for Mathias, memory that brings back the pain of loss also demands that justice be rendered to the dead. While visiting historical places invariably provokes a self-questioning which finds him wanting in comparison with the dead, justice requires that he questions the dead, too, even the craftsmen he greatly admires, like Charlie Stones, or John Abel, the king's carpenter, in 'Sarnesfield'. But the most remorseless questioning is reserved for himself, and his celebrations or commemorations of others are likely to include a self-condemnation, as at the end of 'They Have Not Survived':

> For this dark cousinhood only I
> Can speak. Why am I unlike
> Them, alive and jack in office,
> Shrewd among the plunderers? (*BB*, 96)

The Puritan conscience is reinforced by his sense of isolation in a country where he can call nothing his own; indeed, it is relevant to ask whether, in a situation in which tradition has been largely eroded and the future of the community is in doubt, the 'puritan seriousness about the purpose of living' does not focus too narrowly on the self, with morbid results for a poet whose strongest castigations are of himself.

To expect from Roland Mathias anything other than a poetry that questions himself and implicitly questions the reader is an impertinence. His art is Puritan; it is suspicious of everything that is natural and everything that is human, including itself. He shares with Emyr Humphreys what he calls 'the old Puritan distrust of beauty'. As he said in an interview with Cary Archard, 'Beauty in itself doesn't save.'[27] In 'The Mountain' he asks: 'Give me the punishment that saves' (*BB*, 37), and in a much later poem, 'The Green Chapel', which is the first movement of 'Tide-Reach', he writes:

> the fear within
> Is the worst, the horror of separation
> From meaning. (*BB*, 147)

Distrust of beauty is one thing he has in common with Geoffrey Hill (another is his historical sense), and in 'Memling' he shows his awareness that art can be a subtle form of moral evasion, safely transposing 'the ravisher and ravished' (*BB*, 142). While he has affinities with R. S. Thomas and Geoffrey Hill, Mathias is closest to

Humphreys among his contemporaries. The novelist remorselessly exposes the deceptions of the word in his country's most cherished places: bardic chair, pulpit, political rostrum; Mathias, for his part, is quick to confess what in 'The Fool in the Wood' he calls 'the cost and bloat / I have of words' (*BB*, 108). His aim, applied first to himself, is to lay 'the action bare' ('Freshwater West Revisited', *BB*, 85).

Mathias is not a poet to make concessions to those who patronize Wales with Anglocentric ideas of 'Welshness'. One consequence of his loyalty is that he has taken his Anglo-Welsh situation far more seriously than all but a small handful of writers, including Glyn Jones, Raymond Garlick and Tony Conran, with whom he shares it. He has done this partly out of his humble sense of himself as an outsider who cannot claim to be fully Welsh, and who must earn his place in Wales by his effort and understanding. This, indeed, accounts for the passion informing the meticulous care of his historical sense, and evident equally in his poems, criticism and historical writings. Care of this order is both an emotional need and a moral obligation, and its object is justice. As I have already implied, the discomfort at not belonging which reinforces his Puritan conscience is the very thing that makes him much more of an insider than he would ever claim to be. As both explorer and representative of the Puritan tradition, Mathias is one of the small group of Welsh writers in English who reveal Wales from the inside.

As the conclusion to his powerful poem, 'Brechfa Chapel' shows, Mathias has no confidence that the tradition he has inherited will survive:

> Is the old witness done?
> The farmers, separate in their lands, hedge,
> Ditch, no doubt, and keep tight pasture. Uphill
> They trudge on seventh days, singly, putting
> Their heads to the pews as habit bids them to,
> And keep counsel. The books, in pyramid, sit tidy
> On the pulpit. The back gallery looks
> Swept. But the old iron gate to the common,
> Rusted a little, affords not a glimpse
> Of the swan in her dream on the reed-knot
> Nor of the anxious coot enquiring of the grasses.
> The hellish noise it is appals, the intolerable shilly-
> Shally of birds quitting the nearer mud

> For the farther, harrying the conversation
> Of faith. Each on his own must stand and conjure
> The strong remembered words, the unanswerable
> Texts against chaos. (*BB*, 145)

Here, 'the strong remembered words' curiously echo 'the sweet remembered demarcations' and 'the remembered things' of David Jones's 'The Tribute's Visitation': 'things' which are, either in fact or by analogy, Celtic. Yet Mathias's 'words' and 'texts' also contrast with the Catholic poet's 'things', which embody his sacramental religion, and are also the 'matter' of cultural tradition. The Puritan heritage, by contrast, is based upon the word: the word of God in the Bible, the word God speaks to the individual heart. It is this, too, which, in 'the conversation of faith', binds people together in small communities centred upon the chapel. It is interesting to note this fundamental difference, rooted in different religious traditions, between the two Anglo-Welsh poets who have entered most deeply into the Welsh past. For David Jones, the things of Wales retained a hope of cultural order, albeit 'sleeping' like Arthur in the land itself, in opposition to the chaos of modern Britain and the secular state. They belonged more to his idea of a Catholic, Arthurian Wales than to post-Reformation, historical reality. As a symbol, however, they belonged also to the live current of Welsh nationalist thought associated principally with Saunders Lewis, and they invoked something of the incarnational sweetness, the integration of soul and body, and human and divine love, that we find in the world of Dafydd ap Gwilym. Roland Mathias, by contrast, is a poet of a later tradition, which sets man as a spiritual warrior at enmity with his own nature. For him, it is not things that bind people together and unite them with God, but words; it is not things that stand against chaos, but texts. Tragedy arises, however, from the fact that 'the strong remembered words' are no longer the conversation of a faithful community. Now, they are the support of 'each on his own', as the farmers, 'separate in their lands', trudge 'singly' to chapel on Sundays. It is the waterbirds that stand in the poem for the present state of society, for a people who have lost their tradition; and 'the hellish noise it is appals'.

There is no denying the emotional and rhetorical force of this angry and pessimistic conclusion. It is possible, though, to think the symbol of the birds too weak, and even too contrived, to carry such a burden of significance. It is possible also to be reminded by it of the fascination with birds of Emyr Humphreys's bard, John Cilydd More, which I take to be, among other things, a prophetic portrayal of the marginalization of the poet in modern Wales, whereby the bard, deprived of a role at the centre of his society, tends to project all that he has to say about man, God and nation on to a nature that can scarcely bear the pressure of the displacement. In terms of a parallel process, it is also possible to see in the conclusion to 'Brechfa Chapel' a reflection of the alienated individualism that the poem laments. But if these suggestions seem to limit the power of the poem, this would be to ignore a conviction implicit in my criticism: that a good poet is not known by the 'correctness' of his answers according to any dogma, but by the integrity and intensity with which he lives the questions.

It is in this context that we should understand the paradox that Roland Mathias's poetic achievement is best defined by negatives. Not possessing a world, not being at home in his country, not being able to stand self-confidently alongside his ancestors, not having a truth that words can adequately name – these are all one experience, and it is this that has produced some of his finest poems. Fundamentally, it is an experience of separation, not of the ego from the community, but of the soul convicted of sin, and answerable to the God from whom it is separated. The feeling proper to the experience is awe, a compound of dread and exhilaration at being made nothing, as the human order is shattered, yet at the same time it affords a glimpse of the greater reality with which ultimate meaning lies.

In its negative aspect the experience is fictionalized in 'Ffynnon Fawr', in which the man returning home – in fact, to the ground of his ancestral religion – fails to meet the challenge of its meaning. More positively the experience is dramatized in poems such as 'Freshwater West Revisited' in which the poet faces the sea:

> This is no place of secondary forms,
> Pretty distractions, heights of cliffs
> Or trees, not far-out ships puffing
> Irrelevantly of other shores and clashes,
> Here the brute combers build the waterhead
> And grass girds up the dunes the shock washes. (*BB*, 85)

The place of confrontation is the shore or coast, the place where, as the last line of the poem puts it: 'Sea is, and land, and bloodwreck where they meet.' This is a frontier between the known world, the human world, and all that it is not. It is a locus which, with the decay of traditional religious language as a medium for poetry, Roland Mathias shares with a number of other modern poets. These include T. S. Eliot (especially in 'The Dry Salvages'), Geoffrey Hill, and R. S. Thomas in his later poems: poets who differ considerably from each other both in 'voice' and in degree of scepticism, but whose poetic impulse is fundamentally religious, within the Protestant tradition that emphasizes spiritual conflict and man's distance from a God to whom he is personally answerable. Of all modern poets, Mathias is most conscious that man – which first means specifically himself – is the being questioned by God, and least inclined to be God's questioner.

It would be too neat a conclusion to look back from the frontier of the sea as it occurs in his poetry to the image of the ruined farmhouse, his original home, standing by the desolate water. It would be too neat and too limiting, for it is one purpose of this conclusion to suggest that a poetic achievement whose terms belong consciously to a particular, Anglo-Welsh, tradition is not narrowly confined by it; nor is that tradition narrow. But if sea and reservoir are not to be neatly identified in the writings, and least of all in association with a backward-looking, child's-eye view of a Wales which the man could never fully re-enter, they may be understood in terms of the religious truth to which Roland Mathias has consistently devoted himself. That is the truth that man is responsible for his world as he receives it from his ancestors, but has no abiding place in it or final knowledge of what his contribution is worth. All he can do is keep faith, crying with Elijah, 'I am not better than my fathers.'[28]

8

'Possibilities of Song': The Poetry of Gillian Clarke, Hilary Llewellyn-Williams and Anne Cluysenaar

The emergence of Gillian Clarke as a poet in 1970 brought something new into poetry in Wales. Sam Adams remarked on this in his Introduction to *Snow on the Mountain*, her pamphlet in the Triskel Poets series: 'She takes as her main themes areas of life infrequently explored in poetry and very rarely indeed illuminated with such honesty and insight – the interplay of relationships within the family, and the family observed against the background of nature.'[1] Adams correctly identifies Clarke as a poet of relationships but his 'background of nature', although appropriate to some of her poems, does not do justice to her inwardness with nature, which is one of the chief distinguishing features of her poetry.

The revolutionary effect of Clarke's illumination of certain 'areas of life', in the Welsh context, is best understood in relation to what Tony Conran describes as the 'overwhelmingly masculine' nature of Welsh poetry, and his view that its 'lack of a feminine voice' is 'its most severe limitation'.[2] In his opinion, Clarke 'is trying to redress the balance and to make the land of her mothers (as it were) visible for the first time'.[3]

This view is based on Clarke's achievement by the early 1990s, and its emphasis upon the land of her mothers needs to be qualified by the fact that, as M. Wynn Thomas has demonstrated, it was not Clarke's own mother but her father who 'acted as her muse'.[4] In thinking about Clarke's early poems, it should also be borne in mind that the political dimension of her work only came into full view with her second collection, in the title poem, 'Letter from a Far Country'. In other respects, however, Conran's words apply to Clarke's early work, which introduced a new sense of possibility into the predominantly male world of Welsh poetry. Clarke's validation of women's experience as a subject for poetry should be understood also in relation to social history, in the context of the patriarchal values of Nonconformist, industrial and agricultural Wales in the nineteenth and twentieth centuries. In this respect, 'making the land of her mothers . . . visible' was a riposte to the injustice described by Deirdre Beddoe in 'Images of Welsh Women', which begins with the succinct statement: 'Welsh women are culturally invisible.'[5]

From the beginning, there is nothing invisible about Clarke as a Welsh woman. In 'Dyddgu Replies to Dafydd', for example, in her first full-length collection, *The Sundial* (1978), she dares (through her persona, a lover Dafydd ap Gwilym addressed in his love poems) to speak of a woman's influence on the great medieval Welsh poet. 'Original sin I whitened from your / mind' (*CP*, 21), Dyddgu says, thus claiming a central influence upon the natural (pagan) sensibility of the male, Catholic poet. Moreover, despite the sadness and submissiveness in Dyddgu's voice, she effectively claims equality with her lover:

> All year in open places, underneath
> the frescoed forest ceiling,
> we have made ceremony
> out of this seasonal love. (*CP*, 21)

Already, at this early stage in her poetic career, Clarke is laying claim to her part as a woman in the tradition of Welsh poetry, and in the genealogy dominated by men stretching from her father back to the Age of the Princes that she was to draw up in 'Cofiant', in *Letting in the Rumour* (1989).

The strong erotic element in 'Dyddgu Replies to Dafydd' should not obscure its fundamentally religious nature. Clarke (through Dyddgu) is challenging the puritanical subjection of women to male authority and their identification, as daughters of Eve, with original sin. But she is doing so in Catholic terms, or rather in the terms of a Catholicism hospitable to the spirit of paganism, and far removed from the attitude towards women and sexuality of puritan Wales. Possibly because criticism at present seems to lack the will or interest to tackle religious themes or influences upon poetry, this aspect of Clarke's work has been little noticed. K. E. Smith, however, is an exception. He links Clarke with the three Thomases, Edward, Dylan and R.S., whom he describes 'as embodying the distinctively post-Protestant . . . yet still questingly spiritual sensibility so characteristic of modern Wales'.[6] While this offers a generally important idea, it follows from my remarks about the Catholic influence upon Clarke that I see it, in its placing of her in a 'post-Protestant' context, as offering a potentially misleading emphasis.

Clarke was educated at St Clare's Convent, Porthcawl, between 1948 and 1955, and in 1956, while a student at Cardiff University, she became a Catholic. While she later ceased to practise the religion, she is far from being hostile to its sacramental vision. By a nice irony in the light of 'Dyddgu Replies to Dafydd', Clarke would now describe herself as 'a Dafydd ap Gwilym Catholic'; an anti-Puritan, one who 'says yes to life'. But the anti-Puritan strain in her poetry should not be taken to imply a hostile attitude towards all that Nonconformity stands for. Chapelgoing, a regular event in her family while she was growing up, was also a potent influence upon Clarke as a child and young woman. The Welsh language of the chapel, the Welsh hymns and the Bible in Welsh made a strong contribution to her sense of the music of language, as also did the King James version, Shakespeare and English literature. What we see in her poetry might be described as a naturalizing of religion, in which the new nature associated with the Gaia hypothesis, and a new sense of kinship between humans and the rest of the natural world, harmonizes with the sacral feeling for love and nature that she ascribes to Dyddgu, and finds in the poetry of Dafydd ap Gwilym.[7]

The influence of Catholicism on Clarke's poetry is to be seen in its language. One of the many instances occurs in 'At Ystrad Fflur': 'the young Teifi / counts her rosary on stones' (*CP*, 23); another in 'Burning Nettles': 'Fire / Buried in flower-heads, makes / Bright ritual of decay / Transubstantiates the green / Leaf to fertility' (*CP*, 27). Clearly, neither metaphor is merely ornamental. In the second in particular, the poet is concerned with a process, which is essentially the sacramentalizing of nature and human experience. This is present also in the lists that form an important part of Clarke's poetry; domestic lists that become litanies in 'Letter from a Far Country', for example. These are associated with women's work:

> It has always been a matter
> of lists. We have been counting,

> folding, measuring, making,
> tenderly laundering cloth
> ever since we have been women. (*CP*, 48)

This is an aspect of the 'ceremony' Dyddgu speaks of, and ultimately it sacralizes – makes life (including domestic chores) sacred.
 This relates centrally to Clarke's perception of the woman poet's role. Again in 'Letter from a Far Country' she writes:

> It is easy to make of love
> these ceremonials. As priests
> we fold cloth, break bread, share wine,
> hope there's enough to go round. (*CP*, 50)

(The last line nicely brings the religious imagery down to earth, undercutting any possible suggestion that women have miraculous powers!) Clarke, like the other women poets with whom I am concerned in this chapter, has a strong sense of disorder in the modern world, whether it is 'some terrible undoing' that she fears at the death of elms ('Cardiff Elms', *CP*, 65), or the threat of war or war's violent destructiveness, or the disaster at Chernobyl, which made us all citizens of 'the democracy of the virus and the toxin' ('Neighbours', *CP*, 86). But she has, too, in her sense of the sacramental role of the woman poet/priest, a perception of an essentially ordered universe. It is interesting in this context to recall Saunders Lewis's view 'that the chapters on the Chain of Being in Tillyard's book [*The Elizabethan World Picture*] are the best available English introduction to the matter of the great classical poetry of medieval Wales from the time of Einion Offeiriad'.[8] We may think of Shakespeare's impact on Clarke's growing imagination which she recalls movingly in 'Llŷr';[9] but it is not only a literary influence with which we have to deal here. What is at issue, I think, is more than the idea of the Chain of Being which may, as Saunders Lewis thinks, shape 'the matter' of medieval Welsh poetry, and, as the American poet and critic Wendell Berry says, 'seems to lie under English poetry like a root'.[10] The fundamental issue is Clarke's sense of human and natural bonds, which she experiences in primary relationships and in the life of neighbourhood centred upon her home, Blaen Cwrt, in west

Wales, but which in her later poems she increasingly extends to the world.[11] That this is not only a woman's sense of things is clear enough from the ideas Lewis and Berry espouse. It is worth saying, however, that especially in relation to Lewis's formulation of the idea, Clarke's sense of connections within an ordered universe places her firmly within the Welsh poetic tradition and at the same time subverts its male bias.

The mythologizing of woman's poetic function in priestly terms begins early on in Clarke's poetry and helps to shape its stance towards reality – not so much its stance, as if it were a standing outside, more its participation in the fundamental realities of life and love and death. In this respect, the Catholic influence, as I have suggested, turns back towards pagan origins – the rites that a Catholic poet such as David Jones saw as prefiguring the sacred mystery, but Clarke celebrates for their channelling of natural energies. Another way of putting this would be to say that she invokes the power of the Mother Goddess. In 'Sheila na Gig at Kilpeck', for example, she speaks of 'restlessness' and 'second sight', that spring from her physical being as a woman, and of sharing with the Mother-figure 'premonitions'. We 'are governed by moons / and novenas', she says, 'sisters cooling our wrists / in the stump of a Celtic water stoop'. The poem embodies a sense of premonition, and issues in a powerful expression of natural, and more-than-natural, force:

> Not lust but long labouring
> absorbs her, mother of the ripening
> barley that swells and frets at its walls.
> Somewhere far away the Severn presses,
> alert at flood-tide. And everywhere rhythms
> are turning their little gold cogs, caught
> in her waterfalling energy. (*CP*, 66)

The premonitory restlessness is shared by the woman poet and the 'mother' 'that swells and frets' in the barley, and is 'alert' in the Severn 'at flood-tide'. Something of the 'rhythms' and the 'water-falling energy' is contained within the charged, rhythmic language of the poem itself. It is not only about this sharing, it is haunted by it, as Emily Dickinson might have said. Here, the woman poet shares in the energy of the Earth Mother who participates in the sacred, and, for now, the specifically Christian purpose of the Church is forgotten. Clarke herself has commented on the frequency with which she has 'used falling water, or simply falling, to praise the giving of the self'.[12] That giving is here intimately connected to 'long labouring', in two senses: giving birth and working/making.

One of the things that marks Clarke's early poems indelibly as a woman's poems is the fact that many are, directly or indirectly, palpably birth poems. They are poems charged with the emotional, psychological and visceral knowledge of a woman as mother: knowledge of gestation, giving birth, nurturing, and of conflict between mother and child, as in her struggle with her daughter over 'the tight / Red rope of love' ('Catrin', *CP*, 16). From this intimate, participatory knowledge there comes a sense of connection to nature that is, as far as I am aware, new in Welsh poetry. 'Calf' provides an obvious example:

> I could feel the soft sucking
> Of the new-born, the tugging pleasure
> Of bruised reordering, the signal
> Of milk's incoming tide, and satisfaction
> Fall like a clean sheet around us. (*CP*, 15)

This is original writing, springing from experience that had rarely, if ever, been dealt with by poets in English (or Welsh) until the women's movement of the late 1960s and 1970s. It brings into poetry a new sense of the human bond with nature – a theme that Clarke extends in other poems. Thus, in 'Nightride', the poet, watching her sleeping child who is holding an apple and resting against her in the car, reflects 'that a tree must ache / With the sweet weight of the round rosy fruit, / As I with Dylan's head, nodding on its stalk' (*CP*, 16). Clarke is here using an ancient metaphor of the tree of life, of course; but she makes it new. She enables us to feel the fragility and vulnerability of the child's life, its naturalness, and the organic connection between mother and child. She renews the metaphor by giving it actuality, so that we feel the affinity between the tree aching with its fruit and the mother with the weight of her child's head. The tree metaphor becomes peculiarly intimate. In the skin-to-skin contact with nature, and the sense of empathy with nature, that we find in

Clarke's poetry, and again in Hilary Llewellyn-Williams's, there is, I think, the realization of a new sense of possibility in poetry: a possibility of subject, but more especially of inwardness with it, and of the energies that result. It has some affinities with 'incarnational' poetry, with its blood-and-flesh-and-bone know-ledge of being 'made', that we find in Gerard Manley Hopkins and David Jones, the main difference being the women poets' sense of connection to nature from within.

The same intimacy with which the woman apprehends the tree metaphor in 'Nightride' gives force to 'Lunchtime Lecture', in which Clarke, contemplating a prehistoric skeleton, reflects: 'I, at some other season, illustrate the tree / Fleshed, with woman's hair and colours and the rustling / Blood, the troubled mind that she has overthrown' (*CP*, 21). Again, the theme of mortality is traditional; what makes Clarke's treatment of it so fresh and immediate, and disturbing, is her sense of participation in the rhythmic cycle of life and death. Once more, one is aware of her Catholicism. Here, it is the perception of a wound at the heart of creation, so that human and natural life is in need of restoration. With Clarke, however, there is no theological consolation. As she says of 'The Hare', perhaps her finest single poem, she is capable of shocking herself with her 'sense of our animal mortality'.[13] She is capable of shocking the reader, too.

Both the immediacy and the sensuous notation that distinguish Clarke's poetry from the beginning evidently owe a great deal to the journals she keeps. As she herself has said of her early work: 'Each poem is a journal entry to record the way I thought, what I saw.'[14] She has spoken, too, of images that 'have been in my memory since early childhood. I have kept journals and diaries since I was fifteen, and I re-read them and things spring to life and poetry from those pages.'[15] In another place, she has sketched an equivalent movement from the private to the public in women's creative work: 'Women's art certainly has risen from obscurity: the diarists and letter-writers of the past are now poets.'[16] Her own journals, we may surmise, have been Clarke's imaginative matrix, the source from which she has learnt to hear her own voice. They have helped to generate both creative expression and poetic shaping, which nevertheless retains the impression of sensation becoming thought.

We can see this at the beginning of 'Miracle on St David's Day', for example:

> An afternoon yellow and open-mouthed
> with daffodils. (*CP*, 36)

The image has the immediacy of an impression recorded in a journal, but it also provides the metaphor, 'open-mouthed', from which the poem as a whole unfolds. Clarke's idea of the Welsh poet as 'voice of the tribe' is given extra poignancy when she says: 'The two literatures of Wales, the one far older, of course, than the other, have been the people's journal.'[17] On the one hand, this may be to read an essential privacy, the result of a marginalized existence, back into the Welsh poetic tradition. But on the other, it nicely suggests another side to the formality of Welsh verse: the pressure of experience that animates the channels of poetic expression.

Linden Peach takes me to task, rightly, for my attempt, in an earlier essay on Clarke, to 'shoehorn her' (as he says) into 'the male, Romantic tradition'.[18] I hope that what I was trying to do there, too cryptically, in placing Clarke in a 'Romantic tradition', will be clearer from my argument in the present book about the influence of a Romantic 'poetry of earth' upon Welsh poetry in English. All the same, however, and in spite of Clarke's debt to a number of English-language poets from Shakespeare and Wordsworth to Seamus Heaney, her originality as a woman poet is central to her achievement.

This may be seen, for example, at moments when her work challenges comparison with that of male poets. The following passage from 'Letter from a Far Country' offers an opportunity for us to see this:

> We are hawks trained to return
> to the lure from the circle's
> far circumference. Children sing
> that note that only we can hear.
> The baby breaks the waters,
> disorders the blood's tune, sets
> each filament of the senses
> wild. Its cry tugs at flesh, floods
> its mother's milky fields. (*CP*, 55)

It is instructive to compare Clarke's woman-as-hawk with W. B. Yeats's falcon in 'The Second Coming'. There, the trained bird that 'cannot hear the falconer', spirals beyond his control, providing Yeats with an image of the broken 'centre', and the loosing of anarchy upon the world. Clarke's woman-hawk, by contrast, returns from circumference to centre, and is effectively, despite 'disorders' in 'her blood's tune', the one who brings order. Or consider Ted Hughes's masterful hawk of 'Hawk Roosting' (*Lupercal*, 1960), the hawk holding 'Creation in my foot', which boasts: 'My manners are tearing off heads.' Clarke's woman-hawk obeys nature's inner demands; the male poets' hawks are, in different ways, 'free' of nature – free to initiate chaos, or be instruments of destruction.

A comparison closer to home is with R. S. Thomas, with whom Clarke has certain affinities. But her distance from him may be measured by the poem in which she invokes him, 'Fires on Llŷn'. Here, with her companion, she climbs

> to a land's end
> where R. S. Thomas walks, finding
> the footprint of God
> warm in the shoe of the hare. (*CP*, 92)

She shares a landscape with Thomas, but her image is entirely her own. It is not only that the hare is one of Clarke's most personal symbols, but that the image of 'God / warm in the shoe of the hare' speaks not of absence or emptiness, like Thomas's empty church where he nails 'his questions / One by one to an untenanted cross' ('In Church, *Pietà*, 44), but of presence. And presence that manifests itself as body-warmth, the divine still filling the print God has made.

There is plenty of evidence in Clarke's poetry of what she and others call 'feminine sensibility'. Hilary Llewellyn-Williams says Clarke gives 'a voice to female experience'.[19] Christine Evans seems to express a contrasting view when she sees 'poetry by women not as a separate development . . . but perhaps as part of the latest renewal of poetic sensibility'.[20] Linden Peach discusses Clarke in relation to 'the "feminine principle" of holding opposites together'.[21] K. E. Smith also emphasizes her reconciliatory imagination, claiming that she moves from Edward Thomas's 'watchful male stance' 'towards a woman's sense of fluidity, relationship, changing boundaries'.[22] Smith speaks also of her 'green feminism'.[23]

There is no irreconcilable difference between these views, unless one happens to think 'feminine sensibility' is exclusively the preserve of women, as Clarke herself does not. As she has said in an interview:

> A poet like Seamus Heaney has a tremendously feminine sensibility, and because Seamus Heaney is such an extremely good poet, he admitted possibilities that weren't there before, which women are now exploring. To put it another way, more women began to be published, which enabled us to see a poet like Seamus Heaney. I wonder whether he would have been as well received by an earlier generation, when feminine values were less noticed and admired.[24]

It is also pertinent to note that the period in which Clarke has come to prominence is also that in which Emyr Humphreys, in his 'Land of the Living' sequence of novels, has given effective expression to women's power and women's experience. In this respect, a comment by K. E. Smith on 'Letter from a Far Country' is especially apt. The poem, he remarks, suggests 'that it is women's actions, at least as much as men's preachings, that have put the culture in touch with the ultimate sources of life'.[25]

M. Wynn Thomas is certainly right in my view to claim that Clarke 'raises gender issues in terms that allow them to be ultimately subsumed within an all-embracing concept of the human' and to suggest 'two main, and closely interconnected, reasons' for this, the first concerning 'her relationship with her father; the second relates to Wales'.[26] Clarke's mythologizing of herself as Branwen in 'The King of Britain's Daughter' shows clearly how her father and the stories he told her first made the landscape of Wales magical to her. In 'Rocking Stone', for instance, where she writes of 'Bendigeidfran's stone', known to her as it balanced on the headland when she was a child, but now fallen in the sea:

> It purred in wind, was warm against my back
> with all the summer in it.
> Apple out of legend,
> slingstone of Brân's rage against Ireland.
> Or so my father said. (*CP*, 170)

The adult woman can be affectionately sceptical about her father's stories, but the poet has been in part shaped by their effect upon her imagination when she was a child. For this reason, while Clarke has come to write the poems of a much-travelled woman, it is still Welsh landscapes to which she has a sense of both historical and magical connection – the traditional stories from the *Mabinogion* having received an extra resonance from her father's telling of them. Thus the Llŷn, associated with Bendigeidfran, is for her indeed a giant's country. It would be untrue, however, to say that she imagines it in an exclusively 'feminine' way. Further to what she has said about the 'feminine sensibility' of a male poet, it is interesting to reflect that what happened to awaken Clarke's passionate amd imaginative attachment to her native landscapes was similar to what happened to John Cowper Powys, according to the story he tells, in *Autobiography*, about the influence of *his* father's life and tales upon the young John Cowper's perception of West Country landscapes and of Wales. We may also recall that Powys's imagination was possessed by the figure of the giant Brân.

Hilary Llewellyn-Williams has paid tribute to the part played by Gillian Clarke and her writers' workshop at Lampeter in starting her writing again after a period of self-doubt and uncertainty. Llewellyn-Williams, who was born in Kent in 1951 and is of mixed Welsh and Spanish parentage, moved to west Wales in 1982. She was inspired by a *Guardian* feature on Clarke in which the older poet is reported as saying:

> it wasn't too late, that women are often late-comers to poetry through force of circumstance, and that women's writing and women's concerns were important. Women should write from their own lives, she said, and this was every bit as valuable as anything men had to say.[27]

Subsequently Llewellyn-Williams met Clarke and joined her workshop, which she attended over a period of five years. The impact was immediate; as Llewellyn-Williams says, 'I realised by the end of the evening that I had a reason to write, and the impetus to keep me at it. I wasn't invisible and wordless any more.'[28]

There are affinities between the poetry of Clarke and the poetry of Llewellyn-Williams, but also considerable differences. Llewellyn-Williams, too, was convent-educated; she became an ex-

Catholic in her second year at university, and has reacted strongly against what she sees as the life-denying aspects of Christianity, while retaining positive feelings towards the spiritual tradition of the Catholic Church.[29] She is like Clarke, too, in having rooted herself imaginatively in west Wales landscapes, although she does not have Clarke's sense of historical and ancestral continuity – indeed the continuity she invokes is a different one. Llewellyn-Williams, with the influence of her English and Spanish backgrounds, is more detached, and one form her detachment takes is that she draws more consciously upon worldwide mythological and religious sources of women's spiritual power, such as shamanism and witch lore. For her, Robert Graves's *The White Goddess* has been an influential book. Significantly, she speaks of 'this urge to write poems', in the spring of 1984, as 'an act of assertion, a way of fighting back with some kind of counterspell'.[30]

Llewellyn-Williams's first major cycle of poems, 'The Tree Calendar', is in a way a book of spells. It draws upon *The White Goddess* and is 'based on an ancient Celtic 13-month calendar' and reaffirms 'the widespread ancient belief that trees and language (especially writing) were mystically linked'.[31] 'The Tree Calendar' might be described, however, without suggesting that it intends any disrespect to Graves, as an example of the muse writing back. That is to say Llewellyn-Williams draws upon an ancient tradition of female shamanism to feminize the bardic role. She rejoices in her function as the representative of wisdom-traditions, such as witchcraft that patriarchal attitudes have turned against women, to demean and destroy them. Her poems are counter-spells against a bad time. As she (or the female bardic voice) says in 'Rowan/Luis', 'I rest my fingers on a rowan tree / for a wand and a brand to avert / evil' (*TC*, 14).

'The Tree Calendar' contains a good deal of learning in myth and traditional lore. As the voice in 'Ash/Nion' says: 'All ash-lore, ash-mythologies run through / my brain in twisted threads' (*TC*, 15). The risk Llewellyn-Williams runs, in fact, is that of overwhelming poetic magic with book-learning, and in my view the poems are most successful where her strong personal need coincides with her ability to ground the ancient lore in her west Wales landscapes. 'Alder/Fearn', for example, recalls a specific social occasion:

> Up here, in a stone barn
> this Easter, a straggle
> of children and adults saw
> the outlawed story retold
> of an old resurrection:
>
> a grain reborn as a child
> (as we sat in the straw) . . . (*TC*, 16)

Here, the story of Gwion Bach who is reborn as Taliesin, the fabulous bard, is given a local habitation in a modern setting. The retelling is a social event, rather than an invention of the solitary imagination. Partly in consequence of this, the poem's conclusion carries conviction:

> Now I visit my alder stream
> in a double life, knowing
>
> that nothing's been lost. A raven
> croaks *Brân* overhead:
> banished westward, but still
> surviving. And alder flowers
> green as thieves, still growing. (*TC*, 16–17)

The effect is complex: the survival of a tradition (at once social and the story of a god implicitly made available to the woman poet's imagination) is affirmed as a living reality, 'green' as alder, at the same time as the survival is ascribed to the tradition having been 'banished westward'. A great deal of what I have tried to say about the Welsh mythological imagination in this book is compacted into these lines, which at once affirm the power of that imagination and indicate that it is defensive, dispossessed of a larger sphere of action, and driven back to a margin. It is consequently not surprising to find affinities between Hilary Llewellyn-Williams's vision in *The Tree Calendar* (which has *Vexilla Regis* as its cover illustration) and that of David Jones. In 'Reed/Ngetal', for example, the words 'Water / seeps upwards patiently' (*TC*, 26) recall 'What's under works up' from *The Anathemata*. More than a verbal similarity is at issue. The affinity between the poets inheres in their faith in underlying sacred powers of renewal and resurrection, which are signified by aquatic locations or imagery.

A polemical element outcrops throughout Llewellyn-Williams's poetry. In *The Tree Calendar* it emerges, for example, in 'Contradicting the Bishop', in which the poet retorts upon the TV pundit: 'I do not believe / . . . in the hollowness of created things.' Her answer is her female being:

> no part of me
> is empty, void or hollow; no not even
> that female part you might call hollow
> is wholly so, but is crammed
> with muscle and sweet fluids,
> dark fluids, tidal fluids
> which I rock in me as the moon rocks
> the sea that rocks the world. (*TC*, 39)

As Francesca Rhydderch has said of Menna Elfyn, and as I have shown in discussing Gillian Clarke, Hilary Llewellyn-Williams has an 'interest in the female body as the medium of a specifically feminine apprehension of the world'.[32] Here, her body is the medium of cosmic connection, bodily fluids corresponding to ocean fluids. It is with this that she contradicts 'That old proud cold belief, / cutting you off from this encircling earth / ground of our being' and urges the bishop not to be afraid, but 'be whole, not hollow, holy, hale' (*TC*, 40). Again, in the way of green feminism, holiness/wholeness is taken back from the Church and restored to the earth and the body.

Passion and wordplay together carry the poem and its message into the reader's mind. It is a strength of Llewellyn-Williams, however, that she risks directness and an overt poetry of ideas, reclaiming a tradition of wisdom. This is not, of course, exclusively women's wisdom; no true wisdom, surely, could be the sole possession of one sex; it is, rather, a tradition patriarchy has attempted to outlaw or inter. It is fitting, then, that, as Llewellyn-Williams's more embodied poetry sometimes suggests the upwellings in David Jones's work of what The Lady of the Pool in *The Anathemata* calls 'the deep fluvial doings of the mother', her sense of an ancient wisdom buried in the land should recall John Cowper Powys. In 'Elder/Ruis', for instance, her evocation of 'that massive mound built by the elder / tribe, the dark ones, thieves and dancers' (*TC*, 28), recalls Powys's preoccupation, in *Owen Glendower* and *Porius*, with an ancient matriarchal tradition driven underground, but still surviving in the prehistoric mounds in north Wales – and in some sense recoverable as an imaginative power.

Llewellyn-Williams's interest in magic also recalls Powys. What needs to be said here is that she reclaims magic as a woman poet, with a woman's sense of participation in the rhythms and processes of nature, at the same time as she acknowledges a debt to male practitioners and thinkers. Thus, in the major title sequence of poems, 'Book of Shadows', in her second collection, she adapts the thought of the sixteenth-century philosopher, magician and poet Giordano Bruno to her exploration of 'the old relationship between poetry and magic, and between magic and love'.[33] Bruno's thought as she employs it merges seamlessly with new nature in the age of the Gaia hypothesis: 'not only did he claim that the earth and the whole of Nature was alive and divine . . . but he predicted the fall of the Christian order and its replacement with a new religion based on a revival of paganism' (*BS*, 45).

Llewellyn-Williams opposes Bruno to genetic science, the Renaissance magician to 'that gene-magician in his white coat' and his kind, those who 'still say *Mother-Nature* – / meaning a woman, weak and pliable, / limited, passive, open to be explored, / discarded, raped'.

> But among us, *da noi*, Nature is called
> the inner artificer. And she's everywhere,
> strong, steadfast: power in the womb
> of matter, the spirit that shines
> through things. (III 'The Inner Artificer', *BS*, 53)

Another poem in the sequence, 'Alchemy', which begins 'Wonderful what will come out of darkness', invokes 'power in the womb / of matter', and things through which the spirit shines. This is palpably a different 'darkness' from that which Alun Lewis both feared and desired. This darkness, as Llewellyn-Williams apprehends it, is closer to Powys's idea of the imagination as a cauldron of rebirth, an inner power to shape identities. In 'Alchemy',

> Base matter

> becomes gold: in the Cauldron
> of Annwn, in the crucible of mind

> we're all magicians. (*BS*, 77)

A major difference between Llewellyn-Williams's thought and Powys's, however, is that she feels no need to think in terms of sterile sexuality, or of the energy of frustrated sex redirected to imaginative ends, as he does. In her world, the wonders that come out of darkness include

> stars, owl voices, sleep;

> water, green shoots, bird's eggs
> with their own curved darkness;

> gemstones; a whole and perfect child
> from my own unseen recesses; delight

> from behind shut lids, finding each other,
> fingers and tongues made delicate by night. (*BS*, 76)

As in Gillian Clarke's poetry, but, here, more explicitly, female creativity embraces giving birth to babies and writing poems; the former is not undergone at the expense of the latter; and creativity encompasses sexual love.

Hilary Llewellyn-Williams's third and most recent book of poems, *animaculture*, continues the replacement of Christianity with 'creative magic'. In the title poem, for example, she brings the angels down to earth, as her mishearing of 'guardian angels' in childhood becomes her 'gardening angels'. In a phrase that suggests 'deep feminism' and 'deep ecology', she develops her 'deep song' in the poem of that name. Here, she recalls singing at school, rising with the notes, 'hovering on plumes of pure sound, / the shriven vowels of nuns'. Losing that voice, she lost 'all angelic strivings':

> having descended

> to earth, my substance.

> Now when I sing the sound rises
> not from my throat, but lower,
>
> from my centre, from the ground.[34]

Again, it is integral to the risk she runs, that a poem or part of a poem, sounds like a credo – language stretched over the bones of thought. The clear self-knowledge Llewellyn-Williams brings to her creativity, the steady understanding she has of her 'darkness', could be a danger for her as a poet, tempting her to repetitive and schematic writing. There are, however, three things that work in her favour: her ability to invent or discover objective correlatives for her sense of the sacred; her poetic learning in the fields of myth and magic and traditional lore; and her embodiment of a woman's feelings through identification with nature and other creatures. One image for the object of her poetic quest is 'my blazing grail' in 'A Nun in the Dunes' (*a*, 71); another is what the bear, in 'Ursa', is intent on:

> Something found only by digging, a glow in the dirt,
> in the forest floor. Under rocks, under roots, what my heart
> needs, what my soul feeds on. I will turn every stone
> on earth, until I find what I'm looking for. (*a*, 13)

The movement downwards, into a landscape and into the earth, is also characteristic of Anne Cluysenaar's later poetry. Cluysenaar, however, in her background and in her work, differs in important respects from both Clarke and Llewellyn-Williams. For one thing, her relationship to Wales is more tangential, and more subject to a sense of displacement, than that of either of the other poets. Her family and personal background is all important here. She has spoken in an autobiographical essay of the influence of her parents, and especially her father, who was an artist, upon her. Born in Belgium in 1936, Anne Cluysenaar came to England just before the outbreak of war in 1939. This 'crossing' was true to her pattern of experience:

> . . . early on, my family may have encouraged in me an addiction to crossing boundaries, a liking for the liminal in life, in art, in perception, in character. I had also moved, during my first years, from

French to English, from Belgium to Britain. Then, having learned Gaelic in the final years of my schooling, in southern Ireland, I chose in my twenties to take Irish citizenship. Each language gave me a different world.[35]

Coming to Wales 'some thirteen years ago', Cluysenaar settled on a smallholding in Gwent, so that, like both Clarke and Llewellyn-Williams, she has had daily experience of life in rural Wales, and close working knowledge of the land with its weathers and seasons. Knowing different worlds, however, means living at an angle to any particular one, or perceiving the unfamiliar in familiar things. It is thus partly in the experience of not belonging completely that she discovers her poetry; and it is for this reason that she finds 'Wales unfamiliar and exciting, like a world before language'.[36] As Cluysenaar says of her evocation of the prehistoric Welsh coast in 'Landfall', the first poem in a sequence of poems, 'Timeslips':

. . . a world overlaid with many languages, like a world without language, is one whose reality remains beyond anything but fleeting perceptions of otherness. In Wallace Stevens' words, 'It is not only that the imagination adheres to reality, but, also, that reality adheres to the imagination and that the interdependence is essential'. Edges and boundaries are where this interdependence is most keenly felt, keeping us alive to the world as a wonderful and dangerous place.[37]

This helps us to understand the 'place' in which Cluysenaar's poetry occurs; her 'sense of the numinous' arises from a state of not belonging, in the gap between self and world. This is, however, a gap bridged by 'matter', which is the stuff of life for both self and the world it inhabits.

Another respect in which Cluysenaar differs from Clarke and Llewellyn-Williams is that she is a more intellectual poet. I do not mean by this to denigrate the thought of the other two poets. My intention, rather, is to indicate that Cluysenaar thinks *in* her poems, or uses her poems to think with; they are explorations, processes of discovery, more than in the case of Clarke, who is primarily a poet of feeling, or of Llewellyn-Williams, who usually gives the impression of starting from a firm base of intellectual conviction.[38] Cluysenaar, moreover, has a particular interest in philosophical questions about the relationship between language and reality, and in the part language plays in the evolution of human life.[39] Thus, in 'Timeslips', she shows the involvement of language in the making of the land, and that both language and land are subject to erosion:

> Our latest language, English,
> quickly erodes on contact
> with incoming word-waves.
> After learning *dŵr* I hear *uisge*
> break on the narrow palate
> of ridged sand, new soil
> in the painful making.[40]

Clearly, what is being said here about the part played by language in the making of a land is quite different from Clarke's use of the same word, 'dŵr', in 'The Water-Diviner', where she hears water speaking its native name. Clarke is concerned with cultural continuity, Cluysenaar with the dissolutions and evolution human life shares with the world of matter in time.

'Timeslips', in particular, conveys a strong awareness of geological time. This is the context for vision:

> We are early
> humans, between glaciations, trying
> to see. (*Ts*, 102)

The poems are concerned with continuities of human experience, but also with discontinuities. Thinking of tribal life in 'In a Gap of Light', Cluysennaar says: 'It's the same sun that we see, / and the brain is the same. But our thought / is different: everything changes' (*Ts*, 93). Out of context, the last two words would be a commonplace of the elegiac tradition. In their place in the poem, they subtly relate the sameness of brain structure to the difference of thought-worlds. In the title poem of the sequence, as the poet sees swifts and thinks of them migrating to Africa, her mind 'migrates . . . downward':

> Neanderthal's larger brain
> makes me fear my own in its cave

> of bone. Space behind the eyes,
> where the swifts swoop among trails
> of uncertain thought, among words
> whose alternatives must be jettisoned
> to make a sentence. (*Ts*, 108)

Such a passage shows us that the poet, in a sense that owes more to evolutionary history than to the Psalms, is a fearful wonder to herself, and a person who wonders over time, and feels pity and horror at its wastes. The writing also enables us to enter into its process of composition (verbal pattern-making and verbal choices) that is the discovery of thought.

As Cluysenaar's 'Timeslips' are about seeing – not just observation of natural phenomena but mind watching its own evolution – so she also places herself in nature, where she can be seen. One way in which she does this is by imagining how other creatures see her. An obvious example of this occurs in a separate poem, 'Yellow Meadow-ants in Hallowed Ground':

> I need to displace myself. I need to see,
> when the tip of my finger disturbs the alignment of dust
> over their open holes, how a human hand
> might seem (as to them) nothing more than the foot of a vole.
>
> (*Ts*, 172)

This way of seeing things/being seen is a gift of displacement: the 'need to see' that comes to one who is not part of what she sees, but separated from it. But the idea has more than personal relevance; it also applies to the displacement of the human being from the central position in the universe, to that humbling that enables us, as a life-form among other life-forms, to feel a kinship with other creatures, such as ants. While this may be standard Gaia doctrine in some quarters, Cluysenaar in her poems walks with nature, seeking to know the life around her – the life with which human life has evolved – and to know herself in relation to 'perceptions of otherness'.

The phrase 'walking with nature' calls to mind the seventeenth-century poet Henry Vaughan in response to whom Cluysenaar has written her most impressive poems to date. 'Vaughan Variations' was evidently inspired in part by the landscape Cluysenaar now, as it were, shares with Vaughan, and by his presence in it. But the poems also arise out of a deep feeling for a religious poet with a sensitive awareness of nature who lived in dark times, and a strong sense of the difference between Vaughan's beliefs and poetic language and her situation as a present-day poet without access to those beliefs or that language, but with a sense of the numinous. Given Cluysenaar's sensitivity to nature's mutability and 'quickness', it is easy to see that she would be drawn to the poet who wrote:

> . . . that's best
> Which is not fixed, but flies, and flows . . . [41]

In another essay, she has said:

> In the words of Henry Vaughan, the 17th Century Breconshire poet, there are within nature 'hymning circulations' (a phrase reminiscent of the intertwined clarities of Celtic art) and we may feel within our-selves, as we respond to them, 'bright shoots of everlastingness', a sense of the fragility and the intensity of being alive, the strangeness of matter evolving to 'watch itself' through us.[42]

It is clear that Cluysenaar owes to living in Wales, to sharing a landscape with Henry Vaughan, so to speak, her sense of the numinous, 'of the world as a liminal place' – in terms of the Celtic tradition, 'the notion of a world within the world – not above the clouds but here, all around us'.[43]

Vaughan, as she says in the third part of the sequence, speaks to her need:

> How I need your frankness here!
> A stuttering permission
> (though all the *but's* crowd in) to praise.
> Standing at the window, I hear you say
> quietly, 'Mornings are mysteries.'
> Despite the disgraces that mark our century,
> still the page calls for difficult honesties.
> And would pass them on, from here to there. (*Ts*, 132)

The sense of responsibility expressed here is strong in Cluysenaar – responsibility to be frank (which requires not just frankness of attitude, but writing which avoids meretricious effects that distract from the process of discovery), to render 'difficult honesties', and to 'pass them on'. Responsibility, then, is integral to her idea of continuity, and is something like good faith, rather than one truth that can always be discovered and expressed in the same language. In 'Solstice', from 'Timeslips', she says: 'Distant, / the minds that made us. Sacred, / our present, to their memory, the press / of desire in us for futures' (*Ts*, 99). Among other things, the responsible poet is a channel: aware of the source from which her life flows, and using her creativity to keep it open for the future.

Seeing and being are equally important in Cluysenaar's conception of 'matter':

> With which we make, of which we are made.
> Ancient and new, unpredictably changing.
> It strikes through the robin's wing,
> through the pruned rose, through the stare
> of the dog, the thrust
> of the weed, from a heap of domestic dust.
> Day things. Among them, familiar, the human word. (*Ts*, 148)

The poem concludes by focusing upon a guest in the house 'who carries her first child'.

> With us already, it awaits the doom
> of particular time and language, possibilities of song.

An impressive feature of Cluysenaar's poetry, as it is of that of Clarke and Llewellyn-Williams and other women poets, such as Jean Earle, is the way in which it recreates 'possibilities of song' from the art of 'day things'. This is the tradition that finds great value in the humble object, the tradition that Henry Vaughan shared with George Herbert, and the Dutch and Flemish realist painters honoured, and *Lyrical Ballads* renewed, and passed on to George Eliot and Thomas Hardy and John Ruskin. Resuming this great tradition, Cluysenaar emphasizes not matter alone, but the making of matter, and the interrelationship of matter and 'the human word'.

Cluysenaar sees Vaughan, doctor and poet, as a healer:

> He would work, to heal himself
> and others, with words or herbs. (*Ts*, 142)

This is, perhaps, a peculiarly difficult poetic role to translate into contemporary terms. In the light of John Barnie's view in *No Hiding Place*, his book of 'essays on the new nature and poetry', it would seem to be impossible.

> In the end, neither Robinson Jeffers nor Ted Hughes is what might be termed a healing poet, as Wordsworth was. But perhaps this is impossible in our times. There is a growing air of defeat about us which all the business of politics and economics, the momentous events in Eastern Europe, Russia and the European Community, can hardly disguise. It is not just that we are poisoning the environment or may destroy ourselves in a nuclear war, but that we do not know what to do with our minds. No poet, it may be, can tell us that.[44]

Barnie writes admiringly mainly about male poets who are tough pessimists, and his acceptance of Neo-Darwinism and socio-biology leads him to take a hard line with those who find sanction for religious ideas in the Gaia hypothesis.[45] Certainly, none of the poets I have discussed in this chapter is an apostle of Robinson Jeffers's 'Inhumanism' or shivers 'with the horror of Creation', like Ted Hughes's Crow. All of them are, nevertheless, acutely aware of the horrors and threats to which Barnie refers, as well as of the evils of a Baconian science intent on torturing nature to wrest her secrets from her. And they are more aware than the male poets of patriarchal oppression. Each has, too, a special inwardness with death as a natural phenomenon, and a sensitivity to waste. There is no doubt however that they all 'know what to do with [their] minds'. Different though their poetries are, each has a powerful energy. This arises from a participatory relationship with nature in the case of Gillian Clarke and of Hilary Llewellyn-Williams, and from a perception of mind and matter as interdependent, evolving forms in that of Anne Cluysenaar. In each case their assertions and affirmations are grounded upon humility: in relation to nature, and in relation to our debt to our ancestors, and in our responsibility to our successors. Whether or not we are able to identify a 'new sensibility' which all share, there are I think grounds for claiming that they are all healing poets.

9

'The Roles are Greater than We Know':
Tony Conran's Religious Scepticism

Tony Conran is a poet of great ambition and great accomplishment, as *A Gwynedd Symphony*, the book which completes his *Welsh Commoedia*, amply testifies.[1] It is not easy to come to terms with a poet who, over many years, has been highly inventive, achieving varied work on a grand scale; nor should it be. It can take several generations of readers and critical commentators to arrive at the terms that open up a major poet's work. This continues to be the case with David Jones; one could argue that, after two hundred years, it is still the case with William Blake. There is also the fact that reading important poets is – or should be – a constant process of re-vision, by a reader during his or her lifetime, and by different readers at different times, who will bring their own needs and ideas to the work, and, ideally, an open-minded attentiveness. But even the latter can result in misreadings, and is rarely entirely free of self-interest. I make this point in the context of Tony Conran's poetry with some feeling, since I published my first essay on it more than twenty years ago, and my second in 1995, and I have subsequently come to realize that each was, at best, a step towards understanding, but an uncertain one.[2] In this present chapter I want to look mainly at *A Gwynedd Symphony*, but also to consider Conran's work in the light of my earlier partial understanding. With this revisionary aim in view and with my focus mainly upon *A Gwynedd Symphony*, my underlying concern will be to demonstrate and define the religious scepticism which I now take to be fundamental to Conran's vision.

Tony Conran has expressed surprise that certain things in his earlier poems, which he sees as being 'modernist', could have given me 'the initial impression' that he 'was a late Romantic'.[3] I had admitted in my first essay on his poetry that 'a superficial reading of his *Poems 1951–67*' could leave one with this impression. Evidently, what I had in mind was that he could be seen, superficially, as 'primarily a love poet who explores his universal themes through use of ancient mythology, and a private mythology created from a landscape of slate, water and fern, and in language strained by its combination of archaic and modern elements'.[4] Although it is not clear from the essay itself, I was responding to difficulties that I found in the work, and interpreted as occlusions due to expression of private experience, and also to his self-presentation as a muse poet, who found inspiration in the 'darkness' of certain girls.[5] What I had not grasped fully was his use of kinaesthetic imagery, of which Conran has written: 'As for me, being physically spastic has made most of my imagery kinaesthetic – I have been forced to feel in terms of physical movement rather than sight or hearing' (*VPM*, 190). Looking back, I can see that I had tended to read his poetry more in terms of modes with which I was more familiar. It is also probable that I had at the back of my mind T. E. Hulme's definition of Romanticism as 'spilt religion'.[6] Hulme's idea is, initially, a suggestive one, but it can have crass effects upon our understanding of poetry that operates outside the 'classic' terms of any religious orthodoxy, but is, nevertheless, religious. This, as I shall show later, is the case with Tony Conran's poetry.

Conran himself, although a great admirer of Wordsworth in particular, takes a tough line with English Romanticism. In *Frontiers in Anglo-Welsh Poetry*, for example, he writes as follows:

> Ever since Wordsworth, the philosophy of empiricism (the doctrine that all knowledge comes to us through our senses) with its total emphasis on the individual's experience of the world in a social vacuum, has dominated the English tradition – and still does – so drastically that English poetry has become insular and self-contained, difficult for other traditions to approach or use . . .[7]

In my opinion, there is a good deal to be said for this view if one applies it to fashionable post-war English poetry, the poetry of 'self-expression' – that is to say, the kind of poetry that has dominated the market during Conran's lifetime, and is emphatically *not* the kind he is writing. But the view leaves out a great deal, including most significant English poets from Wordsworth to the present. What it omits from Romanticism itself are 'the poetry of earth', to which I have frequently referred in this study; the social and political engagement of early Wordsworth and other Romantics (albeit an engagement resumed by prose writers, such as Dickens and George Eliot and Ruskin, more than by most later English poets); and Wordsworth's description of the 'the Poet' in the Preface to *Lyrical*

Ballads: 'He is the rock of defence of human nature; an upholder and preserver, carrying every where with him relationship and love.' I make this point not in an attempt to prove Conran a Romantic against his will, but in order to suggest that he is a poet of 'relationship and love'. He is this, however, within the Welsh poetic tradition as he has interpreted it, rather than in the empirical mode.

As with different interpretations of the notoriously polysemous word 'Romantic', nomenclature is a problem in respect of Conran's poetry. He calls himself a modernist, and, on the whole, I think he is right to do so. Ian Gregson favours 'retro-modernist', which he applies to poets who 'owe their most important allegiance to the classic modernism of the 1920s'. Gregson argues that, for retro-modernists, 'the nature of the real is always in question and the experimental forms of their writing are evolved in an attempt to grasp it while simultaneously acknowledging its elusiveness'.[8] I can see the point of placing Conran in this context, and recognize that it helps to explain his concern with poems as 'imaginative constructs' (*VPM*, 88), which relates to his perception of the 'madeness' of Welsh poetry, and to his own lively and inventive formal experimentation. However, placing Conran among poets who interrogate and defamiliarize 'the real' does have one major – paradoxical – drawback: it is a view insufficiently sceptical of scepticism. By this I mean to point to Conran's powerful religious imagination, and his need to construct models of order in relation to Wales.

Octavio Paz has described the theme of *The Waste Land* as 'the nostalgia for a universal order whose model is the Christian order of Rome', and said that its 'poetic archetype is a work that is the culmination and the most complete expression of this world: *The Divine Comedy*'.[9] In my view, Conran's own *Commoedia*, but also his work as a whole, corresponds to this archetype. There is a problem, however, with the pejorative connotations of the word 'nostalgia', which people hostile to religion tend to use of the human desire for wholeness. In an earlier essay, Ian Gregson criticized me for projecting nostalgia on to Tony Conran. The main poem at issue was Conran's 'Elegiac Ode, for R. Willams Parry'. I had quoted the following verses:

> Wherever, in the yellow bones
> Of speaking, phrase turns its fingers
>   To touch our bodies,
>   Your immanent ghost
> Walks proudly in bright eyes.

Whether a gypsy begs water;
Whether old quarrymen debate
  By ramshackle bus
  Football or bible,
Or grumble about cold;

Whether the new teacher forgets
His children no longer listen;
  Whether ovation
  Ends the charm, or no,
Or the bard goes hungry;

In all gay words, in all complaints,
Blasphemies or valedictions,
  The eyes tell their tale,
  Poet, whose homeland
Harks to the summer stars![10]

Had I known it at the time, I would probably have invoked Saunders Lewis's idea that the Chain of Being is 'the best available English introduction to the matter of the great classical poetry of medieval Wales'[11] and applied it to these lines. As it was, I wrote rather clumsily about 'the common culture embodied in a common language' as 'an organism in which men and women know themselves and know each other as parts'.[12] Gregson has a point when he says that I highlight moments in the poem 'in a distorting way', making Conran seem a believer in 'the organic view of community'. I also partly concede the truth of Gregson's: 'Conran is not expressing here any longing for lost origins but a sense of the poet's survival in the Welsh language.'[13] The point about the language, in particular, is important. However, while I accept Gregson's treatment of Conran's modernism as a corrective to my loose notion of organicism, I have to say the fundamental difference between us is that between a political reading of Conran and one that emphasizes his religious imagination. Gregson seems to be more interested in the Marxist in Conran – the radical concern with social and political structures, which include the ways in which poems are made, and serve ideological ends. This has been, undoubtedly, an important part of Conran from quite early on. My interest, on the other hand, is more in the religious desire for wholeness, a desire which does not see Taliesin's claim that his 'original country is the region of the summer stars' (to which Conran refers in the lines quoted above) as representative of reactionary nostalgia, but as an archetype, or model of universal order, on the lines expressed in *The Divine Comedy*. To be more specific than this would be to impose a religious orthodoxy on Conran and take away his freedom as a poet. By speaking of an archetype, or model of universal order, I have in mind, rather, Conran's idea of what was embodied in Welsh civilization. If there is indeed a suggestion in my earlier essay that Conran's nostalgia is backward-looking, it is wrong; his sense of the Welsh past energizes the desire for a renaissance of Wales, to which he contributes as a poet.

Conran has not been shy to speak of his experience of religion or his need to belong. Describing his unhappy time when, as a young man, he was a clerk in Chelmsford, he has said: 'I sat in the public library every evening translating Welsh poetry, and I was received into the Church of Rome. These things at least made me feel I belonged' (*VPM*, 22). In his autobiographical writings, he is disarmingly frank about himself. He describes himself in one place as 'an indeterminate English Welshman of Irish descent'.[14] The threat to his integrity of this indeterminacy helps to account in part for the strength of feeling with which he distances himself from England:

> Welsh poetry impinged on me first as a way out of empiricism – not that I would have put it like that, but English empiricism (and all the other things about English culture that I hated, the class-structure, the 'there there' attitude of superior sympathy) was intensely claustrophobic to me. (*VPM*, 98)

His choice of Wales, together with his disclaimer of 'pure' Welshness, is what makes Conran one of the most astute analysts of Anglo-Welsh poetry as a product of 'frontiers'. He claims that it 'differs from other poetry in the English language in three main respects'. These are: the background of 'a different civilization' that lies behind it; the fact that 'it shares its territory with another linguistic community which regards its tongue as the right and natural language of the country'; and its derivation 'from a special sort of society'.[15] 'Anglo-Welsh literature', he says, 'is not books written by Anglo-Welshmen . . . but books written within earshot of a frontier. It is the literature of a March.'[16]

Over the years, Conran has developed an idea of Welsh civilization, which is 'radically different from the English'.[17] He describes 'the tradition of Taliesin, the great poetry of the Welsh middle ages', as 'the defining art of Welsh civilization'. It is a tradition of poetry of which 'the second person – you – is its main subject'.[18] In his 'Ars Poetica', in *Spirit Level*, he wrote:

> A third person poetry can no longer enact a
> civilization. The
>   poet cannot stabilize his art
> in the tarnishing medium of I and IT.[19]

I do not know whether Conran was influenced in his thinking by Martin Buber's philosophy of I and Thou, which has been highly influential among modern theologians. What is clear is that Conran himself ascribes his belief in 'second-person poetry' to Welsh poetry. Hence his note on 'Gifts' in *Spirit Level*:

> Welsh poetry is second-person poetry. A poem praises, satirizes or laments within the magnetic field of I and Thou. The giving and receiving of gifts, like the giving and receiving of poetry itself, formed the central arch of Welsh civilization; and the celebration of gift and giver an important sub-division of the Welsh poetic art.[20]

It would be easy to see this idea as responding to Conran's own deep need – and why should it not? This would not mean that it was, therefore, historically untrue. For where do ideas come from, if not from human needs and desires? It is not, however, my concern here to judge Conran's idea of Welsh poetry or Welsh civilization against historical facts. My focus, rather, is upon Conran's modernism; in this instance, on his construction or interpretation of a tradition that has nourished his self-making as a poet. In this respect, it is clear that his ideas have arisen through his practice of parallel, and related, arts: his art as a poet, and his art as a translator of Welsh poetry into English.

A fuller account of the relationship between second-person poetry and Welsh civilization occurs in his Preface to *Welsh Verse*:

> [Welsh poetry] brags of its subject who is nearly always imagined as listening, and in fact probably did listen. It was, then, real – if highly crafted – speech. And as such it is itself a fulcrum for us. One can get a purchase from it. It gives one a criterion of whole speaking, of making

poetry as a private person, a social being and an objective observer – all at once. It allows one to judge the imagism of contemporary English poetry for what it is – partial speaking merely, framing bits of experience for sale as commodities.[21]

It would probably be a simplification to say that, if Conran had gone on living and working in Chelmsford instead of finding his way back to Wales, he would have become an English imagist. Other factors would have made this impracticable. As he has said of himself (in words that I quoted earlier), 'being physically spastic has made most of my imagery kinaesthetic – I have been forced to feel in terms of physical movement rather than sight or hearing.' This is one reason why dance is so important to him, and why he is hostile to the primarily visual mode of imagism. He has developed this hostility into a political critique of non-participatory modes of perception. As he writes in *A Gwynedd Symphony*:

> I have always distrusted views – vistas
> Like autobahns and Cathedrals
> And the master-race.
>
> A great view's so one-sided, you forget
> You're part of it.
> You survey it like an empire . . . (*GS*, 48–9)

Castles turns partly on the contrast between artists who have exploited Wales with their vision and those who have contributed to Wales with their participatory imaginations. Thus he sees Turner, with his 'prospecting eye', as an artist who 'launches the bolt of commodity / Deadly down the slatey stream', collaborating with the industrialists who exploited Wales in the nineteenth century.[22] And Conran celebrates his friend, the late Victor Neep:

> Came, in due season, Neep. He centred us.
> His cottage was the hub of North Wales.
>
> Bethesda, Caernarfon, Rhosgadfan. Metropolitan
> Of painters, poets, dramatists
>
> In the two languages.[23]

The words give the lie to the metropolitan view of Wales – the view from London, the view of all those (wherever they live, including Wales) who adopt Anglocentric values. They see Wales as provincial, or see Welsh regions or localities as parochial. It was the painter Victor Neep who was a true metropolitan, an artist in the spirit of a Welsh renaissance, who participated in the life of the land. In *A Gwynedd Symphony* Conran contrasts the imperial view with being 'lookable at // Part of the land' (*GS*, 49).

Ritual has played an important part in Conran's thinking over many years. It is evidently one of the things that has drawn him to W. B. Yeats with his sense of 'ceremony', and his commemoration of his people (Conran's 'Elegy for the Welsh Dead, in the Falkland Islands, 1982' is the Welsh equivalent of Yeats's 'Easter 1916'). *A Gwynedd Symphony* is, as it were, bracketed by Yeats. Its epigraph is from 'Among School Children': 'O brightening glance, / How can we know the dancer from the dance?' The back cover quotes 'Nineteen Hundred and Nineteen': 'Man is in love, and loves what vanishes. / What more is there to say?' Between them, the quotations encapsulate the major themes of *A Gwynedd Symphony*: the dance and love. Conran rarely sounds like Yeats, however – or like anyone other than himself. As I shall later argue, David Jones is a stronger influence upon *A Gwynedd Symphony* than Yeats, while Conran's Marxism, together with the strong communal element within Welsh society through the ages, excludes from his work the snobbery based on hierarchical values that we find in Yeats's poetry.

Dance is, of course, a form of ritual. So is poetry in the tradition of Taliesin, poetry as 'whole speaking', and poetry as a giving of gifts. Marriage, too, as a ceremony uniting man and woman, and the marriage feast, have been important themes of Conran from the beginning. One of his finest earlier poems is 'The Harbour'. Like a number of Conran's poems, 'The Harbour' places the poet among his friends. Here, he has come, with friends, to a small seaside town to attend a wedding of two of their friends. For the poet,

> Bride and groom are almost any bride and groom,
> Their histories forgotten, condensed by the two candles
> And folded into the paired image I now see.

The 'anonymity' extends beyond the bridal pair:

> Anonymous, all enter the whitewalled town,
> And with a sweet lack of the heart's concern
> Meditate here on what has been, what is,
> What shall be: for till you leave this seaport
> All's timely true, nothing is unforeseen.
> A legend has it that this town, called Cana,
> Was where Adam first saw Eve; and therefore
> The anonymous is sweet here, and no trouble
> Of being alone vexes the heart's unnaming
> Of what was known, and now is strange as childhood
> For ever transfixed in the harsh yelp of gulls.

With its concern for the archetypal relationship between a man and a woman, and between time and the timeless, this does not seem to me significantly different in meaning from the more sophisticated 'Winter at Llanddwyn' in *A Gwynedd Symphony*, in which a man and a girl 'danced':

> Time was created in the first moments
> When their eyes met. Like a dance
> In its peformance, nothing
>
> Before that counted. (*GS*, 15)

In both poems love is an absolute; it is the meaning or pattern of human existence. In 'The Harbour' 'anonymity' is not synonymous with alienation, or loss of the self in a uniform mass; it is, rather, the being achieved in participation in the original mystery, a home-coming to universal order. Strangeness, here, is restoration of original innocence; 'the heart's unnaming / Of what was known' transcends the human limitations of language and knowledge. The ritual opens upon a mystery.

The feast and the dance both have behind them the form of the Catholic Mass. Before saying more, I should say that I do not know what literal religious beliefs, if any, Conran holds. Nor am I sure that 'literal', in the context of poetic imagination, is a meaningful concept. Certainly Conran not infrequently mentions his experiences of religion, as in the passage quoted above where he refers to his reception into the Catholic Church as a young man. In the same book, referring to 'Three Swans on the River of Death', a poem which he wrote at the age of twenty, he says: 'For many years after that, the struggle in my soul was between the Muse and Christ, poetry and God' (*VPM*, 16). The very least we may infer, not from this comment alone, but from the whole tenor of Conran's poetry and thought, is a profoundly religious sensibility. He is not, however, exclusively religious in any narrow sense, as the following remark indicates: 'Ritual is the art of community: it is by no means limited to religious rites' (*VPM*, 190).

He has written, too, about the influence of the Roman Mass upon him: 'I became a Catholic just in time to participate in the Roman Mass before it was swept aside by the Second Vatican Council. There was a sense of drama pregnant in it even then . . .' (*VPM*, 188). Evidently the Mass provided Conran with a model of ritual drama, for which, he says, Yeats 'searched all his life' (*VPM*, 189). Inevitably, one thinks of David Jones, for whom (in Saunders Lewis's words) 'the Mass *makes sense* of everything',[24] and who modelled *The Anathemata* upon the form of the Mass. It would not be possible to talk about *A Gwynedd Symphony* in these terms. The Mass is, nevertheless, centrally important in Conran's Paradiso. This should be borne in mind, at the same time as we recognize that a major difference between Conran and Jones turns on the importance for the former of play-acting.

To say that Conran values the Mass as an archetypal form of drama is not to suggest that he therefore devalues its meaning for the orthodox faithful. On the contrary. In one poem in *A Gwynedd Symphony* the poet places himself among the people attending Mass. Here, in terms of the thinking behind the *Commoedia*, the priest is seen as 'the tragic actor', to whom the people respond:

> 'Sir,' we say,
> 'The roles are greater than we know.' (*GS*, 20)

This seems to me to be a key moment in Conran's work, fore-shadowed by the anonymity of the man and woman, and the poet and his other friends, in 'The Harbour'. Here, the poet humbly participates in the sacred ritual. It can be seen, I think, that the whole drive of Conran's thinking has been towards such participa-tion – from the 'darkness' of his muse poems through the 'I–Thou' relationships of his Gift Poems to the act of imagining Wales by placing himself in the land of Wales and in the Welsh tradition, that

he accomplishes in his *Commoedia*. In each phase the poet, through
his art, has situated himself in an order that is larger than himself,
an order modelled upon a universal archetype. By these means
Conran has completely transcended the limits of empirical lyricism,
while experimenting with the 'music' of verse on a grand scale. As
he has said of the Catholicism Raymond Garlick came to reject: it
'does at least have the function of opening up I–thou relationships
. . . As poetry the experience he was in when he wrote *A Sense of
Time* was so much greater than himself.'[25] What he says about
Garlick in this context is crucial to the understanding of Conran's
own work that I am offering here: 'His faith in Christianity may only
have been imagination, but imagination is what poetry is made of.'[26]

It would be going too far to say that this view makes it irrelevant
whether a poet influenced by Catholicism, such as Conran, actually
believes it is 'true' or not. It does, however, help to explain the
importance of drama and acting in his work. Although it would be a
misleading simplification, 'Pilgrimage' in *A Gwynedd Symphony*
could be read as a poem about the poet's baptism not as a Christian,
but as a poet in the tradition of Taliesin. The poem is in four parts.
The first is about the children of Fatima and their vision of the Lady
of the Rosary. The second is about the poet and two college friends –
'He gay, she / In love with him / And I halfway / In love with her' –
going on pilgrimage to Our Lady of Fatima at Bala. The third is
about time – the time taken by the journey, and the time taken by a
prayer. The fourth part continues the theme of love and knowledge.
Conran here describes 'this hag's cauldron, // Bala, by Llyn Tegid',

> Where it boiled and spat at me
> Five tired minutes
>
> And perhaps it was then
> I put my divining finger in my mouth
> To suck off the scald
>
> And I heard language
> Of love and grief
> Colour the whiteness
>
> Before I ran to my changes,
> Hare, fish, bird,
> Grain of wheat

> And the hag after me,
> Greyhound, otterbitch, falcon . . .
> Black, scratching hen. (*GS*, 33–4)

His pilgrimage, it seems, has its consummation in this way, as he is initiated into the mystery of poetry by 'becoming' Gwion Bach who 'becomes' Taliesin. But in a sense he 'becomes' Ceridwen, too, the 'black, scratching hen' who swallows him in the form of a grain of wheat. So the story has a kind of circularity, in which it is magic which gives birth to imagination, without thereby offering a disproof of the children's vision. And perhaps this is to say that imagination is all the poet can know, source and transformative principle of his art. But, if so, it is knowledge that brings with it a distrust of all knowledge, including the certainty of the sceptic that religious belief is 'only a myth'. Understood in this way, the poetic imagination (as Conran understands it) is inherently sceptical, but its deconstructions and demystifications do not bereave us of everything except radical uncertainty, or a vacuum signifying nothing. Instead, they leave love and desire for wholeness intact, as an energy and an aspiration. Rather than being bound up with nostalgia for origins, these inspire all civilized living – human relationships, poetry, religion, community, Wales.

David Jones is a presence in *A Gwynedd Symphony*, more than an influence upon it. One is aware of him in the treatment of geology (Conran's 'Silurian putsch' (*GS*, 10), for example, recalling the similar metaphor from *The Anathemata*). Conran's concern with the land of Wales, as well as linking him to Jones, also places him among other modern poets in a, broadly speaking, Celtic tradition, poets such as Hugh MacDiarmid, Sorley MacLean, and Irish poets (for example, W. B. Yeats, Seamus Heaney, John Montague). These are poets with strong national affiliations, who have turned from the parochialism of Britain towards Europe and the world, and whose poetry, in different degrees, is rooted in a land with an ancient, non-English, culture. The 'rooting' is in some cases highly physical, drawing nourishment from landscapes and their underlying geology, and intimate with local fauna and flora (as in Conran's expert knowledge of ferns). But land, in this sense, is not landscape alone; it is ground of a culture or civilization, and a sovereign realm, or a realm, with memories of independence, that aspires to sovereignty. Land, for poets in this tradition, is the place of a people.

Conran's deployment of dance and drama in *A Gwynedd Symphony*, and his conscious connection of them to the Mass, are also reminiscent of Jones, and especially of the following passage from *The Anathemata*:

> Who knows at what precise phase, or from what floriate
> green-room, the Master of Harlequinade, himself not made,
> maker of sequence and permutation in all things made, called
> us from our co-laterals out, to dance the Funeral Games of
> the Great Mammalia, as, long, long, long before, these
> danced out the Dinosaur?[27]

There is an affinity between Jones's idea of God as 'the Master of Harlequinade' who, from his 'floriate green-room', called us (mankind) out to take our place in the dance of life, and Conran's presentation of the dance in *A Gwynedd Symphony*. The affinity is, to some degree, a matter of echo. More importantly, it points to dance and drama as symbolic forms of universal order which lie behind both poems, as they did behind a significant body of Renaissance poetry. Jones and Conran both give the archetypes a modern application, and their treatments differ significantly from each other. The difference may be seen especially in the poem in *A Gwynedd Symphony* which is about the Mass.

'The Rhiwledyn Mass of Blessed Willam Dai' is, as Conran's note tells us, about a priest who, with other Catholics, 'founded a secret press in a cave of Rhiwledyn (the Little Orme) and produced the first book ever to be printed in Wales: Y *Drych Cristianogol*, "The Christian Mirror"' (*GS*, 20). Within the symphonic structure of the book as a whole, this motif relates to 'the green room – the actors' common room in a theatre – [which] in the Noh theatre opened onto the playing area and contained a large mirror where the actor-dancers checked their make-up and settled themselves before a performance' (*GS*, 81). Conran's use of the motif, therefore, emphasizes its archetypal nature, rather than limiting it to the specific Catholic context:

> Y *Drych Cristianogol* –
> Mirror in the green room,
> The cave on Rhiwledyn
> Where they set up the Type. (*GS*, 20)

Clearly, 'Type' refers to the first Welsh book, but also to the religious archetype, or universal model, which is the pattern underlying the idea of Welsh civilization that Conran invokes as a memory and an aspiration. As I have said earlier, Conran presents himself as a participant, a member of the chorus, 'the tragic chorus dance' (*GS*, 21), who 'crowd round' the priest as he says Mass. At the Mass the priest becomes 'Remembrancer / Of a holy people'.

> A second time the chorus dances.
> Hurrying feet affirm what we know –
> God's oneness, the carpenter,
> The only begotten . . .
>
> We're replying to the messenger
> With what he knows and we know,
> Or what he thinks he knows
> And what we think we believe.
>
> Amen . . . (*GS*, 21–2)

The balance of affirmation ('what we know') and scepticism ('What we think we believe') in these lines is one that Conran maintains, so that it would not be correct to speak of him, as one does of David Jones, as a devotional poet. Yet the scepticism is not an end in itself, as, here, the affirmative 'Amen' shows. It would be very hard to give a prose rendering of the spirit of these lines, which seem to me to affirm not literal belief, but a profoundly religious unknowing – indeed, a religious scepticism.

Conran's priest, then, is an actor, 'Christ's impersonator' (*GS*, 24), and he offers the host 'for all Gwynedd, / For Britain, Christendom / And everywhere, men and women' (*GS*, 24). As in *The Anathemata* and 'The Sleeping Lord', the universality of the redemptive sacrifice commemorated in the Mass is emphasized; and it starts with the here and now, in Gwynedd, extending from these particular people to 'everywhere, men and women'. As in David Jones's thinking there is an analogy between the role of priest and the role of poet, so is there in Tony Conran's. The main difference, it seems to me, turns upon the word 'performative'. Conran is a performative poet – not a performance poet, in the sense now commonly understood – but a poet whose work performs a function in his society, initially in Bangor. The experimental nature of his work over the years, involving actors and drama, dancers and dance, musicians and music, and combinations of these 'players', has explored possibilities, and pushed back the boundaries, of the poet's involvement in his society. Conran's modernism serves a traditional function: his participation as one who gives and takes, creating rituals that confirm community.

Preoccupation with ritual does not mean that Conran is anonymous, of course. On the contrary, his espousal of forms of impersonality, like that of T. S. Eliot and other modernists, enables him to be more personal, rather than less. He is able to bring more of his humanity to his poetry, releasing it at a greater depth, than he would be able to do if confined to empiricism. Instead of being a solipsist gazing at his face in the mirror, he acts as a man in the fullest sense – son, lover, husband, father, social and political being: a full member of the human chorus. At the level of autobiography the *Welsh Commoedia* is rich and complex, and true to the tensions of various relationships, as well as celebratory of varied love. Thus, again in *A Gwynedd Symphony*, Conran writes about his parents, and deals with difficult feelings. In 'The Gardeners', for example:

> My father in the hallway
> Welcomes me, smiling. The call
> Signals of claustrophobia
> Touch nerves like a dentist's probe.
> Nineteen years this December
> He died. But despite that, when
> I haunt him, I'm the phantom –
> He's the too too solid man. (*GS*, 44)

This is writing of considerable psychological and emotional subtlety and force. It expresses love and regret, giving what is due to both father and son, but not shirking the uncomfortable truth of 'claustrophobia'. Consider also the echo in 'too too solid man' of *Hamlet*, another work that has a good deal to say about relationships between fathers and sons, which are loving but also overwhelming, bringing destructive pressures to bear. Nor is the meaning contained only in the passage or in the poem from which it comes, for the structure of *A Gwynedd Symphony*, as its title implies, is symphonic. This means, among other things, that motifs are repeated or developed in different keys. The claustrophobia associated here with Conran's father and his world contrasts with the openness that Conran found in Wales. This is one of the things he celebrates in 'Sending a Harrier to Llaneilian', his poem in memory of the Welsh scholar Bedwyr Lewis Jones:

> I've lost a key
> From my ring –
> A key to openhanded
> Welshness,
>
> A key to the hospitality
> Of Tywyn and Nannau. (*GS*, 36)

It is perhaps worth repeating at this point that what Conran seeks is wholeness. Hence the importance for him of the dance:

> . . . my poetry I've always thought of as a dance for the tongue and the vocal chords: ultimately, since tongues and vocal chords don't occur in a vacuum, for the whole body, the whole mind. But then, all good dance is an intelligent and knowledge-giving activity; all good art is that. (*VPM*, 190)

Wholeness includes emotional wholeness, of course, and in 'Sending a Harrier to Llaneilian' in particular, Conran praises and laments, expressing the whole range of emotion occasioned by the death of a friend who was also, as a scholar and a host, a key to Welsh civilization. The private and the public are not compartmentalized in the *Welsh Commoedia*, which is able, therefore, to draw on experience in depth, while transcending the limits of the empirical.

Conran's achievement in this respect could be described as political – the catchphrase 'the personal is the political' comes to mind. There is no doubt that he is, like Yeats, a political poet. In the present critical climate, however, we are more in danger of failing to recognize his achievement as a religious poet. His deployment of impersonal modes, for example, serves a vision of religious wholeness. In this respect, Conran's thinking has more in common with Jacques Maritain's than it does with T. S. Eliot's. Whereas Eliot's early concept and use of impersonality, in his poetry and criticism, seem to express a fear of human wholeness – a fear of women, for example, and of male and female sexuality, Maritain insisted that poetry 'proceeds from the totality of man, sense, imagination, intellect, love, desire, instinct, blood and spirit together'.[28] He argued that Eliot, in his essay 'Tradition and the Individual Talent', 'missed the distinction between creative Self and self-centred ego'.[29] Maritain's distinction between individuality and personality is crucial to his philosophy, and also, in my view, to Conran's rejection of empiricism:

> In each of us, individuality, being that which excludes from ourselves that which other men are, might be described as the narrowness of the ego, always threatened and always eager to grasp for itself. Personality, on the other hand, is rooted in the spirit inasmuch as the spirit holds itself in existence and superabounds in existence . . . Personality means interiority to oneself and requires at the same time the communications of knowledge and love.[30]

Jacques Maritain was a religious philosopher, Tony Conran is a poet, and I would not want to bind him to Maritain's terms, despite the fact that he has read Maritain with sympathy. It is evident, however, that for Conran the dance is the primary form of self-giving, in which the poet is joined with others in a supreme affirmation of human wholeness. Poetry is the art of a person, but, like dance, it is a participatory art, the art of a community, which communicates 'knowledge and love'. The quotation from Yeats that forms the epigraph to *A Gwynedd Symphony* has a special aptness. The ego reveals itself in its separateness, cut off from others and alone in the universe; in the case of the whole human being, however, how can we know the dancer from the dance?

Afterword: On Being a Critic of Welsh Writing in English

As I was coming towards the end of writing this book, and thinking it would be fitting to conclude with an account of what it has felt like to be involved as a critic in Welsh writing in English, a feature in *A470*, the information magazine of Yr Academi Gymreig, cast my mind violently back into the past. The feature is by Mario Basini, and is called 'Surveying a Blasted Landscape'. Its tone is well illustrated by the following quotation:

> I find the English-language literary scene in Wales pockmarked by the problems created by isolation and inbreeding. I detect a fatal lack of self-belief and enterprise among some of our writers, perhaps because they do not have the confidence generated by challenge of making a living in a more competitive market.[1]

Of course, anything can be alleged against 'some of our writers', since the phrase is vague enough to suggest anything. Or nothing. If one takes the charge seriously, however, one response would be to ask: Isolation from what? And the answer would seem to be: A more competitive market. Basini begins his article by recalling that when he 'arrived in Cardiff to work as a journalist in the late Sixties it seemed that Welsh writing in English was on the verge of a major breakthrough'. 'A clutch of novelists and short story writers had earned themselves spots on the lists of important London publishers and through them had won small but significant international sales and reputations.' It is clear from the outset, then, that Mario Basini judges literary worth with what Bobi Jones calls 'the mentality of slant towards London'.[2] The language with which Basini supports this is remorselessly Thatcherite: aggressive, competitive, masculinist. He tells us that, subsequently, he was disappointed not to see 'a procession of major writers striding purposefully down the trails those pioneers had blazed'. He regrets that Emyr Humphreys and R. S. Thomas are 'without even the most timorous challenger to their authority'.

Basini has a point when he says 'what I feel we are in desperate need of is evaluation'. Unfortunately he makes it at the expense of literary criticism that is 'academic in origin', when in fact the new criticism of Welsh writing in English has come mainly from dedicated individuals working in higher education; he also displays predictable prejudices against Arts Council bursaries for writers and subsidies to their publishers in Wales, and his description of 'slim, pretty collections of verses' shows familiarity with book covers but not their contents.

Whether Basini's point about evaluation applies to Welsh-language criticism, I am unable to judge, but it remains true of criticism of Welsh writing in English, despite the notable maturing of such criticism over recent years. It is not however a simple point, a palpable hit, as it may initially seem. In the first place, good evaluative criticism is an art that is always in short supply, and in recent years, with the rise of smart literary journalism and the intellectual ascendancy of literary theory in the academy, serious criticism of poetry and novels has become rare everywhere. In the second place, Basini's request for 'something which tells me whether a novel, a short story or a poem is worth reading and why' both dispenses with the need for independence of mind on the part of the reader and replaces it with a passivity which makes the reader defenceless against the prejudice or blindness of critics. If I seem to be making heavy weather of a polemical feature that might, after all, have the beneficial effect of waking 'some of our writers' up, that is because independence of mind is one of the qualities I have come to value most through my critical engagement with Welsh writing in English, and reliance on external authority one of the things I have come to reject.

With its tone and its lack of specificity, Mario Basini's article gave me a strong sense of *déjà vu*. I arrived in Wales shortly before he did, in 1965, and, as I became engaged as a critic with what was then generally called 'Anglo-Welsh' literature, I became all too familiar with dismissals or denigrations of that literature which rarely showed interest in or knowledge of actual writings. The only difference from Basini's present polemic was that in those days Dylan Thomas was the 'giant' against whom other writers were seen as pygmies. Moreover, without doubting Welsh readers' love of Dylan Thomas's work, it can be confidently asserted that the supremacy of his reputation in Wales had something to do with the 'inferiority complex' that required confirmation of the quality of English-language Welsh writing to come from outside Wales, before it was widely acknowledged in Wales. In the main the dismissals of other Welsh writers in English came from two sources: from English critics based mainly in London who looked down their noses at what they saw as a provincial literary scene, and from critics in Wales who, like Mario Basini, judged Welsh literary success by what was published and praised in London. The irony of the latter position is that it negates the independence of judgement requisite for evaluation, even while demanding it.

It was, however, precisely the independent-mindedness of Welsh writers in English that drew me to what was then a beleaguered group, passionate about a Wales that did not always value them. When I first arrived in Wales, I had no idea that there was a living literature in Welsh or a significant English-language Welsh literature, since my knowledge was confined to a few individual writers, such as Dylan Thomas, R. S. Thomas and Alun Lewis. What began for me in 1965 was, therefore, an education. One of my main teachers was David Jones, through whose writings I discovered the Welsh past. Not as past, however; for, as I wrote in 1969:

> David Jones's learning can be valuable to us now, surely, by showing how the imagination immersed in history can give both depth and perspective to its interpretation of man's life in the present; while it reveals for us the significance of our own Celtic past.[3]

That 'our' was, I later came to see, at once tendentious and telling, revealing as it does the extent to which, at that time, I had accepted David Jones's idea of the heritage of these islands – the common human ground, as it were, shared by the Welsh and English soldiers in *In Parenthesis*. I was also influenced, no doubt, by the Celtic groundwork of Hardy's Wessex, which is not a recovered culture, as it is in David Jones's work, but a presence that survives in folklore and in the landscape of Egdon Heath. A further influence is apparent in my early indignant reaction to the idea that Edward Thomas was an 'Anglo-Welsh' poet, since for me at that time he was identified with the landscapes of southern England. The idea of 'our own Celtic past' did, however, enable me to begin to recognize how decisive an influence his Welshness had had upon him.

Another of my teachers was Roland Mathias. It was he who ensured my involvement as a critic in Welsh writing in English, initially by asking me to review *The Lilting House* for *The Anglo-Welsh Review*, and subsequently by encouraging my critical writing and poetry. Without wishing to denigrate the enhanced production and design qualities of the magazines in Wales that have succeeded it, I have to confess a particular affection for the old *Anglo-Welsh Review*: a block of a magazine that periodically thudded on to the floor among the morning post, and was itself, often through Roland Mathias's reviews, an education in the Welsh past, as well as a quarry of modern writing. The quarry metaphor may seem eccentric, but for me it exactly captures the sense of a literature and a history being hewn out of resistant materials, which so appealed to me in *The Anglo-Welsh Review*. First through my contributions to this magazine, therefore, and then in writing for *Poetry Wales* and attending Academi Gymreig conferences, I came to play a part as a critic in English-language Welsh literature during the 1970s.

It was inevitable that, in a small country, I should meet most of the writers during that period, and I will concede that I *have* sometimes wondered whether acquaintanceship, and in some instances friendship, took the edge off my ability to evaluate. The answer, I think, is that interpretation, and dedication to a task, imply evaluation. As well as meeting writers in their maturity, as a lecturer in the English Department at the University College of Wales at Aberystwyth, I enjoyed early contacts with some who would later establish themselves as poets and critics and short-story writers, such as John Davies, Mike Jenkins, David Annwn, Katie Gramich, Glenda Beagan, Greg Hill, Julian May and Linden Peach. Later, after leaving Aberystwyth in 1984, I continued to play a part as a critic. By then the scene had changed – in poetry, as I indicated in an essay on *The Bright Field*, the emphasis had shifted, with some notable exceptions, from a concern with national identity to a concern with the threat posed by the ecological crisis to the future. But still, I maintained, 'human brotherhood . . . has remained, through all social and cultural changes, a major concern of Welsh poetry.'[4] And, I was able to say: 'Fortunately, one has nowadays to speak of sisterhood also, in the context of poetry from Wales.'[5] In introducing *Green Horse* in 1978, Roland Mathias had doubted whether the 'future will long contain what could meaningfully be called "Anglo-Welsh poetry" '.[6] Given the continuing existence of an alternative poetic tradition in Wales – in effect a range of different poetic possibilities than those that are present in mainstream contemporary English and American poetry – and given the unpredictable creativity of poets, I do not share this doubt.

In so far as I am able to recall the view that I held when I first came to Wales, it was that London was the 'centre', where I, as a young poet, hoped to publish. It then seemed to me that to be taken seriously by Ian Hamilton at *The Review* and to be published by Faber, publishers of Ted Hughes and Thom Gunn, were the apex of achievement. I also had a vague idea, which probably owed something to my reading of T. S. Eliot, that the object of a poem was to express a state of mind. From that time, the process began by which I came to think the opposite – that poetry, instead of imprisoning poet and reader in a state of mind, should work towards liberation from the narrowly conceived ego, and open upon shared depths – depths known as need for meaning, if not as the encompassing order of whose existence we can no longer be sure. By an allied process, what also happened through my involvement in Wales (not just in writing, but in my growing sense of the culture) was that I came to reject a metropolitan idea of 'the centre' and replace it with the conviction that any place was potentially a centre for a writer who was prepared to explore it in depth, free from fashionable assumptions about its marginality.[7] One aspect of this thinking was radically democratic, and it corresponded with what I felt to be a Welsh tradition which some Welsh writers in English, such as Glyn Jones, espoused.

Much later, in reviewing the new edition of Tony Conran's *Welsh Verse*, I used a phrase translated from the Welsh of Waldo Williams, 'brotherhood's country', to describe what I took to characterize the whole Welsh poetic tradition. I quoted Conran's translation of Ann Griffiths's 'Full of Wonders': God is 'Giver of being, abundant sustainer, / Governor of all that is, / In the manger a swaddled baby' and went on to say:

> Her poems embody a complete, passionate theology, but it is not fanciful, I think, to relate her sense of the infinite contained in the very small to an early and persistent habit of feeling among Welsh poets, whose essentially religious order was founded on small settlements in a hostile world. Hence the transition without much strain from tribal kinship and aristocratic comradeship to a sense of brotherhood, which is Christian and democratic, with socialist aspirations, within the one poetic tradition.[8]

I am aware that this was to make a large claim, and, although I do not intend now to take it back, I do want to acknowledge that I approached Welsh literature (in both languages) with an outsider's idealism, which led me, on occasions, to make misreadings. There are three instances in particular of which I am aware, and I shall deal with them now, not in the spirit of *mea culpa*, but because I believe that a critic, provided he or she remains open-minded, can learn a great deal from recognizing his or her misreadings.

The first occurred in my essay on Emyr Humphreys's *Outside the House of Baal*, where I simplified the 'goodness' of the main male character, J. T. Miles.[9] This was a case of finding what I wanted to find, and of failing to recognize the full complexity of Humphreys's treatment of character or of the Welsh Nonconformist tradition. He is a much sharper and more subtle psychologist, with a more rigorous moral vision, than I had recognized. It is probable, moreover, that I had deceived myself with my reading of what I now call the poetry of religion, without sufficiently taking into account the male idealist's capacity for unconsciously using verbal eloquence to blind himself to his self-deception and to the sacrifices he exacts of others, especially women. I had not understood Humphreys's Christian vision because I had not realized the extent to which it makes him question the behaviour and values of characters – Welsh nationalists and Nonconformists – whose values he shares. To say the same thing differently: he tests to breaking point the very things about Wales he most cherishes, because he is concerned with the souls of his characters and the soul of the nation.

The second instance was my reading of Tony Conran's *All Hallows*, in which I understood the first part, 'The Shadow: Notation for Raymond Garlick', as exclusively comradely in intention.[10] I read it, in effect, as a sequence of poems in Yeatsian mode, with Conran mythologizing Garlick along with himself and other friends for the part they had played together in the political struggle that ended, disastrously at the time, in the Devolution referendum of 1979. Once it was pointed out to me that this was a misreading, I saw at once that it was my own sense of 'brotherhood', which I had projected in an idealized form on to Conran and his friends, leading me to overlook his criticism of Garlick for subsequent defeatism. In Tony Conran's own words about Raymond Garlick:

> As poetry the experience he was in when he wrote *A Sense of Time* was so much greater than himself. To deal with it as he does in the *Collected Poems* amounts to a deliberate slighting of his vision, as castles were

'slighted' or destroyed by their defenders to prevent them being captured and used by the enemy. Why has he limited himself in this way? For survival's sake? Or for identity? Both of these deities seem to me to be another name for the ego – its opinions, its images, its fight to gain equilibrium and calm.[11]

This is not evaluative criticism as it is normally understood. Irrespective of whether one thinks it is just or not, it is a profound questioning of the turn taken by a poet's imagination, and it pays tribute to the importance of poetry as lifework, as personal vision that is also a shaping vision of Wales.

The third instance arose from my early reading of David Jones, when I abstracted a political sentiment from *In Parenthesis* – in effect a comradeship or brotherhood consonant with socialism – and was subsequently deeply troubled to discover that his writing requires a very different political interpretation. I have written about this else-where[12] and will not dwell on it now, except to say that what was at issue was a misunderstanding of the terrible tension in David Jones's mind. Only in reading *The Dying Gaul* did I finally realize how a deeply charitable and humane man, with his understanding of what is truly human and his perception of the dominance of utilitarian-ism in the modern world, was being forced by his own ideas to see fellow human beings as virtually subhuman. The position at which I have currently arrived on this complex issue is that David Jones is indeed the most humane of writers, but with an impossibly demand-ing religious ideology in respect of man-the-artist – as distinct from the love and devotion that permeate his religious feelings.

Being a critic of 'Anglo-Welsh' literature in the 1970s was not an easy option. One memory in particular from the early years of the decade invokes for me the feelings of that time. I am walking across a field with a friend, a fellow academic, when I ask him, gloomily, whether he thinks writing about John Cowper Powys is a way of committing 'academic suicide'. He replies that he thinks it probably is, and I agree. The name of Powys attracted a particular odium in academic circles, mainly because of F. R. Leavis's dismissal of his work. But my question might have applied equally to other writers tarred with the brush of 'Anglo-Welsh' or to the subject as a whole. The memory comes to me with a curious sense of shame, because academic success was not my motive for teaching or writing, and this anecdote may suggest that it was. It is worth recalling, nevertheless, to indicate the feeling of being embattled, and the consequent anxieties, that resulted from being a critic of Welsh writing in English at that time.

Teaching or study of the literature was not encouraged in the English Department at the University College of Wales, Aberystwyth, and it was not until the later 1970s that Ned Thomas was able to establish an optional course in Welsh Writing in English, which enabled translations from the Welsh to be studied alongside English-language Welsh writings. In literary and academic circles in and outside Wales, the subject commonly elicited hostility or disdain. The reactions were difficult to deal with in that they were usually unspecific, taking the form of 'if these writers were any good, we would have heard of them', or, more insidiously, of seeing their promotion as the plot of a minority of mediocrities avid to achieve publication and gain Arts Council subsidies. It was generally assumed, as Mario Basini has done, that there were two or three good writers from Wales, who could be discussed adequately in the context of English literature, while the rest were no good because they were not published in London.

The injustice of this view was one of the things that turned me into a critic. Justice, in fact, became one of my main motivations in writing criticism. Like most young poets who are also academics, I had difficulty reconciling my two functions. In order to write criticism I had to believe in it as an activity, and the romantic received wisdom is that critics are parasites on literature. More seriously, there are problems, involving time and energy, for the person who aspires to be a poet and a critic in reconciling the different demands of the arts. The justification at which I arrived for writing criticism was on two grounds: that it is valuable to bring to light unjustly neglected writings and writers, and that criticism is a necessary function in a civilized literary society. Tony Conran and others have evolved ideas of a specifically Welsh civilization. On a smaller scale, I came to believe that a civilized literary society did exist in Wales, and that its survival was a matter of importance. In this spirit, I added my support to that of the few critics working in the field. It is also relevant to record that I was by this time at war with what I thought of as 'alienation' as an easy fashion. This did not apply to a genuine existential crisis, which compelled the writer to personal expression, but also to exploring its cultural and historical roots, as for example D. H. Lawrence did in examining the 'disconnection' resulting from the First World War, or Samuel

Beckett in his plays and novels, or even the first 'confessional' poets. It applied to the adoption of a conventional romantic individualism, which by a superior isolation of the self effectively denied common humanity. Behind my ideal of playing a part as a critic lay an idea similar to that which A. M. Allchin expresses, when he says that the purpose of words is 'to establish communication, communion between people and between the world and God. The Romanian word for "word" is helpful to us here, it is *cuvint*, from the Latin *Conventum*; a word is a meeting place.'[13] I was far from being unsympathetic towards genuine expression of psychic or cultural breakdown; it was, rather, my sense of the shared crisis of the word as a meeting place that made me react against its fashionable simulacra, that could become profitable selling lines in *angst*.

In my experience, hostility towards Welsh writing in English and its critics came mainly from people who knew little or nothing about the subject. But one could also be unsettled by those with informed opinions. For me, this was principally the case with Bobi Jones's famous essay 'Anglo-Welsh: More Definition'. There, he argues that 'Anglo-Welsh writing finds its source and inspiration' in the 'colonialist predicament'.[14] In terms of this political perspective he describes Trevor Fishlock and myself as examples of 'the good old English liberal' and proceeds as follows:

> On the whole the Welsh are very receptive to such liberalism, and I feel a contrast in Wales to what one may notice amongst some other colonialised groups. Sometimes, for instance, in a 'black-power' group, an English ban-the-bomb, colour-bar-opposing, anti-apartheid liberal – with all the required externalities and right basic sentiments – will suddenly find himself faintly despised. He goes along burgeoning with noble principles, and lo and behold he is not accepted. He's even shouted down: they hate him. He's a hanger on.[15]

The passage is craftily worded but, with my 'liberal' sensitivity, I could not help reading it as suggesting that, as an Englishman who interested himself in Welsh writing in English, I deserved contempt. As far as being 'a hanger on' was concerned, I have to say there did not seem much to hang on to, at that time when 'Anglo-Welsh' literature had no powerful friends inside or outside Wales.

The portrait Bobi Jones painted was not less hurtful for being a caricature. From another direction, while I developed an ideal of

Welsh literary culture, I have sometimes been presented with an idealized portrait of myself. Thus, Tony Conran, in *Frontiers in Anglo-Welsh Poetry*, wrote of 'Jeremy Hooker, who of course approaches Anglo-Welsh writing from the firm ground of his English roots'.[16] The comment was kindly meant, but to me it is highly ironic. After all, I had been at pains in my criticism to problematize the metaphor of 'roots', while my poetry should have shown that I experienced Englishness, not as a 'firm ground' to which I belonged, but as a question, even a predicament. Indeed, the question of identity which I had been living seemed to me to have affinities with that of my Welsh friends. Whether I was the 'colonialist' or not, it seemed to me that we were all living in a post-imperial world, and one in which defence of the human involved defence of marginalized people and places against the forces of placelessness. While I do not have a fully thought-out attitude to what Tom Nairn called 'the break-up of Britain', I understand and largely agree with J. R. Jones's thinking about 'Britishness' and its baleful influence in Wales.[17] At the same time, I am drawn to the idea of the 'Briton', as applied by T. S. Eliot to David Jones,[18] in whose work love of country reaches out to embrace the whole of 'these islands',[19] and I respond with particular sympathy to Welsh writers, such as Waldo Williams, whose love of Wales coexists with affection for English places. My emotional reaction is to value cultural differences, and, therefore, to avoid stereotyping and caricaturing other people, and my anti-centralist thinking is based upon that.

I would like at this point to quote A. M. Allchin again:

> The inability of the British government to hear what was being said by the tragic events in places like Handsworth, Brixton and Tottenham was ultimately rooted in our age-old English refusal to hear and learn the languages of others, and in particular of our western neighbours. The ancient history is linked with the new. A deep and genuine change in English attitudes towards Welsh could be, I believe, an important precondition for a more human, more sensitive, more constructive approach to the urgent problems of our multi-cultural inner city areas.[20]

Unlike the ruralism and medievalism implicit in David Jones's nostalgia for a Britain that was part of Catholic Europe, this view seems to me both necessary and practical, although, as a mainly monolingual Englishman, my agreement with it is not accompanied by complacency. As far as I am concerned, the operative words here are 'more human'. This is what I found embodied in the Welsh poetic tradition, in for example modern Welsh poems which I read in translation (especially Gwenallt's 'Rhydcymerau' and Waldo Williams's 'In Two Fields', translated by Tony Conran), and in Welsh writing in English, in *In Parenthesis*, in Alun Lewis's poems and stories and letters, in the work of Glyn Jones and Gwyn Thomas, and in the new women's poetry that began to appear in Wales in the 1970s.

I found it too, at a critical moment, in John Cowper Powys's novels and *Autobiography*, which enlarged my sense of the possibilities of being human, and gave me a larger air to breathe. His work might be seen as old-fashioned in the light of the anti-humanism that has become the dominant academic intellectual trend in recent years.[21] Or it might be seen as prophetic of the eco-logical awareness that has been gaining ground since his death, an awareness that enlarges human consciousness by humbling human pride. Here, a brief illustration from *Porius* must suffice. In answer to Neb ap Digon's question 'What turns a god into a devil, master?', Myrddin Wyllt answers:

> 'Power, my son. Nobody in the world, nobody beyond the world, can be trusted with power, unless perhaps it be our mother the earth; but I doubt whether even she can. The Golden Age can never come again till governments and rulers and kings and emperors and priests and druids and gods and devils learn to un-make themselves as I did and leave men and women to themselves!'[22]

This is Powys's answer, too – his antihumanism, if one cares to put it in those terms. But in fact he is showing the way to a new human empowerment, through the un-making of powers that separate humankind from the rest of creation and fetter the imagination in its capacity to remake human identity. Powys himself was convinced that he found the inspiration for his vision in Wales. One of the things of which I have become especially aware is the way in which certain writers – most notably David Jones and Powys himself – who were either English or spent their formative years in England, chose Wales as their imaginative matrix, because they found in its 'matter' a numinous aura, or a historical or mythic connection to the past, that they did not find in England. While I have emphasized the literary potentialities of such choices, I recognize the attendant danger of political distortion – at worst, the Arnoldian romance of Wales that negates real Welsh independence.

When Tony Conran speaks of Glyn Jones 'coming to English poetry as a relative foreigner, delighting in its wonder world, and at the same time separated from everything that gave it social relevance',[23] I can only exclaim *'Everything!'* Perhaps an outsider does see some things a 'native' is unable to see. Certainly H. D. Thoreau thought so: 'A stranger may easily detect what is strange to the oldest inhabitant, for the strange is his province.'[24] Conran himself was an outsider who chose to become Welsh, a man who in shaping himself has shaped a vision of Wales; and he is one who sees more than most. In his case, as a pioneer 'Anglo-Welsh' writer – a term he has done more than almost anyone else to make meaningful, indeed, to make ring like a boast – there was perhaps a need to emphasize the differences between Anglo-Welsh and English poetry. For my part, living in Wales was a progressive experience of seeing differences. Yet it might reasonably be alleged that I have brought different needs to the study of Welsh writing in English. I have already indicated that this was probably the case with my early reading of Edward Thomas. And no doubt part of the appeal for me of John Cowper Powys is the link that he makes between Wales and Wessex. In no instance, however, do I wish to read 'Welsh' under 'English', or to substitute a uniform 'human' for national or local particularities. But neither can I accept the difference Conran apparently posits between English and Welsh in his comments on Glyn Jones, since it leaves no ground between English and Welsh for shared human experience.

On a memorable occasion when Meic Stephens took me with my then wife to meet our neighbours Gwyn and Daisy Williams at Trefenter, he seemed to suggest that I could 'become Welsh'. I scarcely knew what he meant then, though later I met people who by birth and upbringing were as English as I was and who now thought of themselves as Welsh. That struck me as being one way for an English person to live in Wales. Another, more common, way was to assert one's English difference, becoming, perhaps, like the parishioners who so annoyed R. S. Thomas when he lived at Eglwys-fach.[25] As far as I was concerned neither was an option, though there is no doubt that I became more conscious of my English origins through living in Wales. The underlying experience, however, was inseparable from that creative uncertainty which is one of the main reasons why I write – the blindness in which one strives to become partially sighted, the unknowing that one wins from deceptive knowing, the breaking of false images. The one certain thing was that in Wales, in people, in the Welsh language but also in English, in the culture, in the landscape, I came up against differences, and what I made, as poet and critic, was in one way or another an attempt at forming a relationship with what was not myself, but in which I could find something of common human ground.

As I have discussed earlier in this book, the 'frontier', or 'border', is a metaphor which different writers apply differently to the situation of Welsh writing in English. The actual border is at once socially diverse and a *limes* with a magical atmosphere, as we see in such contrasting works as the writings of Thomas Traherne, *The Diary of Francis Kilvert*, the books of Margiad Evans, the novels of Raymond Williams, the 'Welsh' poems of Anne Stevenson, and other writings. Some of these rich materials have been explored in the Border Lines series of books edited by John Powell Ward for Seren. The existence of this series, together with the Writers of Wales series established earlier by University of Wales Press, represents the great change that has affected the situation of criticism of Welsh writing in English since I first became involved with it. In the case of John Cowper Powys, for example, there were two critical books to which I could refer when I wrote my study of his work in 1973. Now there are numerous studies, in some of which, as in articles in *The Powys Review* and *The Powys Journal*, the critical and theoretical approaches are far more sophisticated than those of earlier critics. The same is true across the whole field of Welsh writing in English since Glyn Jones's pioneering *The Dragon Has Two Tongues* was published in 1968, as we see in work by Roland Mathias, Tony Conran, M. Wynn Thomas, John Pikoulis, Jane Aaron, Belinda Humfrey, Walford Davies and others, and in the annual *Welsh Writing in English* edited by Tony Brown. Indeed, I scarcely recognize the subject that, with Ned Thomas and Robin Young, I began to teach at Aberystwyth. Then, for teachers and students alike, part of the excitement of the course was its pioneering nature. There were no shelves of books to consult, as there were if one were lecturing or writing an essay on D. H. Lawrence or James Joyce; there was not much choice except to be independent-minded.

To return for the last time to the 'border', its great interest for me is that it offers a writer choices that are not available in more insulated societies. In a sense, with their larger multicultural populations, England and America may be said to be more open to challenges that will shape the future; but in other ways, they are more insulated, more closed, than Wales. To say that Wales is more open to the past is not to imply that it lives on memory alone. On the contrary, as, in their very different ways, both David Jones and Raymond Williams knew, the past in Wales contains a hope for the future, a living ideal. For all the destruction of communities by market forces, the country which has embodied ideals of brotherhood, and in which sisterhood has become a living force in recent years, offers ways of apprehending common experience that we do not find in Middle England. It is not only the spirit of a different politics that lives on in Wales, but, as I have shown in this book, religious or spiritual resources that are not available in a mainly secular society. This does not mean that the poet as competitor – Mario Basini's favoured model – cannot exist in Wales; he or she can, and does. Only it is more difficult in Wales to ignore the claims of the word as a meeting place; more difficult for the writer to be insulated from his or her kind, and from social and cultural and ecological issues. This is more than a matter of social consciousness, involving as it does a sense of connection between the living, and between the living and the dead. The relationship between the visible and the invisible continues to exist in Wales as a viable alternative to materialistic and solipsistic insularity, and is felt in flesh and blood. It is a tradition known in words that are meeting places. Owing to the ties that still bind a writer to people and place in Wales, it is more likely that in making a personal vision he or she will, in some way, be shaping a vision of Wales, and thereby imagining a larger human world.

Notes

1 Twentieth-Century Welsh Writing in English

[1] David Jones, *In Parenthesis*, 1937 (London: Faber, 1963), 79.

[2] Ibid., 207.

[3] David Jones, *The Anathemata*, 1952 (London: Faber, 1972), 10.

[4] Quoted in Glyn Jones, *The Dragon Has Two Tongues* (London: Dent, 1968), 34.

[5] See Harri Webb, 'Thanks in Winter', *The Green Desert* (Llandysul: Gomer, 1969), 45.

[6] Raymond Garlick and Roland Mathias (eds), *Anglo-Welsh Poetry 1480–1980* (Bridgend: Poetry Wales Press, 1984), 39.

[7] Gwyn Jones, *Being and Belonging*, BBC Wales Annual Radio Lecture (Cardiff: BBC Publications, 1977), 7.

[8] Emyr Humphreys, *The Taliesin Tradition* (London: Black Raven Press, 1983), 168.

[9] R. S. Thomas, *What is a Welshman?* (Llandybïe: Christopher Davies, 1974), 12.

[10] Tony Conran, *Welsh Verse* (Bridgend: Poetry Wales Press, 1986), 286.

[11] John Tripp, *Collected Poems 1958–1978* (Swansea: Christopher Davies, 1978), 111.

[12] John Davies, *At the Edge of Town* (Llandysul: Gomer, 1981), 37.

[13] Tony Curtis, *Selected Poems* (Bridgend: Poetry Wales Press, 1986), 135.

[14] *Being and Belonging*, 17.

[15] J. R. Jones, 'Need The Language Divide Us?', *Planet* 49/50 (January 1980), 25.

[16] Tony Curtis, *Selected Poems*, 134. Curtis is here partly quoting and partly paraphrasing Gwyn A. Williams's *When Was Wales?* (Harmondsworth: Penguin Books, 1985), 304.

[17] Bobi Jones, 'Anglo-Welsh: More Definition', *Planet* 16 (Feb./March 1973), 11–23.

[18] Tony Conran, 'Anglo-Welsh Manqué?', *Planet* 76 (August 1989), 67–73.

[19] Tony Conran, *Frontiers in Anglo-Welsh Poetry* (Cardiff: University of Wales Press, 1997), 259.

[20] Tony Conran, *The Cost of Strangeness* (Llandysul: Gomer, 1982), 27.

[21] For a discussion of this significant Irish writer and thinker, with a strong south Wales background, see Jeremy Hooker, 'The Sun Centered in Darkness: The Poetry of Gerard Casey', *Planet* 95 (Oct./ Nov. 1992), 83–9.

[22] 'The Dissident Condition', Emyr Humphreys interviewed by Murray Watts, *Planet* 71 (Oct./Nov. 1988), 29.

[23] Published as *On the Study of Celtic Literature*, 1867.

[24] Emyr Humphreys, 'Arnold in Wonderland', *Miscellany Two* (Bridgend: Poetry Wales Press, 1981), 98.

[25] Ibid., 99.

[26] John Cowper Powys, *Autobiography*, 1934 (London: Macdonald, 1967), 334–5.

[27] John Cowper Powys, *Owen Glendower* (London: John Lane/The Bodley Head, 1941), 889.

[28] Powys began to publish his poetry in the late 1890s and an early influence upon him was W. B. Yeats. Seamus Heaney's description of Yeats's reaction against the materialistic spirit of the Victorian age provides a context for Powys's outlook.

> At a time when the spirit of the age was becoming increasingly scientific and secular, when Sir James Frazer's *Golden Bough* was seeking to banish the mystery from the old faiths and standardize and anatomize the old places, Yeats and his friends embarked upon a deliberately counter-cultural movement to reinstate the fairies, to make the world more magical than materialistic, and to elude the social and political interpretations of society in favour of a legendary and literary vision of race. (Seamus Heaney, *Preoccupations: Selected Prose 1968–1978* (London: Faber, 1980), 135)

[29] Arthur Machen, *Far Off Things* (London: Martin Secker, 1922), 8–9.

[30] Dylan Thomas, 'Poem in October', *Collected Poems 1934–1952* (London: Dent, 1952), 103.

[31] Alun Lewis, *Raider's Dawn* (London: Allen & Unwin, 1942), 87–8.

[32] *Selected Poems of Glyn Jones* (Llandysul: Gomer, 1975), 30–3.

[33] Raymond Williams, *Border Country* (London: Chatto and Windus, 1960), 75.

[34] 'Gwalia Deserta' XXIX, *Collected Poems of Idris Davies* (Llandysul: Gomerian Press, 1972), 44.

[35] *Collected Poems of Idris Davies*, 175.

[36] For this and the following story I consider, by Gwyn Thomas, see Gwyn Jones (ed.), *Welsh Short Stories* (London: Oxford University Press, 1956).

[37] Quoted in Glyn Jones, *The Dragon Has Two Tongues*, 109–10.

[38] See Raymond Williams, *Politics and Letters* (London: New Left Books, 1979), 279.

[39] *Border Country*, 32–3.

[40] Raymond Williams, *The Country and the City* (London: Chatto and Windus, 1973), 197.

[41] *The Collected Poems of Idris Davies*, 39.

[42] Gillian Clarke, 'Voice of the Tribe', in Lothar Fietz, Paul Hoffmann and Hans-Werner Ludwig (eds), *Regionalität, Nationalität and Internationalität in der zeitgenössischen Lyrik* (Tübingen: Attempto Verlag, 1992), 174–5.

[43] Emyr Humphreys, *A Toy Epic*, 1958 (Bridgend: Poetry Wales Press, 1989), 17.

[44] Anne Cluysenaar, 'Growing-Points', *Second Light Newsletter V1*, 29.

[45] Ruth Bidgood, 'All Souls', *Lighting Candles: New and Selected Poems* (Bridgend: Poetry Wales Press, 1982), 34.

[46] Lynette Roberts, *Collected Poems* (Bridgend: Seren, 1998), 66.

[47] Raymond Williams, *The Fight for Manod* (London: Chatto and Windus, 1979), 97–8.

[48] Ned Thomas, *The Welsh Extremist* (London: Gollancz, 1971), 126.

[49] See Ned Thomas, 'From Raymond Williams to Post-Modernism?', *Planet* 81 (June 1990), 19.

[50] Waldo Williams, *The Peacemakers: Selected Poems*, translated by Tony Conran (Llandysul: Gomer, 1997), 130–1.

[51] David Jones, *Epoch and Artist* (London: Faber, 1959), 86.

[52] David Jones, *The Sleeping Lord* (London: Faber, 1974), 96.

2 R. S. Thomas, David Jones and Gillian Clarke

[1] R. S. Thomas, *Autobiographies*, translated by Jason Walford Davies (London: J. M. Dent, 1997), 10 (hereafter *As*).

[2] Matthew Arnold, *On the Study of Celtic Literature and Other Essays* (London: J. M. Dent, 1976), 13–14.

[3] R. S. Thomas, *An Acre of Land* (Newtown: Montgomeryshire Printing Co. Ltd, 1952), 23.

[4] Ibid., 26.

[5] R. S. Thomas, *The Stones of the Field* (Carmarthen: The Druid Press, 1946), 14.

[6] *An Acre of Land*, 12.

[7] Iago Prytherch proved to be a fertile and flexible symbol for R. S. Thomas both in respect of the materialism/spirituality opposition and of the Welsh/English culture wars. In 'Too Late', for instance, the man originally of vacant mind is described as 'drawing your strength / From membership of an old nation // Not given to beg' (*Tares* (London: Rupert Hart-Davis, 1961), 25).

[8] *The Stones of the Field*, 12.

[9] 'H. Idris Bell, in 1922, toyed with the notion of a new "Anglo-Welsh movement" headed by a Welsh Yeats, an idea which R. S. Thomas himself took up in 1946. In the same year the nationalist historian A. W. Wade-Evans looked to an "Anglo-Welsh literary movement . . . on the Anglo-Irish model" for the "resurrection of Wales"' (Tony Bianchi, 'R. S. Thomas and His Readers', in Tony Curtis (ed.), *Wales: The Imagined Nation* (Bridgend: Poetry Wales Press, 1986), 75).

[10] R. S. Thomas, *What is a Welshman?* (Llandybïe: Christopher Davies, 1974), 12.

[11] 'The Creative Writer's Suicide', in Sandra Anstey (ed.), *R. S. Thomas Selected Prose* (Bridgend: Poetry Wales Press, 1983), 173.

[12] R. S. Thomas, *Not That He Brought Flowers* (London: Rupert Hart-Davis, 1968), 26.

[13] *Not That He Brought Flowers*, 26.

[14] *The Stones of the Field*, 29.

[15] R. S. Thomas, *Later Poems* (London: Macmillan, 1983), 194.

[16] *R. S. Thomas Selected Prose*, 43–7.

[17] *An Acre of Land*, 19. For a discussion of 'The Tree' as 'the first announcement of a recurring motif in Thomas's poetry', a motif representing 'a "something unnameable, a lost Eden"', as well as for a perceptive treatment of important aspects of Thomas's poetry as a whole, see Tony Brown, 'Language, Poetry and Silence: Some Themes in the Poetry of R. S. Thomas', in William Tydeman (ed.), *The Welsh Connection* (Llandysul: Gomer Press, 1986), 159–85.

[18] *An Acre of Land*, 16.

[19] Ned Thomas, 'R. S. Thomas: The Question about Technology', *Planet* 92 (April/May 1992), 54.

[20] 'Postscript', *H'm* (London: Macmillan, 1972), 22.

[21] *Frequencies* (London: Macmillan, 1978), 19.

[22] *Later Poems*, 214.

[23] 'Welsh Landscape', *An Acre of Land*, 26.

[24] The original version of 'Welsh History' was included in *An Acre of Land*, 23; the revised version was published in *Song at the Year's Turning* (London: Rupert Hart-Davis, 1965), 61.

[25] 'Abercuawg', *R. S. Thomas Selected Prose*, 164.

[26] M. Wynn Thomas makes a rather similar point about Abercuawg differently, when he says:

> Yet it is actually presented as an image of dream which is the opposite of Romantic escapism, and is intended to be the prelude to serious engagement with present unsatisfactory realities in the name of 'Abercuawg' – that is, in the name of other, fuller ways of living, memories and hints of which are preserved in the 'obsolete' terms that

haunt the margins of current, debased speech. (*Internal Difference: Literature in Twentieth-century Wales* (Cardiff: University of Wales Press, 1992), 122)

27 David Jones, 'In illo tempore', *The Dying Gaul* (London: Faber, 1978), 26. David Jones discusses the Celtic 'defeat-tradition' in his essay 'The Dying Gaul' in the same book.

28 Ibid., 23.

29 For an account of this period in David Jones's life see Jonathan Miles, *Eric Gill and David Jones at Capel-Y-Ffin* (Bridgend: Seren Books, 1992).

30 David Jones, *In Parenthesis* (Faber: London, 1937), 49 (hereafter *IP*).

31 Kathleen Henderson Staudt discusses David Jones's 'struggles' with Spengler in 'The Decline of the West and the Optimism of the Saints: David Jones' Readings of Oswald Spengler', in John Matthias (ed.), *David Jones: Man and Poet* (Orono, Me.: The National Poetry Foundation, 1989), 443–63.

32 The reference here is to the 1961 edition of *In Parenthesis*.

33 Crucial to all David Jones's writings (implicitly in *In Parenthesis*) is his comment in a letter to his friend Saunders Lewis, 'as you once said to me "the Mass *makes sense* of everything"' ('Saunders Lewis Introduces Two Letters from David Jones', *Mabon* 1, 5, 18). David Jones was a metaphysical poet in the sense in which he understood the metaphysical poets of the seventeenth century:

> Who wrote a poetry that was counter-Renaissant, creaturely yet other-world-ordered, ecstatical yet technically severe and ingenious, concerned with conditions of the psyche, but its images very much of the soma; metaphysical, but not un-intrigued by the physics of the period; English, but well represented by names hardly English. (Preface to *The Anathemata*, 17)

The only word here that does not apply to David Jones himself is 'English', for while he is a great poet in the English language, his achievement is, in a special sense, distinctively 'Anglo-Welsh'.

34 My treatment of David Jones's work in this book is necessarily limited. For a comprehensive understanding of his poetry Thomas Dilworth's *The Shape of Meaning in the Poetry of David Jones* (Toronto: University of Toronto Press, 1988) is essential reading.

35 David Jones, *Epoch and Artist* (Faber: London, 1959), 216.

36 Ibid., 54.

37 Ibid., 259.

38 *The Dying Gaul*, 165.

39 Alwyn Rees and Brinley Rees, *Celtic Heritage* (London: Thames and Hudson, 1961), 94. Liminality has become an important literary

concept in recent years, the main influence upon it being the thinking
of the anthropologist Victor Turner which he developed in *The Ritual
Process* (1969) and other books. For David Jones, the important
thinker in this respect was W. F. Jackson Knight in his books *Cumaen
Gates* (1936), and *Vergil's Troy* (1932). I discuss the influence of
Jackson Knight's idea of the labyrinth and its close connection with
the ritual pattern of initiation upon David Jones in 'In the Labyrinth:
An Exploration of *The Anathemata*', *David Jones: Man and Poet*,
263–84. See also Tom Goldpaugh, 'The Labyrinthine Text of David
Jones', *The David Jones Journal* (Summer 1997), 78–90. I compare
David Jones's treatment of the symbolic borderland of Welsh myth
and legend with John Cowper Powys's imaginative use of the same
symbolic location in *John Cowper Powys and David Jones: A
Comparative Study* (London: Enitharmon Press, 1979), 28–30.

40 *Epoch and Artist*, 237.

41 Ibid., 238–9.

42 'Moreover, there is, they said, an island in which Cronus is imprisoned,
with Briarius keeping guard over him as he sleeps; for as they put it,
sleep is the bond of Cronus. They add that around him are many
divinities, his henchmen and attendants' (Plutarch, *De Defectu Oracul-
orum*, quoted in *Epoch and Artist*, 218).

43 David Jones, *The Anathemata* (London: Faber, 1952), 163 (hereafter
Ana).

44 *Epoch and Artist*, 82.

45 *The Dying Gaul*, 38.

46 David Jones, 'The Tutelar of the Place', *The Sleeping Lord* (London:
Faber, 1974), 59. Thinking in terms of 'feminine' and 'male' principles
is a hazardous undertaking, tainted by the history of patriarchal
attitudes, and vulnerable to criticism from a feminist point of view.
(There is, however, a feminism which speaks positively of the
'feminine' principle.) Kathleen Henderson Staudt, in what I think is the
most balanced treatment of David Jones's thinking in terms of gender
opposites, writes that: 'Beginning with *The Anathemata*, his later
poetry explores and develops the implications of a view of culture and
history rooted in bodily experience and hence responsive to the
feminine principle as an integral force in human affairs. The female
figures in Jones's work reflect this unusually androgynous sensibility.'
Staudt goes on to say:

> I do not claim that Jones gives any particular evidence, in his personal
> life or his writing, of supporting feminine power as a political pro-
> gram or even of eschewing the basic social stereotypes of women that
> prevailed in his day. I would not call him a feminist writer in any sense.

But the originality of his vision is obvious if the female speakers in *The Anathemata* are compared to some of the better-known female figures of Jones's modernist contemporaries. (Kathleen Henderson Staudt, *At the Turn of a Civilization: David Jones and Modern Poetics* (Ann Arbor: The University of Michigan Press, 1994), 143)

Staudt recognizes the fundamental fact that 'in Jones's work these multiple female voices lead back to a silent female archetype who is at once mother earth and Mary, the human mother of the Incarnate God, much as the activities of priest, poet, and "man-the-artist" all lead to the silent person of Christ' (134). It should be observed that Jones never forgets the interdependence of the 'male' and 'feminine' principles in all forms of human creativity.

[47] 'There is a key line in Aneirin's poem *Beird byt barnant wyr o gallon*. The bards of the world appraise the men of valour. One could hardly put it more clearly than that. The poetry of the "first-bards" was concerned with a recalling and appraisment of the heroes in lyric form. It is my view that something analogous to this belongs to the arts as such' ('Welsh Poetry', *Epoch and Artist*, 57–8).

[48] *Epoch and Artist*, 81.

[49] Gillian Clarke, *Collected Poems* (Manchester: Carcanet, 1997), 54–5 (hereafter *CP*).

[50] Jean Earle, *Visiting Light* (Bridgend: Poetry Wales Press, 1987), 11. I discuss Jean Earle's poetry rather more fully in 'Ceridwen's Daughters: Welsh Women Poets and the Uses of Tradition', in Tony Brown (ed.), *Welsh Writing in English*, 1 (1995), 138–9.

[51] 'Blaen Cwrt', *Collected Poems*, 13–14.

[52] Gillian Clarke, 'Language Act', *Five Fields* (Manchester: Carcanet, 1998), 83.

[53] R. S. Thomas, 'The Small Country', *Frequencies*, 19.

3 Emyr Humphreys's 'Land of the Living'

[1] The novels comprising the sequence in order of publication are: *National Winner* (London: Macdonald, 1971), *Flesh and Blood* (London: Hodder and Stoughton, 1974), *The Best of Friends* (London: Hodder and Stoughton, 1978), *Salt of the Earth* (London: J. M. Dent, 1985), *An Absolute Hero* (London: J. M. Dent, 1986), *Open Secrets* (London: J. M. Dent, 1988), *Bonds of Attachment* (London: Macdonald, 1991). I have incorporated page references to these original publications into my text using the following abbreviations: *National Winner*, NW; *Flesh and Blood*, FB; *The Best of Friends*, BF; *Salt of the Earth*, SOE; *An Absolute Hero*, AH; *Open Secrets*, OS; *Bonds of Attachment*, BA.

The seven volumes in the chronological order in which they should be read are as follows: *Flesh and Blood*, *The Best of Friends*, *Salt of the Earth*, *An Absolute Hero*, *Open Secrets*, *National Winner*, *Bonds of Attachment*.

The whole sequence has now been reprinted in paperback by University of Wales Press: *Flesh and Blood*, *The Best of Friends* and *Salt of the Earth* in 1999, *An Absolute Hero*, *Open Secrets* and *National Winner* in 2000, and *Bonds of Attachment* in 2001.

[2] Emyr Humphreys, 'Arnold in Wonderland', *Miscellany Two* (Bridgend: Poetry Wales Press, 1981), 94.

[3] 'Welsh Literature and Nationalism', in Alun R. Jones and Gwyn Thomas (eds), *Presenting Saunders Lewis* (Cardiff: University of Wales Press, 1973), 144.

[4] 'A Protestant View of the Modern Novel', *The Listener*, 2 April 1953, 558.

[5] '*Ulysses*, Order and Myth', *Dial* (November 1923). Reprinted in Frank Kermode (ed.), *Selected Prose of T. S. Eliot* (London: Faber, 1975), 177.

[6] *The Taliesin Tradition* (London: Black Raven Press, 1983), 3.

[7] 'Notes on the Novel', *New Welsh Review* 35 (Winter 1996/7), 10.

[8] *In Parenthesis* (London: Faber, 1937), 2.

[9] *The Crucible of Myth* (W. D. Thomas Memorial Lecture, University College of Swansea, 1990), 19.

[10] '*Outside the House of Baal*: The Evolution of a Major Novel', in Sam Adams (ed.), *Seeing Wales Whole* (Cardiff: University of Wales Press, 1998), 136.

[11] Preface to a new edition of *Outside the House of Baal*, 1965 (Bridgend: Seren, 1996), 8.

[12] *The Listener*, 2 April 1953, 558.

[13] Ibid., 559.

[14] 'In Memory of W. B. Yeats', *W. H. Auden Collected Poems* (London: Faber, 1976), 197.

[15] *Seeing Wales Whole*, 126.

[16] 'Options and Allegiances', *Planet* 71 (Oct./Nov. 1988), 34.

4 *Alun Lewis: A Study in Poetic Courage*

[1] Alun Lewis, 'The Journey', *Collected Poems*, ed. Cary Archard, (Bridgend: Seren, 1994), 133 (hereafter *CP*).

[2] 'Religion' is in my view a necessary word to use in this context, but I do not want to give the impression that I think Lewis was a believer in a religious orthodoxy. The following passage from Robert Graves's *The White Goddess* should indicate where Lewis stood.

The rediscovery of the lost rudiments of poetry may help to solve the question of theme: if they still have validity they confirm the intuition of the Welsh poet Alun Lewis who wrote just before his death in Burma, in March 1944, of 'the *single* poetic theme of Life and Death . . . the question of what survives of the beloved'. Granted that there are many themes for the journalist of verse, yet for the poet, as Alun Lewis understood the word, there is no choice. The elements of the single infinitely variable Theme are to be found in certain ancient poetic myths which though manipulated to conform with each epoch of religious change – I use the word 'myth' in its strict sense of 'verbal iconograph' without the derogatory sense of 'absurd fiction' – yet remain constant in general outline. (*The White Goddess*, 1948 (Manchester: Carcanet, 1997), 17)

Lewis's religious disposition found expression in his 'theme', and had more in common with 'certain ancient poetic myths' than with the dogmas of any 'epoch of religious change'.

[3] John Pikoulis, *Alun Lewis: A Life* (Bridgend: Poetry Wales Press, 1984), 30 (hereafter *Life*). I am indebted to this biography for my knowlege of the facts of Alun Lewis's life.

[4] See Brenda Chamberlain, *Alun Lewis and the Making of the Caseg Broadsheets* (London: Enitharmon Press, 1970). Linda Adams in her illuminating article 'Fieldwork: The Caseg Broadsheets and the Welsh Anthropologist' (in Tony Brown (ed.), *Welsh Writing in English: A Yearbook of Critical Essays*, 5/1999) links the populism of the venture with Welsh anthropological theory.

The Broadsheets are a manifesto which aims to reunite the *gwerin* and the working class through rediscovery of their shared cultural identity, seeking roots and continuity in the land and traditions of Wales. Alun Lewis's agenda is also an assertion of difference, based on that sense of a unique culture under threat, which had motivated Welsh anthropological studies from the early years of the century onward. (Adams, 65)

[5] In October 1943 he wrote to Brenda Chamberlain: 'There's a maniac in me that cries out only to be sensitive to hurt. He's more concerned with poetry than normal human happiness and patience and he drives me to odd places' (*Life*, 239). The following month, writing to Freda Aykroyd, he said:

At other times in these long inadequacies I suffer I think I want it to go a little further, that I might explore the fields of insanity. That is a temptation that attracts & repels me with like force & I don't act towards it; it's just a thought in me, not an impulse. I know it's danger; but it's very closely connected with the bit of poetry there is in me, the writing and creating mystery that wants to break down the last barriers and explore the deep involutions of trouble & complexity & relationship of things. But I don't really know whether the great poems were really written in madness. I think they were written in intervals of sanity. Madness I fear is chaos, a greater bewilderment, a worse darkness. (*Life*, 244)

This is, of course, a highly rational, lucid exposition of the risks Lewis knew he was running in being the kind of poet he was.

6 Alun Lewis, *Letters to My Wife*, ed. Gweno Lewis (Bridgend: Seren, 1989), 410 (hereafter *LTMW*).

7 Alun Lewis, *In the Green Tree* (London: Allen & Unwin, 1948), 58.

8 *Alun Lewis: A Miscellany of His Writings*, ed. John Pikoulis (Bridgend: Poetry Wales Press, 1982), 134.

9 *In the Green Tree*, 51.

10 Alun Lewis, *Selected Poetry and Prose*, with a Biographical Introduction by Ian Hamilton (London: Allen & Unwin, 1966), 46.

11 *Alun Lewis: A Miscellany of His Writings*, 119–20.

12 In 1940 Lewis described the army as 'a test of endurance – long term qualities – not courage or alacrity so much as the ability to conceive and maintain one's courage or faith until it's needed – indefinitely' (*Life*, 106). To Robert Graves he wrote in January 1944, 'India! What a test of a man!' (*Alun Lewis: A Miscellany of His Writings*, 149). For the idea of 'the Test' which haunted the Auden generation, that had grown up hearing constantly of courage and sacrifice during the First World War, see Christopher Isherwood's autobiographical *Lions and Shadows* (1938). It is worth observing in this context that Alun Lewis's father, Tom, had fought and been wounded in the First World War.

13 The quotation from *The Story of My Heart*, 1883, is from Chapter VI. Edward Thomas tells the fictional story of David Morgan in Chapter VIII of *The-Happy-Go-Lucky Morgans*, 1913. For discussions of the influence of Richard Jefferies upon Edward Thomas see my *Writers in a Landscape* (Cardiff: University of Wales Press, 1996).

14 Rainer Maria Rilke, *Letters to a Young Poet*, translation by M. D. Herder Norton (New York: Norton, 1954), 35.

15 Ibid., 67.

16 'I'm deliberately trying to explore the spirit world – I don't mean spooks, but the soul world, space, life, eternity, because I think all the answers to the things that grieve and afflict us today lie there' (letter, 2 February 1943 (*LTMW*, 303)).

17 *Letters to a Young Poet*, 29.

18 J. Maclaren-Ross, *Memoirs of the Forties* (London: Alan Ross, 1965), 233.

[19] As I have indicated above, I do not believe in playing the part of retrospective psychologist to poets, through analysis of their writings, but it would be inhuman not to infer a sense of guilt in Lewis as a result of his divided loyalties to Gweno and Freda Aykroyd, whom he met and fell in love with in India. Freda Aykroyd seems to contradict herself when, in the space of a few lines, she says: 'guilt and "the mind's divisions" haunted him' and 'But he never admitted to guilt' (Freda Aykroyd, 'An Exchange of Love Poems', *The New Welsh Review* 13 (Summer 1991), 15). If there is a contradiction here, however, perhaps that expresses the 'divisions', and in any case guilt does not have to be admitted to work on the mind.

[20] Jacqueline Banerjee, 'Seeking and Still Seeking: Alun Lewis in India', *Poetry Wales* 10, 3 (October 1974) (*Alun Lewis – Special Number*), 105.

[21] W. H. Auden, *The Orators* (London: Faber, 1932), 14.

[22] David Jones, *In Parenthesis* (London: Faber, 1937), 162.

[23] See, however, Freda Aykroyd, 'Echoes in the Work of Alun Lewis and David Jones', *Poetry Wales* 23, 2/3 (October/January 1987–8), where Aykroyd discusses the constantly recurring theme in Alun Lewis's work of 'the goddess of decay and regeneration', and finds 'many resonances' in the works of Alun Lewis and David Jones (72).

In his Editorial Introduction to the new edition of *The White Goddess* (1997), Grevel Lindop observes Graves's relationship with Lewis as one of the influences upon the book's writing. 'In late 1941 Graves began to correspond with the Welsh poet Alun Lewis. They discussed the nature of poetry and poets; the name of the medieval Welsh poet Taliesin cropped up' (viii). As I have shown above, Graves identified Lewis's '*single* poetic theme of Life and Death' with 'the rediscovery of the lost rudiments of poetry', by which he meant that of the muse poet, as distinct from 'the journalist of verse'.

[24] Alun Lewis, *Collected Stories*, ed. Cary Archard (Bridgend: Seren, 1990), 195.

[25] Ibid., 212.

[26] *The Collected Poems of Edward Thomas*, ed. R. George Thomas (Oxford: Oxford University Press, 1981), 122.

[27] Rainer Maria Rilke, 'An Hölderlin', translation by David Luke, in Michael Hamburger and Christopher Middleton (eds), *Modern German Poetry 1910–1960* (London: Macgibbon & Kee, 1962), 31.

[28] *The Complete Poems of D. H. Lawrence*, ed. Vivian de Sola Pinto and F. Warren Roberts (Harmondsworth: Penguin Books, 1977), 697.

5 *John Cowper Powys: 'Figure of the Marches'*

[1] I owe the phrase 'figure of the Marches' to Jerome J. McGann's Foreword

to Denis Lane (ed.), *In the Spirit of Powys* (Lewisburg: Bucknell University Press, 1990), 7.

2 John Cowper Powys, *Autobiography*, 1934 (London: Macdonald, 1967) (hereafter *A*), 104–5.

3 Powys's actual poems are not my subject in this chapter. I do not assume their failure. What I am assuming is that his poetic genius found its finest – and most original – expression in his major prose romances. For a careful study of Powys's poetry, see Roland Mathias, *The Hollowed-Out Elder Stalk: John Cowper Powys as Poet* (London: Enitharmon Press, 1979).

4 The dramatic element in Powys's novels is rooted in what he described in an early philosophical work as 'the inherent duality of all things'.

> Pleasure and pain, night and day, man and woman, good and evil, summer and winter, life and death, personality and fate, love and malice, the soul and the objective mystery, these are the threads out of which the texture of existence is woven; and there is no escape from these, except in that eternal '*nothingness*' which itself is the 'contradiction' or 'opposite' of that '*all*', which it reduces to chaos and annihilation. (John Cowper Powys, *The Complex Vision*, 1920 (London: Village Press, 1975), 95)

5 Emyr Humphreys, *The Crucible of Myth* (Swansea: University College of Swansea, 1990), 1.

6 John Cowper Powys, *The Meaning of Culture* (London: Jonathan Cape, 1930), 34.

7 John Cowper Powys, *Obstinate Cymric* (Carmarthen: The Druid Press, 1947), 45.

8 For knowledge of the 'two Taliesins: one historical and one legendary' (Ford, 3), 'the shape-shifter Gwion Bach, reborn as Taliesin' and 'Taliesin, the bard who is mentioned in the *Historia Brittonum* and who sang the praises of Urien Rheged' (Ford, 9–10), I am indebted to Patrick K. Ford's introduction to his edition of *Ystoria Taliesin* (Cardiff: University of Wales Press, 1992) and Emyr Humphreys, *The Taliesin Tradition* (London: Black Raven Press, 1983). I have also found suggestive the discussion of Taliesin as a 'Celtic shaman' in John Matthews, *Taliesin: Shamanism and the Bardic Mysteries in Britain and Ireland* (London: The Aquarian Press, 1991) and Oliver Davies's treatment of the figure in *Celtic Christianity in Early Modern Wales* (Cardiff: University of Wales Press, 1996). Davies's discussion of the subject is especially germane to my treatment of the Powysian imagination when he links Taliesin's metamorphoses to Keats's 'negative capability', and says that 'the Taliesin tradition is one of the most uncompromising assertions of the claims and powers of the poetic imagination that we will find in any

literature' (78–9). I have retained Powys's spelling, 'Taliessin', when referring to the figure in his writings.

[9] Matthew Arnold, *On the Study of Celtic Literature and Other Essays* (London: Dent's Everyman Library, 1976), 14. The *Study* was first published in 1867.

[10] Emyr Humphreys, 'Arnold in Wonderland', *Miscellany Two* (Bridgend: Poetry Wales Press, 1981), 96.

[11] David Jones, *The Dying Gaul* (Faber: London, 1978), 53. See also Ernest Renan:

> the Celtic race has worn itself out in resistance to its time, and in the defence of desperate causes. It does not seem as though in any epoch it had any aptitude for political life . . . Take the songs of its bards of the sixth century; they weep more defeats than they sing victories. Its history is itself one long lament . . . (*The Poetry of the Celtic Races, and Other Studies by Ernest Renan* (London: Walter Scott, 1896), 7)

[12] See Roland Mathias, 'John Cowper Powys and "Wales". A Limited Study', *The Powys Review* 17 (1985), 11.

[13] Herbert Williams, *John Cowper Powys* (Bridgend: Seren, 1997), 138.

[14] Ned Thomas, 'Obstinate Cymric', *The Powys Review* 4 (Winter/Spring 1978/9), 75.

[15] Ibid., 76.

[16] Richard Cavendish describes 'the attempt to become superhuman or divine' as 'the ultimate aim of magic in the entire western tradition' (*A History of Magic* (London: Book Club Associates, 1977), 3). An interesting recent definition, which could be applied suggestively to Powys as a shamanistic 'figure of the Marches', occurs in David Abrams, *The Spell of the Sensuous* (New York: Vintage Books, 1997), where Abrams describes 'the traditional magician or medicine person' as functioning 'primarily as an intermediary between human and nonhuman worlds' (8). Powys, like his Taliessin and Myrddin Wyllt in *Porius*, could be described as an 'exemplary voyager in the intermediate realm between the human and more-than-human worlds, the primary strategist and negotiator in any dealings with the Others' (Abrams, 7). I must add, however, the caveat that applies generally to perceptions of Powys as a 'shaman': that he was not a 'traditional magician or medicine person' with a well-defined cultural function, but a modern poet working through prose romance who constructed his imaginative role, or life-illusion, from his adoption and transformation of modern interpretations of 'primitive' ideas.

[17] 'John Cowper Powys and "Wales". A Limited Study', *The Powys Review* 17 (1985), 23.

[18] Roland Mathias, 'The Sacrificial Prince: A Study of *Owen Glendower*',

in Belinda Humfrey (ed.), *Essays on John Cowper Powys* (Cardiff: University of Wales Press, 1972), 261.

[19] Jeremy Hooker, *John Cowper Powys* (Cardiff: University of Wales Press, 1973), 74–8.

[20] *The Powys Review* 17 (1985), 23.

[21] John Cowper Powys, *Owen Glendower* (London: John Lane/The Bodley Head, 1941), 3.

[22] Joe Boulter, 'John Cowper Powys's [De]construction of Welsh Identity in *Porius*', *The Powys Review* 31 and 32, 14.

[23] Urien, in *Maiden Castle*, speaks in the spirit of Powys when he says:

> the power of the Underworld that our old bards worshipped, *though it was always defeated*, is the power of the Golden Age! Yes, it's the power our race adored when they built Avebury and Maiden Castle and Stonehenge and Caer Drwyn, when there were no wars, no vivisection, no money, no ten thousand times accursed *nations!* (*Maiden Castle* (Cardiff: University of Wales Press, 1990), 460)

[24] John Cowper Powys, *Mortal Strife*, 1942 (London: Village Press, 1974), 224.

[25] John Cowper Powys, *A Philosophy of Solitude* (London: Jonathan Cape, 1933), 220.

[26] *Mortal Strife*, 157.

[27] See Taliesin's poem beginning 'Primary chief bard am I to Elphin / And my original country is the region of the summer stars' in Lady Charlotte Guest's translation of *The Mabinogion*, 1877 (Cardiff: John Jones, 1977), 482.

[28] John Cowper Powys, 'PREFACE / or anything you like / to PORIUS', *The Powys Newsletter* Four (Colgate University Press), 10.

[29] John Cowper Powys, *Porius* (New York: Colgate University Press, 1994) (hereafter *P*), 423.

[30] G. Wilson Knight, 'Powys on Death', in Belinda Humfrey (ed.), *Essays on John Cowper Powys* (Cardiff: University of Wales Press, 1972), 201–2.

[31] John Cowper Powys, *The Pleasures of Literature* (London: Cassell, 1938), 650.

[32] See my review-article, 'Romancing at the Cave-Fire: The Unabridged *Porius*', *The Powys Journal* 4 (1994), 219. My subsequent discussion of *Porius* in this chapter adapts some ideas from the review-article.

[33] Jeremy Hooker, *Writers in a Landscape* (Cardiff: University of Wales Press, 1996), 96–138.

[34] *The Pleasures of Literature*, 299.

[35] Richard Holmes discusses Coleridge's 'image of Shakespeare's godlike creative power to transform himself into other forms of being', and says:

'Coleridge saw this power of displacement of the self into the other, of self-projection or self-metamorphosis, as central to the workings of the Imagination' (*Coleridge: Darker Reflections* (London: HarperCollins, 1998), 124). Powys's self-identification with Taliessin of the many incarnations is directly in line with this idea of the Romantic Imagination.

36   *The Pleasures of Literature*, 298.
37   William Blake, *The Marriage of Heaven and Hell*, 1790 (Oxford: Oxford University Press, 1975), xx.
38   *Mortal Strife*, 41.
39   John Cowper Powys, *In Spite of* (London: Macdonald, 1953), 161.
40   Alwyn Rees and Brinley Rees, *Celtic Heritage* (London: Thames and Hudson, 1961), 344.
41   John Cowper Powys, *A Glastonbury Romance* (London: John Lane/The Bodley Head, 1933), 771. This passage should be compared with its main 'source' in John Rhys, *Studies in the Arthurian Legend* (Oxford: The Clarendon Press, 1891): 'The name of [Urien's realm] is yr Echwyd, the evening and the dusk, the twilight which is essential to the illusion and glamour on which this whole cosmos of unreality is founded' (259). Rhys's idea of the ancient bards is also significant in relation to Powys's adoption of a bardic role and preoccupation with magicians and poets such as Myrddin and Taliessin:

> the bards thought themselves, as a class, to be under the special protection of the dark divinity under his various forms and names, such as Urien, Brân, Uthr Ben, and others. The dark divinity is the god both of beginning and ending, of life and death: as the former he is the god of plenty, and as the latter he is the god of the departed . . . (260)

42   *A Glastonbury Romance*, 169.
43   Cf. John Keats: 'The poetry of earth is never dead' ('On the Grasshopper and Cricket').
44   John Cowper Powys, *Powys on Keats*, ed. Cedric Hentschel (London: Cecil Woolf: 1993), 36–7.
45   John Cowper Powys, *Dostoievsky* (London: John Lane/The Bodley Head, 1946), 169.
46   John Cowper Powys, *The Meaning of Culture* (London: Jonathan Cape, 1930), 71.
47   John Cowper Powys, *Dorothy M. Richardson*, 1931 (London: Village Press, 1974), 18.
48   *Maiden Castle*, 245.
49   *The Pleasures of Literature*, 591.
50   Ibid., 582–3.

Notes

[51] The idea of the Celts as 'feminine' is a Romantic one. Ernest Renan, for example, remarks: 'If it be permitted us to assign sex to nations as to individuals, we should have to say without hesitation that the Celtic race, especially with regard to its Cymric or Breton branch, is an essentially feminine one' (*Poetry of the Celtic Races*, 8). Arnold followed Renan in finding 'something feminine' in 'the sensibility of the Celtic nature' (*On the Study of Celtic Literature*, 86). In mythological terms, both the land and the Otherworld are closely associated with the feminine among Celtic peoples. This emphasis fitted in extremely well with Powys's thinking. Powys conceived of himself as having 'a feminine sensibility', and his idea of this (as described in his study of Dorothy M. Richardson, for example) is of first importance for our understanding of his art.

[52] *On the Study of Celtic Literature*, 54.

[53] *The Pleasures of Literature*, 436.

[54] *In Spite of*, 231.

[55] John Cowper Powys, 'Emily Brontë', *Suspended Judgments*, 1916, (London: Village Press, 1975), 322–4. In thinking about Powys's 'poetry of the earth' I have found Stevie Davies's *Emily Brontë: Heretic* (London: The Women's Press, 1994) highly suggestive, as well as a powerful argument in its own right.

[56] *Maiden Castle*, 185.

[57] *Mortal Strife*, 148.

[58] John Cowper Powys, *Wood and Stone*, 1915 (London: Village Press, 1974), 1.

[59] Ibid., 3.

[60] John Cowper Powys, *After My Fashion* (London: Picador, 1980), 22–3.

[61] Ibid., 166.

[62] *The Meaning of Culture*, 159, 162.

[63] *A Glastonbury Romance*, 1171.

[64] John Cowper Powys, *Wolf Solent*, 1929 (Harmondsworth: Penguin Books, 1964), 403.

[65] John Cowper Powys, *Weymouth Sands*, 1934 (London: Macdonald, 1963), 271.

[66] *In Spite of*, 145.

[67] *Obstinate Cymric*, 85–6.

[68] Proinsias Mac Cana, *The Mabinogi* (Cardiff: University of Wales Press, 1977), 127.

[69] *Celtic Heritage*, 212.

[70] Nikolai Tolstoy, *The Quest for Merlin* (London: Coronet Books, 1986), 168. For a discussion of Powys's 'shamanic vocation' in connection with his epilepsy, see Robin Wood, 'Queer Attacks and Fits: Epilepsy and Ecstatic Experiences in the Novels of J. C. Powys', *The Powys Review* 31 and 32, 21–9. Powys invites consideration in the terms he applies to the

poet Huw Menai as representing 'that most primordial type of all human soothsayers, the individual in an aboriginal tribe who is at once priest, clown, actor, magician and poet' (*Obstinate Cymric*, 123). In my view, Powys should be seen in the context established by Michael Tucker in *Dreaming with Open Eyes: The Shamanic Spirit in Twentieth Century Art and Culture* (London: Aquarian/Thorsons, 1992), in which Tucker writes that 'it is from the late nineteenth-century onwards that the shamanic spirit in Western art really begins to develop the many formal and spiritual implications of Romanticism's dream of a magical world' (22). That is the *historical* perspective in which to see Powys as 'an aboriginal'.

[71] Letter to Norman Denny, 9 October 1949, quoted in Wilbur T. Albrecht, Foreword, *Porius*, xv.

[72] *Owen Glendower*, 889–90.

[73] Robin L. Wood, 'John Cowper Powys's Welsh Mythology: Gods and Manias', *The Powys Review* 22, 9.

[74] *A Philosophy of Solitude*, 166.

[75] *Dorothy M. Richardson*, 22–3.

[76] Morine Krissdottir, *John Cowper Powys and the Magical Quest* (London: Macdonald & Jane's, 1980), 127.

[77] *The Pleasures of Literature*, 66.

[78] *Obstinate Cymric*, 108.

[79] Ibid., 148.

[80] John Cowper Powys, *In Defence of Sensuality* (London: Gollancz, 1930), 119.

[81] *Owen Glendower*, 777.

[82] H. W. Fawkner, *The Ecstatic World of John Cowper Powys* (London: Associated University Presses, 1986), 37.

[83] John Cowper Powys, *The Inmates* (London: Macdonald, 1952), Prefatory Note, v–vi.

[84] *Obstinate Cymric*, 31.

[85] Emyr Humphreys, *The Crucible of Myth*, 5.

6 David Jones and the Question of Arthur

[1] *Epoch and Artist* (London: Faber, 1959), 237 (hereafter *E & A*).

[2] ' "All must be safely gathered in", as Mr Stanley Spencer said to me, with reference to the making of a picture (a more apt expression of the artist's business I never heard)' (*E & A*, 243).

[3] *Dai Greatcoat: A Self-Portrait of David Jones in His Letters*, ed. René Hague (London: Faber, 1980), 151.

[4] David Jones quotes Julian of Norwich in *The Dying Gaul*, 142 (hereafter *DG*).

⁵ David Jones, *The Roman Quarry*, ed. Harman Grisewood and René Hague (London: Agenda Editions, 1981), 41.

⁶ S. T. Coleridge, *The Friend*. Quoted in Richard Holmes, *Coleridge Darker Reflections* (London: HarperCollins, 1998), 166.

⁷ Fernando Cervantes's quotations from Christopher Dawson's *Memories of a Victorian Childhood* and treatment of Dawson's idea of *pietas* are highly relevant to David Jones:

> his [Dawson's] notion of *Pietas*, in the classical sense of the word, 'which is the cult of parents and kinsfolk and native place as the principles of our being' and which far from being 'a matter of sentiment or social tradition' is in fact 'a moral principle that lies at the root of every culture and every religion, and a society that loses it has lost its primary moral basis and its hope of survival'. (Fernando Cervantes, 'Christopher Dawson and Europe', in Stratford Caldecott and John Morrill (eds), *Eternity in Time: Christopher Dawson and the Catholic Idea of History* (Edinburgh: T. & T. Clark, 1997), 53)

⁸ Walter Pater's famous description of *La Giaconda* occurs in *The Renaissance* (1873). It was made yet more famous, of course, by W. B. Yeats's abstraction of the passage and relineation of it as a poem, which he placed as no. 1 in his edition of *The Oxford Book of Modern Verse 1892–1935* (Oxford: Oxford University Press, 1936): 'She is older than the rocks among which she sits; / Like the Vampire, / She has been dead many times, / And learned the secrets of the grave . . .' The passage I have quoted from David Jones's 'The Myth of Arthur' seems consciously to echo this description. It is also worth noting that Jones's prose is frequently 'poetic' in rhythm and diction, and when this occurs, as in this passage about 'The Bear of the Island', it would not be difficult to treat it as Yeats treated Pater. More to the point, the apparently natural closeness of Jones's prose to his poetry indicates one of the main reasons behind his success in creating forms that combine poetry and prose or afford passages between them.

⁹ *Dai Greatcoat*, 75.

¹⁰ For a discussion of the 'pattern of initiation' in *In Parenthesis*, see my *David Jones: An Exploratory Study of the Writings* (London: Enitharmon Press, 1975).

¹¹ *The Collected Poems of Wilfred Owen*, ed. C. Day Lewis (London: Chatto & Windus, 1963), 58.

¹² *The Collected Works of Isaac Rosenberg*, ed. Ian Parsons (London: Chatto & Windus and The Hogarth Press, 1984), 111.

¹³ Saunders Lewis, 'An Introduction to David Jones' Dream of Private Clitus', in Aneirin Talfan Davies (ed.), *David Jones: Letters to a Friend* (Swansea: Triskele Books and Christopher Davies, 1980), 115–16.

[14] 'Under Arcturus' (included in *The Roman Quarry*) is among Jones's most sustained (and densest) treatments of the Arthurian theme. It typically invokes recessive images behind Arthur, including 'far back a cult-figure called Arctaius'. This fertility god was metamorphosed into the tutelar of 'the men who form in line in battle', his function 'to pile high the bodies pierced by the pitiless bronze'. In this way the cult-figure comes full circle, since he is again involved with 'sustenance of a sort, supposing the mounded dead were left for long enough to become one with the humus of the field where they fell'. The voice speaking here in the poem goes on to say:

> 'tis said that where the battle has been of most contention, there, given time, the grain gives fullest yield. So, may be, the metamorphosis from Lord of the furrowed line to Marmor or Arctaius makes little difference after all – but here [we] are in deeper waters than I care for. (*The Roman Quarry*, 68)

The 'waters', surely, have a deep personal significance for David Jones: in them is hidden the meaning of the deaths of his comrades in the war.

[15] In *A Room of One's Own*, Virginia Woolf reflects on what Coleridge meant when he said that a great mind is androgynous. 'He meant, perhaps, that the androgynous mind is resonant and porous; that it transmits emotion without impediment; that it is naturally creative, incandescent, and undivided. In fact one goes back to Shakespeare's mind as the type of the androgynous, of the man-womanly mind . . .' (Penguin edition, 97). According to Mircea Eliade, 'Androgyny is an archaic and universal formula for the expression of *wholeness*, the coexistence of the contraries, or *coincidentia oppositorum*' (*Myths, Dreams and Mysteries* (London: The Fontana Library, 1968), 176). Nicolas Berdyaev writes:

> The Kabbala contains the profound doctrine of the Androgyne. The Zohar says: 'No form which does not contain both the masculine and the feminine principle is a complete or a higher form. The holy finds its place only where these two elements are completely united. The name person (man) may be given only to man and woman united in one being.' (*The Meaning of the Creative Act* (London: Gollancz, 1955), 65)

Understanding the androgynous mind is as important in our reading of David Jones as in our reading of John Cowper Powys. For somewhat different reasons, neither can be interpreted satisfactorily in Jungian terms, which are currently perhaps the most familiar in respect of this subject.

[16] Paul Shepard and Barry Sanders, *The Sacred Paw* (New York: Arkana, 1992), xv.

[17] *The Roman Quarry*, 17–18. In a note on this passage Jones writes:

> *Gwlad y Hud*: Land of Enchantment; *lledrith*, illusion. The expression
> *hud a lledrith*, 'enchantment and illusion', is an often recurring one in
> the traditional literature wherever the magic processes are referred to.
>   The south-west part of Wales was denominated *Gwlad y hud* by
> tradition, and by the poets, and was particularly associated with the
> earlier mythology . . . (17)

[18] In 'The Myth of Arthur', he says: 'the tradition of Arthur (even when
reintroduced in Angevin disguises) was, for the Welsh, an authentic part
of their historical mythus, whereas for the English it was a literary
convention mixed with locality-traditions as at Glastonbury and elsewhere' (*E & A*, 227).

[19] As he wrote in 'A London Artist Looks at Wales':

> Those who read the 'Stanzas of the Graves', the *Englynion y Beddau*,
> will understand how an actual topography, being commemorative,
> becomes inviolate, like a shrine. Perhaps Cymru has no shrines because
> she *is* one. And it may be no accident that her highest hill is called, in
> Welsh, the Great Burial-Place. (*DG*, 39)

[20] *The Tribune's Visitation* (London: Fulcrum, 1969), n.p. (Also included in
The Sleeping Lord, 51.)

[21] *The Roman Quarry*, 37.

[22] Oliver Davies's comments on a poem by the medieval Welsh poet,
Gwalchmai ap Meilyr, illuminate the fundamental idea. 'Here he uses
some very sophisticated theological material as he explores the theological status of Mary through the imagery of paradox. She is thus both
mother and virgin, mother and daughter to her father, a daughter to her
son and a sister to God by her faith.' Davies observes that 'Material of
this kind is, of course, part of the common medieval inheritance' (*Celtic
Christianity in Early Medieval Wales* (Cardiff: University of Wales Press,
1996), 101–2).

[23] *Dai Greatcoat*, 227.

[24] With regard to the question of war and morality this was especially true
of that tortuous and tortured essay 'Art in Relation to War' (*DG*,
123–66). The comments on Jones's argument in this essay by the pacifist
and Nonconformist Roland Mathias are particularly challenging. For
example:

> 'All art . . . has beauty for its end, without qualification', he [David
> Jones] asserts. An aesthetic which could equate beauty with good with-
> out noticing a loss of moral content and which could by-pass entirely the

Christian refusal to justify bad means even in the cause of a good end was thus flowering dangerously in David's mind as late as 1946 . . . (Roland Mathias, *A Ride Through the Wood* (Bridgend: Poetry Wales Press, 1985), 26)

[25] *The Sleeping Lord*, 70–1.

[26] 'Incarnational' poetry is too large and deep a subject to be dealt with adequately in passing. Here, it may be said that David Jones thought of Gerard Manley Hopkins and James Joyce as 'incarnational' artists, and he evidently saw the metaphysical poets in the same light (*E & A*, 114). Dermot Quinn quotes a summarizing passage by Christopher Dawson that will serve as a useful sketch of ideas that Jones shared with Dawson:

> [Man] is the point at which the world of spirit touches the world of sense, and it is through him and in him that the material creation attains to intelligibility and becomes enlightened and spiritualized . . . Thus the Incarnation does not destroy or supersede nature. It is analogous and complementary to it, since it restores and extends man's natural function as the bond of union between the material and the spiritual worlds. ('Christopher Dawson and the Catholic Idea of History', *Eternity in Time*, 81)

Quinn draws this paragraph from Dawson's *Progress and Religion* (London: Sheed & Ward, 1929), 168–75.

[27] See, for example, Dawson's *Religion and Culture* (London: Sheed & Ward, 1948): 'Throughout the greater part of mankind's history, in all ages and states of society, religion has been the great central unifying force in culture' (49–50).

[28] René Hague, *A Commentary on The Anathemata of David Jones* (Wellingborough: Christopher Skelton, 1977), 260.

[29] *The Sleeping Lord*, 96.

7 *A Portrait of Roland Mathias*

[1] This chapter constitutes a reworking and in places a repetition of substantial parts of two of my previous writings on Roland Mathias: 'Roland Mathias: "The strong remembered words"', in my book *The Presence of the Past* (Bridgend: Poetry Wales Press, 1987), and 'Profile: Roland Mathias', *The New Welsh Review* 4 (Spring 1989). It is not meant as a replacement for the former, from which it differs quite considerably, not least because of the inclusion of new material. Another respect in which these two treatments of the subject differ is that the former dwells

at greater length on the 'difficulties' of Roland Mathias's verse. This is a subject on which I have said enough in the earlier essay. I should also say that I was dismayed to learn from Sam Adams's book on Roland Mathias in the Writers of Wales series that my criticism of Mathias's poetry on grounds of obscurity, in my first essay on his work (*Poetry Wales* (Summer 1971)), had led to the author of a critical survey of his poetry in the *Western Mail* dismissing it 'without troubling to turn the pages' (Adams, 89). It is a galling thought that anything I have written about Roland Mathias, including essays in which I have wrestled with the difficulties of his verse, should be taken to justify carelessness and disrespect.

[2] Roland Mathias, *A Field at Vallorcines* (Llandysul: Gomer, 1996), 9.

[3] 'Craswall' first appeared in *The Roses of Tretower* (1952). My reference to it and to all subsequent Mathias poems, except those in *A Field at Vallorcines*, is to its appearance in *Burning Brambles: Selected Poems 1944–1979* (Llandysul: Gomer, 1983), 44 (hereafter *BB*).

[4] *A Field at Vallorcines*, 59.

[5] Roland Mathias, in Meic Stephens (ed.), *Artists in Wales* (Llandysul: Gwasg Gomer, 1971), 161.

[6] Ibid., 162.

[7] An interview with Roland Mathias, in Susan Butler (ed.), *Common Ground: Poets in a Welsh Landscape* (Bridgend: Poetry Wales Press, 1985), 181.

[8] Roland Mathias, *Vernon Watkins* (Cardiff: University of Wales Press, 1974), 56.

[9] Roland Mathias, *The Eleven Men of Eppynt* (Pembroke: Dock Leaves Press, 1956), 175–88.

[10] Editorial, *The Anglo-Welsh Review* XV, 36 (Summer 1966), 3.

[11] *Artists in Wales*, 163.

[12] Waldo Williams, 'Pa Beth yw Dyn?' Quotation and translation from Waldo Williams, *The Peacemakers: Selected Poems*, translated by Tony Conran (Llandysul: Gomer, 1997), 130–1.

[13] *Artists in Wales*, 166.

[14] Ibid., 163.

[15] Ibid., 167.

[16] Sam Adams, *Roland Mathias* (Cardiff: University of Wales Press, 1995), 63–4.

[17] See Roland Mathias, 'In a Co-educational Grammar School in Wales', in W. O. Lester Smith (ed.), *The School as a Christian Community*, (London: SCM, 1954).

[18] Roland Mathias, *A Ride Through the Wood* (Bridgend: Poetry Wales Press, 1985), 206.

[19] *A Ride Through the Wood*, 303.

[20] *A Field at Vallorcines*, 31.

[21] *Artists in Wales*, 168.

[22] Roland Mathias, *Anglo-Welsh Literature: An Illustrated History* (Bridgend: Poetry Wales Press, 1986), 98.

[23] 'Roland Mathias: An Interview', *Poetry Wales* 18, 4 (1983), 62.

[24] *Common Ground*, 183.

[25] *A Ride Through the Wood*, 206.

[26] *A Field at Vallorcines*, 20.

[27] *Poetry Wales* 18, 4 (1983), 61.

[28] 'Roland Mathias: An Interview', *Poetry Wales* 18, 4 (1983), 60.

8 Gillian Clarke, Hilary Llewellyn-Williams and Anne Cluysenaar

[1] Sam Adams, Introduction, The Triskel Poets Five: Gillian Clarke, *Snow on the Mountain* (Swansea: Christopher Davies, 1971), 6.

[2] Anthony Conran, 'The Lack of the Feminine', *The New Welsh Review* 17 (Summer 1972), 28–9.

[3] Ibid., 29.

[4] M. Wynn Thomas, *Corresponding Cultures: The Two Literatures of Wales* (Cardiff: University of Wales Press, 1999), 194.

[5] Deirdre Beddoe, 'Images of Welsh Women', in Tony Curtis (ed.), *Wales: The Imagined Nation* (Bridgend: Poetry Wales Press, 1986), 227.

[6] K. E. Smith, 'The Poetry of Gillian Clarke', in Hans-Werner Ludwig and Lothar Fietz (eds), *Poetry in the British Isles* (Cardiff: University of Wales Press, 1995), 268–9.

[7] The personal details of Clarke's Catholic background in this paragraph derive from conversations with the poet.
In *Gaia* (Oxford University Press, 1979), J. E. Lovelock described

the development of the hypothesis that the entire range of living matter on Earth, from whales to viruses, and from oaks to algae, could be regarded as constituting a single living entity, capable of manipulating the Earth's atmosphere to suit its overall needs and endowed with faculties and powers far beyond those of its constituent parts. (9)

In view of the importance to the poets discussed in this chapter of their lives in the Welsh countryside, and their contact with neighbours and familiarity with rural working traditions, it is worth noting Lovelock's finding 'that country people still living close to the earth seem puzzled that anyone should need to make a formal proposition of anything as obvious as the Gaia hypothesis' (10–11).

The 'ecological awareness' which the poets share derives in part from this hypothesis, and is well described by Fritjof Capra:

> Ecological awareness and ecological consciousness goes far beyond science, and at the deepest level it joins with religious awareness and religious experience. Because at the deepest level, ecological awareness is an awareness of the fundamental interconnectedness and interdependence of all phenomena and of this embeddedness in the cosmos. (Fritjof Capra, *Belonging to the Universe* (Harmondsworth: Penguin Books, 1992), 70)

Especially relevant to poetry in this context is Jonathan Bate's description of 'Romantic ecology', which

> reverences the green earth because it recognizes that neither physically nor psychologically can we live without green things; it proclaims that there is 'one life' within us and abroad, that the earth is a single vast ecosystem which we destabilize at our peril. (Jonathan Bate, *Romantic Ecology* (London: Routledge, 1991), 40)

[8] *Presenting Saunders Lewis*, ed. Alun R. Jones and Gwyn Thomas (Cardiff: University of Wales Press, 1973), 156.

[9] A beautiful instance of indebtedness may be seen in the following lines from 'Dyddgu Replies to Dafydd': 'The forest falls / to ruin, a roofless minster / where only two still worship' (*CP*, 22), which echo the 'Bare ruin'd choirs, where late the sweet birds sang' of Sonnet LXXIII.

[10] Wendell Berry, *Standing by Words* (San Francisco: North Point Press, 1983), 149.

[11] Of her move from Cardiff to Cardiganshire in 1984, when she 'no longer had a child at home', Clarke has said:

> Nineteen eighty-four was the year of my move away from the family. My children are still important to me, but now they are responsible for themselves. At that time, I began to allow myself to become more interested in things like green issues, science, the New Nature, the winds and the weathers, coming from somewhere and going to somewhere. Our prevailing weather is Atlantic weather. So there's a sense of being one with the world. ('Interview with Gillian Clarke', in David T. Lloyd (ed.), *The Urgency of Identity: Contemporary English-Language Poetry from Wales* (Evanston, Ill.: Triquarterly Books, Northwestern University Press, 1994), 25)

[12] Gillian Clarke, 'Voice of the Tribe', in Lothar Fietz, Paul Hoffmann and Hans-Werner Ludwig (eds), *Regionalität, Nationalität and*

Internationalität in der zeitgenössischen Lyrik (Tübingen: Attempto Verlag, 1992), 172.

[13] Gillian Clarke's note of introduction to her selection of her poems in Meic Stephens (ed.), *The Bright Field: An Anthology of Contemporary Poetry from Wales* (Manchester: Carcanet, 1991), 54.

[14] Ibid.

[15] Interview with Gillian Clarke in Susan Butler (ed.), *Common Ground: Poets in a Welsh Landscape* (Bridgend: Poetry Wales Press, 1985), 198.

[16] Gillian Clarke's contribution to 'Beyond the Boundaries: A Symposium on Gender in Poetry', *Planet* 66 (December/January 1987–8), 60.

[17] *Regionalität, Nationalität and Internationalität in der zeitgenössischen Lyrik*, 173.

[18] Linden Peach, 'Wales and the Cultural Politics of Identity: Gillian Clarke, Robert Minhinnick, and Jeremy Hooker', in James Acheson and Romana Huk (eds), *Contemporary British Poetry* (Albany: State University of New York Press, 1996), 376. Peach is referring to the chapter '"A Big Sea Running in a Shell": The Poetry of Gillian Clarke' in my book *The Presence of the Past* (Bridgend: Poetry Wales Press, 1987).

[19] Hilary Llewellyn-Williams, 'Rooms of the Mind: Gillian Clarke's *Collected Poems*', *Poetry Wales* 34, 2 (October 1998), 16.

[20] Christine Evans in her contribution to 'Symposium: Is There a Woman's Poetry?', *Poetry Wales* 23, 1 (July 1987), 44.

[21] Linden Peach, *Ancestral Lines* (Bridgend: Seren Books, n.d.), 79.

[22] *Poetry in the British Isles*, 269.

[23] Ibid., 270.

[24] *The Urgency of Identity*, 28–9.

[25] *Poetry in the British Isles*, 275.

[26] *Corresponding Cultures*, 193.

[27] Hilary Llewellyn-Williams, 'Through the Telescope', in Menna Elfyn (ed.), *Trying the Line: A Volume of Tribute to Gillian Clarke* (Llandysul: Gomer, 1997), 22.

[28] Ibid., 25.

[29] The details of Hilary Llewellyn-Williams's religious background recorded here are taken from a conversation with the poet.

[30] *Trying the Line*, 20. In the preceding paragraph, she has shown what she was fighting back against: 'It was easy to feel despair then [in the early 1980s], a year after Thatcher's landslide re-election, with the miners embarking on their long hopeless battle and everywhere greed, lies and self-interest.'

[31] Hilary Llewellyn-Williams, *The Tree Calendar* (Bridgend: Poetry Wales Press, 1987), 11 (hereafter *TC*).

[32] Francesca Rhydderch, ' "Between my tongue's borders": Contemporary Welsh Women's Poetry', *Poetry Wales* 33, 4 (April 1998), 41.

[33] Hilary Llewellyn-Williams, *Book of Shadows* (Bridgend: Seren Books, 1990), 46 (hereafter *BS*).

[34] Hilary Llewellyn-Williams, *animaculture* (Bridgend: Seren, 1997), 55 (hereafter *a*).

[35] Anne Cluysenaar, 'Growing-Points', *Second Light/Newsletter V1*, 29. (*Second Light* is a 'Network for Older Women Poets'.)

[36] Ibid., 30.

[37] Ibid.

[38] Anne Cluysenaar has written interestingly about her writing as a process of discovery. For example:

> When I begin to write a poem (as against getting the first inkling of it) I seem to be harking after something to the right, just at the back of my head. To turn as it were directly towards it would threaten to dispel this impression, and with it the possibility of the poem. So I cast about – always with two or more words at a time, because what I am seeking to hear is a stretch of language running like blade along the grain of what remains hidden. Any relationship to my subject may seem quite tangential. But from the rhythm, intonation, sounds and syntax of this first phrase I know that the rest of the poem will develop, provided I continue to keep 'in touch'. ('Poetry as Discovery and Potential', in Jon Silkin, *The Life of Metrical and Free Verse in Twentieth-Century Poetry* (Basingstoke: Macmillan, 1997), 384)

This serves as a useful gloss on the lines, 'The past / is my body now, like layers / of a poem discovering itself' in 'Vaughan Variations' 22, *Timeslips*, 158. Cluysenaar also describes her experience of the process of writing a poem as 'rather like numinous experience itself – a changed way of being that arises imperceptibly out of deep attention but somehow transcends anything that could properly be called attention, because the self that should attend has vanished' ('Growing-Points', *Second Light/Newsletter V1*, 32).

[39] As well as a poet, Cluysenaar is a linguist. See her *Introduction to Literary Stylistics* (Batsford, 1976).

[40] Anne Cluysenaar, *Timeslips: New and Selected Poems* (Manchester: Carcanet, 1997), 90 (hereafter *Ts*).

[41] 'Affliction (1)', in Alan Rudrum (ed.), *Henry Vaughan: The Complete Poems* (Harmondsworth: Penguin Books, 1983), 219. Cluysenaar uses the lines as epigraph to 'Vaughan Variations' 1 (*Ts*, 129).

[42] Anne Cluysenaar, 'A Quarry in the Brecon Beacons', *Landscape & Art, The Newsletter of the Landscape & Art Network* (Spring 2000), 4.

[43] Ibid.

[44] John Barnie, *No Hiding Place* (Cardiff: University of Wales Press, 1996), 92.

[45] For example: 'If the Earth is "Gaia" – "Mother" – then we are both part of "her" and also her "children". It is honey in the rock for the sentimental end of the environmental movement which prefers infantilism to thought' (*No Hiding Place*, 11).

9 Tony Conran's Religious Scepticism

[1] Tony Conran, *A Gwynedd Symphony* (Llandysul: Gomer, 1999). For the purpose of page references, I shall designate this *GS* in the body of my text. The book includes a 'Programme Note', in which Conran outlines the three books that comprise his 'Commoedia':

> *Castles* is largely an Inferno, a hell's eye vision based on the extent we keep faith or not – and largely not. It is about exploitation, cruelty, alienation, fear, suffering, betrayal and the vanity of human endeavour . . . And perhaps sometimes, something else, the ambiguity of suffering, of the Cross, as not simply hellish but a sign of paradise in our midst. *All Hallows* (as the title implies) is a Purgatorio, about hope and about the two great sins against hope, presumption and despair. Both poems are tragic, symphonic attempts at epic scale without a consistency of epic narrative. They are about individuals, certainly, including me; but they are also an epic vision of Wales and a tragic vision of mankind.
> . . . this last of the three poems in my tragic Commoedia, *A Gwynedd Symphony*, is a Paradiso, in the sense that it is about love and the claims of love. (*GS*, 79–80)

[2] My first essay, 'The Poetry of Anthony Conran', was reprinted in my book *The Presence of the Past*, 114–22; my second, 'Conran's Brag', was contributed to Nigel Jenkins (ed.), *Thirteen Ways of Looking at Tony Conran* (Cardiff: The Welsh Union of Writers, 1995), 217–26.

[3] Tony Conran, *Visions and Praying Mantids* (Llandysul: Gomer, 1997), 56 (hereafter *VPM*).

[4] *The Presence of the Past* (Bridgend: Poetry Wales Press, 1987), 115.

[5] See Conran's 'Introduction' to his *Poems 1951–67*, 2nd edition (Bangor: The Deiniol Press, 1974). See also 'The Muse', *Visions and Praying Mantids*, 43–57.

[6] T. E. Hulme, *Speculations*, 1924 (London: Routledge, 1960), 118.

[7] Tony Conran, *Frontiers in Anglo-Welsh Poetry* (Cardiff: University of Wales Press, 1997), 27.

[8] Ian Gregson, 'Tony Conran's "Gift" Poems in Context', in *Thirteen Ways of Looking at Tony Conran*, 120.

[9] Octavio Paz, *The Bow and the Lyre* (Austin: University of Texas Press, 1973), 64.

[10] *Poems 1951–67*, 33–4.

[11] Alun R. Jones and Gwyn Thomas (eds), *Presenting Saunders Lewis* (Cardiff: University of Wales Press, 1973, 1991), 156.

[12] *The Presence of the Past*, 118.

[13] Ian Gregson, 'The Modernism of Anthony Conran', in William Tydeman (ed.), *The Welsh Connection* (Llandysul: Gomer, 1986), 186.

[14] *Frontiers in Anglo-Welsh Poetry*, 251.

[15] *Frontiers in Anglo-Welsh Poetry*, 1.

[16] Ibid., 259.

[17] Tony Conran, *Welsh Verse* (Bridgend: Poetry Wales Press, 1986), 13.

[18] Ibid., 16.

[19] Anthony Conran, *Spirit Level* (Swansea: Christopher Davies, 1974), 80.

[20] *Spirit Level*, 101.

[21] *Welsh Verse*, 16–17.

[22] Tony Conran, *Castles* (Llandysul: Gomer, 1993), 34.

[23] Ibid., 38–9.

[24] 'Saunders Lewis introduces Two Letters from David Jones', *Mabon* 1, 5 (1972), 18.

[25] *Frontiers in Anglo-Welsh Poetry*, 258.

[26] Ibid., 257.

[27] David Jones, *The Anathemata*, 63.

[28] Jacques Maritain, *Creative Intuition in Art and Poetry* (London: The Harvill Press, 1954), 111.

[29] Ibid., 143.

[30] Ibid., 142.

Afterword

[1] Mario Basini, 'Surveying a Blasted Landscape', *A470* (February/March 2000), 7. All subsequent quotations from Mario Basini are from this one-page feature.

[2] Bobi Jones, 'Why I Write in Welsh', *Planet* 2 (October 1970), 21.

[3] Jeremy Hooker, 'Image and Argument', *The Anglo-Welsh Review* 18, 42 (February 1970), 66.

[4] Jeremy Hooker, 'Questions of Identity', *Planet* 87 (June/July 1991), 62.

[5] Ibid.

[6] Roland Mathias, Introduction, in Meic Stephens and Peter Finch (eds), *Green Horse: An Anthology by Young Poets of Wales* (Swansea: Christopher Davies, 1978), 22.

[7] In case I make it seem that the idea of the 'centre' which I touch on here was exclusively the product of my Welsh experience, I should add that it was instinctively, if vaguely, integral to my way of seeing things from an early age. In this respect, my greatest debt was to the English poet-

naturalist Richard Jefferies, as I describe in 'Richard Jefferies: A Personal Discovery', *The Richard Jefferies Society Journal* 9 (2000), 3–17.

[8] Jeremy Hooker, 'Brotherhood's Country', *P.N. Review* 14, 2, 74.

[9] The essay, 'A Seeing Belief', which first appeared in *Planet* 39, was reprinted in my book *Poetry of Place* (Manchester: Carcanet, 1982), 93–105.

[10] The reference here is to my discussion of Tony Conran's treatment of Raymond Garlick in 'Conran's Brag', in Nigel Jenkins (ed.), *Thirteen Ways of Looking at Tony Conran* (Cardiff: The Welsh Union of Writers, 1995), 220–2.

[11] Tony Conran, *Frontiers in Anglo-Welsh Poetry* (Cardiff: University of Wales Press, 1997), 258.

[12] Jeremy Hooker, '"One is trying to make a shape"', *The David Jones Journal* (Summer 1998), 6–19.

[13] A. M. Allchin, *God's Presence Makes the World: The Celtic Vision Through the Centuries in Wales* (London: Darton, Longman and Todd, 1997), 9.

[14] Bobi Jones, 'Anglo-Welsh: More Definition', *Planet* 16 (Feb./March 1973), 11.

[15] Ibid., 15.

[16] *Frontiers in Anglo-Welsh Poetry*, 148.

[17] For a discussion of J. R. Jones's thinking in English, see Dewi Z. Phillips, *J. R. Jones* (Cardiff: University of Wales Press, 1995).

[18] T. S. Eliot, 'A Note of Introduction', *In Parenthesis* (London: Faber, 1963), vii.

[19] I touch on the subject of patriotism in David Jones in 'David Jones and the Matter of Wales', in Belinda Humfrey and Anne Price-Owen (eds), *David Jones: Diversity in Unity* (Cardiff: University of Wales Press, 2000). In brief, my argument is that in expressing his 'love of the things of the Island of Britain', David Jones's 'emphasis is to put England in its place, in several senses' (24).

[20] A. M. Allchin, *Praise Above All: Discovering the Welsh Tradition* (Cardiff: University of Wales Press, 1991), 139.

[21] See, for example, Tony Davies's *Humanism* in the New Critical Idiom Series (London: Routledge, 1997).

[22] John Cowper Powys, *Porius*, new edition (New York: Colgate University Press, 1994), 287–8.

[23] *Frontiers in Anglo-Welsh Poetry*, 146.

[24] Henry David Thoreau, *Cape Cod*, 1865 (New York: Penguin Books, 1987), 224.

[25] See R. S. Thomas, *Autobiographies* (London: Dent, 1997), 74–5.

Index